Appreciation and Evaluation of MGNREGA in Punjab

Appreciation and Evaluation of MGNREGA in Punjab

Dahlia Khaira
Assistant Professor
Khalsa College of Technology and
Business Studies (Amritsar)
Mohali

ADROIT
Adroit Publishers
New Delhi

ISBN : 978-81-87393-55-9

First Published in 2017

Published by
ADROIT PUBLISHERS
4675/21, Ganpati Bhawan, Ansari Road,
Daryaganj, New Delhi-110 002
Phone : 011-23266030

Exclusively Distributed by:

Akhil Book Distributors
4675/21, Ganpati Bhawan,
Ansari Road, Daryaganj
New Delhi, INDIA
Tel: 011-23266030

Typesetting—Gaurav Graphics, Delhi-110002
E-mail: gauravsingh1908@gmail.com
Printed at: Rajyoriya Prints, Delhi.

Dedicated to

My Grandparents and Parents

Contents

Foreword

The core strength of a public policy lies in its implementation in letter and spirit. Implementation glitches can cause financial waste and disruption of services for ordinary citizens and, of course, frustration for policy makers. Thus objective policy implementation evaluations have an important role and can contribute greatly to improve the policy process. I am very pleased that Dahlia Khaira doctoral research engagementhas facilitated this publication on implementation of a social policy, namely, Mahatma Gandhi National Rural Employment Guarantee Act, (MGNREGA) 2005.

It is noteworthy to mention here that MGNREGA was conceived inthe mould of similar wage-employment programmes within India and outsidewith a view to reduce poverty. In India, a spate of rural employment schemes, non-wage and wage, had been launched from time to time. The national level ones were the National Rural Employment Programme (NREP) 1980-89, Rural Landless Employment Guarantee Programme (RLEGP) 1983-89, JawaharRozgarYojana (JRY) 1989-99, Employment Assurance Scheme (EAS) 1993-99, Jawahar Gram SamridhiYojana (JGSY) 1999- 2002, SampoornaGrameenRozgarYojana (SGRY) in 2001, National Food for Work Programme (NFFWP) in 2004. However these programmes could not provide social security to the rural poor. In response to this need, the Central Government merged SGRY and NFFWP with NREGS 2005 and launched NREGA.

MGNREGA is a landmark social legislation that guarantees wage employment on an extraordinary scale, covering the entire country. The Act guarantees the right to work by providing 100 days of guaranteed wage employment in a financial year to every rural household whose adult members are willing to do unskilled manual work. NREGA provides a statutory guarantee of wage employment and is demand driven, thus aiming at providing employment where and when it is most needed. This demand driven, guaranteed rural wage employment programme has the additional focus on building durable rural assets, monetizing the rural economy, empowering women and discouraging seasonal migration; all of this at the grassroots level, at the initiative of the 'panchayat' under the oversight of the Block Development Officer. The expectations from this legislation were to be realized best with effective implementation, hence the significance of this study.

The book has contemporary relevance as its subject is one of the largest ongoing wage employment programme in the world. The demand for work under the programme witnessed an upsurge post-demonetization. Thefindings of the book are of immense importance to students of policy, policy makers and officials involved in implementation, not least the street level bureaucracy.

The book presents the details of MGNREGA, its provisions regarding organizational structure and outreach, an analysis of the effects of the policy on women empowerment; extent of capacity building of officials; efficacy of accountability and transparency mechanisms. The important findings of the book include the improved socio-economic conditions of the women workers; their wages are on par with those of men and they choose what items to spend them on.However, it was noticed that the implementation of the programme suffered from many lacunae. Administrative agencies prescribed under the Act such as Central Employment Guarantee Council, National Management Team, Punjab State Employment Guarantee Council and State Vigilance Cell had not been constituted. By and large lip service was paid to transparency and accountability mechanisms such as proactive information disclosure, social audit and Vigilance and Monitoring Committees; the real essence of the concept was found missing. Shortage of MGNREGA implementation officials at the district and block level led to overburdening the existing staff, delay in preparation of work proposals and wage payments to the workers. Further, inadequate training handicapped the implementation staff.

The conclusions arrived at have found response in a series of suggestions presented at the end.

The study recommends that implementation agencies such as Central Employment Guarantee Council and State Employment Guarantee Council must be in place. Staff appointments should be as per the norms and officials must be trained. Grievance redressal mechanisms should be fully in place to redress the beneficiary's grievances.

I was witness to the onerous task taken on by Dr. Dahlia Khaira and compliment her on publishing a book that would add to the valuable literature in the field.

Prof. Ramanjit Kaur Johal
Chairperson, Department of Public Administration,
Panjab University, Chandigarh
India

List of Tables

List of Figures, Box and Image

A. LIST OF FIGURES

B. LIST OF BOX

C. LIST OF IMAGE

List of Abbreviations

ADC	Additional Deputy Commissioner
ADPC	Additional District Programme Coordinator
APO	Additional Programme Officer
BDPO	Block Development and Panchayat Officer
BNVs	Bharat Nirman Volunteers
BPL	Below Poverty Line
BRC	Block Resource Centre
BRGF	Backward Regions Grant Fund
BRPs	Block Resource Persons
CAGI	Comptroller and Auditor General of India
CAP	Command Area Programme
CB&T	Capacity Building and Training
CBOs	Community Based Organizations
CDP	Community Development Programme
CEGC	Central Employment Guarantee Council
CERD	Centre for Education and Research Development
CFT	Cluster Facilitation Team
CSOs	Civil Society Organizations
CSRE	Cash Scheme for Rural Employment
CVO	Chief Vigilance Officer
DDP	Desert Development Programme

DPAP	Drought Prone Area Programme
DPC	District Programme Coordinator
DRPs	District Resource Persons
DWCRA	Development of Women and Children in Rural Areas
EAS	Employment Assurance Scheme
EGS	Employment Guarantee Scheme
FWP	Food for Work Programme
GAD	Gender and Development
GP	Gram Panchayats
GRS	Gram Rozgar Sahayak
GS	Gram Sabha
HADP	Hill Area Development Programme
IADP	Intensive Agricultural District Programme
IAY	Indira Awas Yojana
ICT	Information and Communication Technology
IEC	Information, Education and Communication
IPC	Interpersonal Communication
IRDP	Integrated Rural Development Programme
IRMA	Institute of Rural Management
IT	Information Technology
IWMI	International Water Management Institute
JBY	Janashree Bima Yojana
JDC	Joint Development Commissioner
JE	Junior Engineer
JGSY	Jawahar Gram Samridhi Yojana
JRY	Jawahar Rozgar Yojana
KVIP	Khadi and Village Industries Programme
M&E	Monitoring and Evaluation
MEGS	Maharashtra Employment Guarantee Scheme
MGNREGA	Mahatama Gandhi National Rural Employment Guarantee Act

MIS — Management Information System

MKSS — Mazdoor Kisan Shakti Sangthan

MNP — Minimum Needs Programme

MoPR — Ministry of Panchayati Raj

MoRD — Ministry of Rural Development

NAN — National Authority for NREGS

NCBF — National Capability Building Framework

NES — National Extension Service

NFW — National Food for Work

NGOs — Non-Government Organizations

NIRD — National Institute of Rural Development

NMT — National Management Team

NRDWP — National Rural Drinking Water Programme

NREGA — National Rural Employment Guarantee Act

NREP — National Rural Employment Programme

NRHM — National Rural Health Mission

NRLM — National Rural Livelihood Mission

NRM — Natural Resource Management

NSAP — National Social Assistance Programme

NSSO — National Sample Survey Organisation

OBCs — Other Backward Classes

PDS — Public Distribution System

PIREP — Pilot Intensive Rural Employment Programme

PMEYSA — Panchayat Mahila Evam Yuvak Sashaktikaran Abhiyaan

PMGY — Pradhān Mantrī Grāmodaya Yojanā

PO — Programme Officer

PRIs — Panchayātī Rāj Institutions

PURA — Providing Urban Amenities in Rural Area

RGPSA — Rājīv Gāndhī Panchāyat Sashaktīkaraṇa Abhiyān

RGSY — Rāshtrīya Grām Swarāj Yojanā

RGVY — Rājīv Gāndhī Vidyutīkaran Yojanā

RLEGP	Rural Landless Employment Guarantee Programme
RMP	Rural Manpower Programme
RSBY	Rāshtrīya Swāsthya Bimā Yojanā
RTI	Right to Information Act
RWP	Rural Works Programme
SAU	Social Audit Unit
SCs	Scheduled Castes
SEGC	State Employment Guarantee Council
SEGF	State Employment Guarantee Fund
SEGM	State Employment Guarantee Mission
SGRY	Sampoorna Grameen Rozgar Yojana
SGSY	Swarṇajayantī Grām Swarozgār Yojanā
SIRD	State Institute of Rural Development
SRPs	State Resource Persons
SRTs	State Resource Trainers
STs	Scheduled Tribes
TA	Technical Assistant
TPDS	Targeted Public Distribution System
TRYSEM	Training of Rural Youth for Self–Employment
UIDAI	Unique Identification Authority of India
UNDP	United Nations Development Programme
UPDS	Universal Public Distribution System
USAID	United States Agency for International Development
VMC	Vigilance and Monitoring Committee
VRPs	Village Resource Persons
WID	Women in Development

1

Introduction of MGNREGA

1.1 Outline

The concept of development is very broad and dynamic. Although, over a period certain well-defined goals of development have emerged, it has not been possible to form a coherent image of the process of development. It is a multifaceted process involving economic development, social advocacy and proper planning to improve the capacity of the existing social systems and institutions to cope with the demands of change and growth. In other words, development is a multi-dimensional process.[1]

Depending upon the pursuits of development relating to various spheres, development has been classified as economic development, social development, regional development, human development, gender development, rural development, urban development and so on. The broader area of study is rural development.

1.2 Concept of Rural Development

Rural development has been receiving increasing attention of the governments across the world. It was an important focus of the World Bank that encouraged its introduction into the Official Development Plan Documents of all the member developing countries. Also, the concept of rural development has been changing over the years. It was considered synonymous with agricultural development. However, it was realized subsequently that rural development was much broader in its scope.[2] Apart from agriculture, rural development is also concerned with the development of infrastructure like roads, transport, power, insurance and banking, cottage industries, rural poverty, employment, modern education, health facilities and decent housing for the rural poor.[3] Thus, rural development is a strategy specifically designed to improve economic and social life of the rural poor.[4]

Rural development is defined in terms of economic betterment of people as well as greater social transformation by the Planning Commission.[5] It is a "strategy designed to improve the economic and social life of a specific group of people – the rural poor. It involves extending the benefits of development to the poorest, those who seek a livelihood in the rural areas".[6]

Further, rural development is defined as a "process through collective efforts aimed at improving the well-being and self-realization of people living outside the urbanized areas. The ultimate target of rural development is people and not infrastructure......one of the objectives of rural development should be to widen the people's range of choices".[7]

Therefore, rural development is a pre-requisite of urban development. Dr. A.P.J. Abdul Kalam advocated adoption of PURA (Providing Urban Amenities in Rural Area) in his Vision 2020. According to him, PURA can be adopted for the upliftment of the rural areas. PURA involves four types of connectivities:

(i) physical connectivity, where 15 to 25 villages are linked to each other through roads. Besides roads, provision of electricity and transport facilities is included;

(ii) electronic connectivity, where villages are linked with modern telecommunication and information technology services;

(iii) knowledge connectivity, in which a school, a higher education centre, a hospital is established on every 5 to 7 kilometres;

(iv) economic connectivity, where good marketing facilities are established to procure commodities and services of daily use and rural people can sell their produce in such markets.[8]

Prof. A.M. Khusro stated that ***"instead of moving human beings where infrastructure exists it is better to take infrastructure to villages where human beings live".***[9] Therefore, ongoing rural development programmes need to be re-oriented to integrate the components of PURA in the rural development, thus enriching the process.

Unfortunately, India has been unable to build rural development as a mass movement. The country requires "rural development in which economic growth is attained along with social justice as well as ecological balance so that the long and short term goals of development are harmonized and percolate to the grassroots that sustain the economic prosperity and socio-cultural beauty".[10]

Therefore, rural development must be organized to utilize the relatively un-skilled human resources that are available in the rural areas by generating adequate employment opportunities. The various employment generating schemes initiated by the government should not only be able to generate employment but also strengthen the livelihood resource base and rural infrastructure simultaneously creating durable assets for the poor.

In the Indian context, rural development assumes special significance. According to the Census of India, 2011, 83.3 crore of population resides in the rural areas and 37.7 crore in the urban areas. This implies that 68.84 percent of the total population is rural and only 31.16 percent is urban (Table 1.1).

Table 1.1: Rural and Urban Population in India

S.No.	Category of Population	Population (in Crores)	Percentage of Population to Total Population
1.	Rural	83.3 crore	68.84%
2.	Urban	37.7 crore	31.16%

Source: Government of India (2011), *Census 2011,* Office of the Registrar General and Census Commissioner, Ministry of Home Affairs, New Delhi.

As more than half of the population in the country lives in rural areas, the development of these areas is important as the backwardness of the rural sector would be a major impediment to the overall progress of the economy.

Keeping in mind, the large rural population base and also backwardness of the rural areas, Government of India implemented various programmes and policies for transforming rural lives and ushering in rural development.

1.3 Rural Development Programmes: Indian Initiatives

Over the years, there is witnessed a shift in the Government's approach towards development policies. Instead of relying only on increase in general affluence to enhance the living standard of people, the approach has been to consider the acquisition of minimum levels of education, health, employment and nutrition as basic entitlements and recognize the key role of the state in providing them to every citizen of the country. There is also a fundamental change in funding and executing the government programmes. More number of key programmes are being funded by the Union Government and executed by state governments to ensure that no entitlement or programme suffers due to resource constraint.[11] Also, the role of rural local bodies in planning and implementation of rural development programmes has been increasing post 73rd Constitutional Amendment Act.

After independence, the Government of India adopted Five-Year plans for realizing the development goals of the country. These plans had a major rural development component for transforming the rural areas. The various Five-Year plans and rural development programmes enshrined in them are discussed briefly here under (Table 1.2).

Table 1.2: Rural Development Programmes

Plan Period	Programme	Year
1st Five Year Plan **(1951-56)**	(a) Community Development Programme (CDP)	1952
	(b) National Extension Service (NES)	1953
2nd Five Year Plan **(1956-61)**	(a) Khadi and Village Industries Programme (KVIP)	1957
	(b) Multi–Purpose Tribal Development Blocks Programme	1959
	(c) Intensive Agricultural District Programme (IADP)	1960
3rd Five Year Plan **(1961-66)**	(a) Applied National Programme	1962
	(b) Rural Industries Projects	1962
	(c)Intensive Agricultural Area Development Programme	1964
Annual Plan **(1966-67)**	(a) Farmer's Training and Educational Programme	1966
	(b) Well Construction Programme (WCP)	1966
Annual Plan **(1967-68)**	(a) Rural Works Programme (RWP)	1967
	(b) Tribal Development Block	1968
Annual Plan **(1968-69)**	(a) Rural Manpower Programme (RMP)	1969
	(b) Composite Programme for Women and Children	1969
4th Five Year Plan **(1969-74)**	(a) Drought Prone Area Programme (DPAP)	1970
	(b) Cash Scheme for Rural Employment (CSRE)	1971
	(c) Pilot Intensive Rural Employment Programme (PIREP)	1972
	(d) Minimum Needs Programme (MNP)	1972
	(e) Command Area Programme (CAP)	1974
5th Five Year Plan **(1974-79)**	(a) Hill Area Development Programme (HADP)	1975
	(b) Food for Work Programme (FWP)	1977
	(c) Desert Development Programme (DDP)	1977
	(d) Training of Rural Youth for Self–Employment (TRYSEM)	1979
	(e) Integrated Rural Development Programme(IRDP)	1979
6th Five Year Plan **(1980-85)**	(a) National Rural Employment Programme(NREP)	1980
	(b) Rural Landless Employment Guarantee Scheme (RLEGP)	1981
	(c) Development of Women and Children in Rural Areas (DWCRA)	1983
7th Five Year Plan **(1985-90)**	(a) Jawahar Rozgar Yojana (JRY)	1989
8th Five Year Plan **(1992-97)**	(a) Employment Assurance Scheme (EAS)	1993
	(b) National Social Assistance Programme (NSAP)	1995
9th Five Year Plan **(1997-2002)**	(a) Jawahar Gram Samridhi Yojana (JGSY)	1999
	(b) Swarna Jayanti Gram Swarozgar Yojana (SGSY)	1999
	(c) Indira Awas Yojana (IAY)	1999
	(d) Pradhan Mantri Gramodaya Yojana (PMGY)	1999
10th Five Year Plan **(2002-07)**	(a) Mahatama Gandhi National Rural Employment Guarantee Act (MGNREGA)	2005
	(b) National Rural Health Mission (NRHM)	2005
	(c) Rajiv Gandhi Vidyutikaran Yojana (RGVY)	2005
11th Five Year Plan **(2007-12)**	(a) Prime Minister Employment Generation Programme	2008
	(b) National Rural Drinking Water Programme (NRDWP)	2009
12th Five Year Plan **(2012-2017)**	(a) National Rural Livelihood Mission (NRLM)	2013

Source: B.K. Prasad (2003), Rural Development: Concepts, Approach and Strategy, Sarup and Sons, New Delhi, pp. 61-64; internet.

An attempt has been made to look into the various factors that lead to the non-achievement of desired goals of these programmes. For this the programmes have been broadly classified into various categories, namely, self-employment, food safety, social protection, rural infrastructure and development, health, women and child development and wage employment programmes (Table 1.3). The focus is on central government schemes only; the difficult task of mapping the numerous programmes of the states could not be undertaken here.

Table 1.3: Classification of Various Rural Development Programmes

Classification of Rural Development Programmes	Programmes	Main Objective	Lacunae / Problems
Self-employment programmes	IRDP, SGSY, NRLM– Aajeevika	To provide vocational training to the unskilled for self-employment	Poor targeting – many non-poor managed to get the benefits. Poor implementation of the programmes. Non-involvement of PRIs. Attempt to develop an entrepreneur out of the unskilled landless labourers having no experience in managing an enterprise. Unviable projects undertaken and sub-critical investments made leading to collapse of micro-enterprises. Banks uninterested in providing credits to poor and landless farmers having no experience in entrepreneurship.
Food safety programmes	PDS, TPDS, UPDS	To provide food subsidy to the poor to tackle malnutrition and create demand for food grains thereby giving price-support to the farmers	Diversion of food grains to the open market. Low purchasing power of the poor made it difficult for the BPL families to buy large quantity of food grains at one time. Non-transparency in the selection of beneficiaries and complicated basis of selection lead to faulty targeting. Being a centralized procurement system, high administrative costs were incurred. Problems of wastage and pilferage.
Social protection programmes	NSAP (NOAPS, NFBS, NMBS), AABY, RSBY	To provide financial and social security to the destitutes and deserted; pregnant women, etc.	Inadequacy of funds. Unsatisfactory coverage and limited reach of the schemes. Under-utilization of funds.

Rural Infrastructure and Development programmes	Bharat Nirman Programme, IAY, PMGSY, Rural Drinking Water, TSC	For achieving higher degree of rural-urban integration and an even pattern of growth and opportunities for the poor and disadvantaged sections of society	Non-participation of beneficiaries in the selection of projects. Inactive involvement of PRIs, civil society in the schemes. Non-coordination between implementing agencies. Inadequacy of funds. Lack of trained manpower with the PRIs. Poor infrastructural development.
Health Programmes	NRHM, PMSSY, AYUSH, JSY	To provide accessible, affordable and quality healthcare to the rural population	Lack of availability of specialized doctors and well qualified staff in the rural health centres. Failure of government in attracting well qualified health practitioners to work in rural areas. Lack of motivation by the government to convince people to go to government health centres rather than traditional daayis, hakims and vaids. Limited access to timely and affordable health care.
Women and Child Development Programmes	ICDS, RGSEAG – Sabla, IGMSY, RSBY	To provide special attention to women and children due to their vulnerability and lack of access to resources	Poor Implementation. Weak Administrative machinery. Lack of infrastructure.
Wage employment programmes	NREP, RLEGP, JRY, JGSY, SGRY, MGNREGA	To provide employment opportunities during the lean agricultural season	Poor targeting. Poor implementation of the programmes. Administrative interferences and delays. Under-utilization of funds. Absence of community participation. Weak Administrative machinery. Lack of human and technical resources with PRIs. Lack of experience and incapacity of the PRIs. Embezzlement of funds.

Source: Compiled from various sources including internet.

It is evident from an above sources that although the nature and objective of the programmes has been different, they suffered from similar kind of short-comings and constraints (Table 1.3). These programmes suffered on account of poor targeting of beneficiaries, administrative delays, untrained human resources, inadequate financial resources, unavailability of technical resources, lack of participation of the people, corrupt practices and faulty implementation. More specifically,

(i) the targeting of the poor was the main problem. Many non-poor or richest among the poor reaped the benefits which resulted in lesser benefits reaching the poor.

(ii) schemes were implemented with poor knowledge about the ground realities. Not much research was done to adjust or fit the programmes as per the local conditions and needs which lead to unviable projects.

(iii) a number of agencies are involved in the planning and implementation of the schemes which lack coordination amongst themselves. Also, there is no central agency or official appointed to establish coordination between them.

(iv) there were too many programmes prevailing under different authorities and agencies. The rural masses had difficulty in understanding the complexity and nuance of the various programmes and approaching concerned authorities for different schemes.

(v) implementing authorities like panchayats lack human and technical resources needed for the implementation of the programmes.

(vi) no effort was made by the government to encourage people to participate in the formulation and implementation of the programmes.

(vii) no separate administrative apparatus was set-up to monitor or evaluate the programmes.

(viii) there was no mechanism to involve PRIs or other implementing agencies in the programme or project plan formulation. In this aspect, top-down approach was followed by the government.

(ix) most of the programmes and schemes were centrally sponsored, so there was lack of will on the part of state governments to implement the programmes properly.

(x) administrative interferences and delays led to under-utilization of funds, high administrative costs and corruption.

(xi) the fund allocation for most of the programmes especially wage employment programmes reduced.

Amongst all the programmes of rural development, wage employment programmes deserve special mention as they are associated with curbing distress migration by providing employment opportunities locally. The wages offered in lieu of work widens the spending choice of rural masses. The wage employment programmes also instill a feeling of confidence and self-respect amongst the people as fear of hunger no longer prevails.

1.4 Wage Employment Programmes

Since the broad area of study focuses on the wage employment programmes, an attempt has been made to look into the historical aspect of the wage employment programmes initiated after independence by the Government of India (Table 1.4).

Table 1.4: Wage Employment Programmes

Programmes	Period	Objectives
Rural Manpower Programme (RMP)	1960-1969	To provide employment to 2.5 million persons in areas exposed to pronounced seasonal employment.
Cash Scheme for Rural Employment (CSRE)	1971-1974	To provide employment to 1000 persons in 350 districts through labour intensive works and create durable assets.
Drought Prone Areas Programme (DPAP), Rural Works Programme (Later restricted as Area Development Programme)	1971-1973	To mitigate the severity of scarcity by organizing labour intensive and production oriented works so as to generate considerable employment.
Food for Work (FWP)	1977-1980	To generate gainful employment to a large number of unemployed and under-employed persons, both men and women in rural areas to improve their income and consequently their nutritional level. To create durable community assets and strengthen the rural infrastructure which will result in high production and better living standard in rural areas. To utilize surplus food grains for development of human resources.
National Rural Employment Programme (NREP)	1980-1989	To generate additional gainful employment; create durable community assets and raise nutritional standards of the poor.
Rural Landless Employment Guarantee Programme (RLEGP)	1983-1989	To provide 100 days of employment to at least one member of a landless household.
Jawahar Rozgar Yojana (JRY)	1989-1999	To generate additional gainful employment for unemployed and under-employed through creation of rural economic infrastructure, community and social assets with an aim to improve quality of life in rural areas.
Employment Assurance Scheme (EAS)	1993-1999	To provide 100 days of assured employment to a person in 1752 backward blocks during lean agricultural periods in the form of manual work.

Food for Work Programme II	2000-2002	To augment food security through wage employment in drought affected rural areas.
Jawahar Gram Samridhi Yojana (JGSY)	1999-2001	Creation of demand driven community village infrastructure including durableassets at the village level and assets to enable the rural poor to increase the opportunities for sustained employment. Generation of supplementary employment for unemployed poor in rural areas.
Sampoorna Grameen Rozgar Yojana (SGRY)	2001	To provide wage employment, food security and creation of durable assets.

Source: Government of India (2002), Drought 2002, Department of Agriculture and Cooperation, Ministry of Agriculture, Government of India, New Delhi, p. 17.

1.5 Selection of the Research Problem

Since the commencement of First Five-Year plan, the concern for rural development has led to the initiation of a number of schemes in this regard. However, inspite of nearly six decades of planning, the battle for rural development remains to be successfully, fruitfully and meaningfully fought. The fruits of economic growth have not benefitted everyone uniformly. There are various reasons for this uneven development in the society.

Modern economy is technology driven and not labour-intensive. A large number of high quality goods and services are produced with fewer hands. In short, modern economy is not generating much employment and sometimes it displaces and replaces labour with machines and tools.[12]

Also, the modern education system is not tuned to the changing economic scenario. The large agricultural work-force in rural areas is not sustainable with dwindling cultivable land and use of modern methods of cultivation. As a result, the rural labour is pushed into cities in search of work; but as they do not have any employable skills in the urban formal sector, they often end up doing jobs in informal sector.[13]

Thus, in this backdrop, the government needs to develop safety nets for such sections of society who have not reaped dividends of the development process and try to mainstream them. They need livelihood security in the form of wage employment to ensure a dignified survival (enshrined in Directive Principles of State Policy) and reduce distress migration.

1.6 Formulation of the Research Problem

As stated earlier, the provision of employment to the unskilled labour force in the rural areas is one of the means to undertake rural development. The development programmes, especially wage employment programmes help in self-sustenance of rural economy by providing employment locally and instilling a feeling of respect among rural population.

But various studies have highlighted that wage employment programmes suffered on account of improper utilization of funds, low coverage of the targeted population, funds being utilized for capital intensive activities rather than labour intensive activities, lower days of wage employment (less than 30 days in a year), elite capture, corruption, lower women participation and so on.[14]

The policies, programmes and schemes that appeared sound on paper could not be translated successfully into practice. The need was to review the planning and implementation aspects of the programmes. An effort in this direction was made for the first time by providing statutory base to an employment programme in the form of Mahatma Gandhi National Rural Employment Guarantee Act (MGNREGA) in 2005.

This study specifically focuses on MGNREGA as it provides guaranteed 100 days of on-demand wage employment to the unskilled labour force locally. The programme has priority for employment provision and creating durable assets for the rural economy. Being a guarantee and rights-based approach, it strengthens the bargaining power of the rural people. Also it ensures that if work on-demand is not provided within 15 days, unemployment allowance is paid.

1.7 Mahatma Gandhi National Rural Employment Guarantee Act, 2005: A Retrospect

Mahatma Gandhi National Rural Employment Guarantee Act (MGNREGA), 2005, has its genesis in the preceding wage employment programmes. The rights-based framework was inherited from Maharashtra Employment Guarantee Act, 1977. MGNREGA made the demand factor, a conscious strategy as a right to obtain employment. Financial obligations of both Centre and the states are a part of the legal framework. The MGNREGA guidelines also detail operational and administrative modalities of implementation seeking to address the limitations of the earlier wage employment programmes and placing greater emphasis on planning processes and Management Information System for improving data management. Apart from guaranteeing 100 days of wage employment, the Panchayati Raj Institutions have been vested with the responsibility of planning, implementation and monitoring of activities taken up under the scheme.

However, since the conditions for implementing the rights-based processes of the Act were not necessarily universally or equally present, the implementation of the Act, became the testing and training ground.[15]

MGNREGA aims at enhancing the livelihood security of the people in rural areas by guaranteeing 100 days of wage employment in a financial year, to a rural household whose members volunteer to do unskilled manual work. The objective of the Act is to create durable assets, strengthen the livelihood resource base of the rural poor and to reinforce the commitment towards livelihood security in the rural areas. "For the first time, rural communities have been given not just a development programme but a regime of rights. The Act will unlock the potential of the rural poor to contribute to the reconstruction of their environment. By doing this it will accelerate the growth of the rural economy. MGNREGA provides for employment, income, livelihood and a chance to live a life of self-respect and dignity".[16]

Earlier MGNREGA provided employment under nine different heads, namely: (i) rural connectivity; (ii) Bharat Nirman Rajeev Gandhi Sewa Kendra; (iii) water conservation and water harvesting; (iv) drought proofing; micro-irrigation works; (v) provision of irrigation facility to land owned by households belonging to the SC/ST, or to land of the beneficiaries of land reforms, or to land of the beneficiaries under (vi) the Indira Awas Yojana/ Below Poverty Line families; (vii) renovation of traditional water bodies; land development and flood-control and protection works. In year 2012, convergence of MGNREGA with other works happened due to which more works related to coastal areas, fisheries, rural drinking water and rural sanitation were added to its ambit along with above mentioned nine types of works.

1.7(a) Salient Features of MGNREGA

- **Rights based Framework –** The adult members of a rural household who are willing to do unskilled manual work can demand employment as their right under MGNREGA.
- **Time bound Guarantee –** The Act provides for 15 days time period within which the employment has to be provided to the applicant otherwise, unemployment allowance has to be paid.
- **Employment** – Every household can seek employment for upto 100 days in a financial year depending on the actual demand.
- **Labour Intensive Works** – The wage and material ratio has to be within 60:40 limits for permissible works at the gram panchayat; no contractors or machinery is allowed under the Act.
- **Decentralized Planning** – The local bodies have been assigned a principal role in planning, implementation and monitoring of the scheme. The gram sabha is mandated to recommend works to be undertaken in the village and at least 50% of works has to be executed by the gram panchayats.
- **Work site facilities** – The workers must be provided with various facilities at the worksites such as crèche, drinking water, first aid and shaded area for rest.
- **Women empowerment** – The Act prescribe that at least one-third of beneficiaries should be women.

- **Transparency & Accountability** – The transparency and accountability mechanisms have been ensured through pro-active disclosure through wall writings, citizen information boards at public places, regular updation of the MGNREGA website, information display boards at the work-sites, vigilance and monitoring committees, social audits and so on.
- **Funding** – The Central Government has to bear 100% cost towards unskilled wages and 75% towards skilled, semi-skilled and material cost while 25 % of skilled, semi-skilled and material cost has to be contributed by the states. In addition, 6% administrative expenses are also to be borne by the Centre for effective implementation of the Act.[17]

1.7(b) Implementation of MGNREGA

The Act came into force on February 2, 2006 and was implemented in a phased manner. In Phase I, it was introduced in two hundred most backward districts of the country. It was implemented in an additional one hundred thirty districts during Phase II in 2007-2008. As per the initial target, MGNREGA was to be expanded countrywide in five years. However, in order to bring the whole nation under its safety net and keeping in view the demand, the scheme was extended to the remaining two hundred eighty-five districts of the country from April1, 2008 in Phase III.

1.7(c)Significance of MGNREGA

The significance of MGNREGA lies in the fact that it creates rights-based framework for wage employment programmes and makes the government legally accountable for providing employment to those who ask for it. It provides statutory guarantee or a legal base for wage employment. In this way, the legislation goes beyond providing a social safety net towards guaranteeing the right to employment.[18]

MGNREGA also marks a paradigm shift from the previous wage employment programmes. For an instance, wage employment programmes were allocation based. However, MGNREGA is not supply driven but demand driven. Employment is dependent upon the worker exercising the choice to apply for registration, obtain a job-card and seek employment through a written application for the time and duration that the worker wants. The legal guarantee has to be fulfilled within the time limit prescribed and this mandate is underpinned by the provision of unemployment allowance. The Act offers an incentive to the states for providing employment as ninety percent of the cost for employment provided is borne by the Centre. There is a concomitant disincentive for not providing employment if demanded, as the states then bear the double indemnity of unemployment and the cost of unemployment allowance. Resource transfer under MGNREGA is based on the demand for employment and this provides another critical incentive to states to leverage the Act to meet the employment needs of the poor.

The public delivery system has been made accountable as an Annual Report on the outcomes of MGNREGA has to be presented by the Central Government to the Parliament and by the State Government to the State legislature.[19]

Table 1.5: MGNREGA National Overview

	2008-09	2009-10	2010-11	2011-12	2012-13	2013-14	2014-15
Total Job Cards issued in crores	10.01	11.25	11.98	12.50	13.06	13.15	13.00
Employment provided to household in crores	4.51	5.26	5.49	5.06	4.99	4.79	3.60
Personsdays [in Crore]							
Total	216.32	283.59	257.15	218.76	230.48	220.22	121.25
SCs	63.36 (29%)	86.45 (30%)	78.76 (31%)	48.47 (22%)	51.21 (22%)	49.79 (23%)	27.5 (23%)
STs	55.02 (25%)	58.74 (21%)	53.62 (21%)	40.92 (19%)	41.00 (18%)	38.23 (17%)	20.18 (17%)
Women	103.57 (48%)	136.40 (48%)	122.74 (48%)	105.27 (48%)	118.23 (51%)	116.24 (53%)	67.32 (56%)
Others	97.95 (45%)	138.40 (49%)	124.78 (48%)	129.38 (59%)	138.27 (60%)	132.29 (60%)	73.57 (61%)
Persondays per HH	48 days	54 days	47 days	43 days	46 days	46 days	34 days
Central Relie in crores	29939.60	33506.61	35768.95	29189.77	30009.96	32743.68	26710.96
Total available fund (including OB) in crores	37397.06	49579.19	54172.14	48805.68	45630.50	42215.67	31467.58
Expenditure in crores (percentage against available funds)	27250.10 (73%)	37905.23 (76%)	39377.27 (73%)	37072.82 (76%)	39778.29 (87%)	38672.40 (92%)	26404.45 (84%)
Expenditure on Wages in crores	18200.03 (67%)	25579.32 (70%)	25686.53 (68%)	24306.22 (69.53%)	27153.53 (72%)	26647.54 (73%)	18859.16 (76%)
Total works taken up in lakhs	27.75	46.17	50.99	80.77	104.62	94.14	95.14
Works Completed		22.59	25.90	27.56	25.53	24.11	9.88
Works break up							
Water conservation	12.79 (46%)	23.43 (51%)	24.26 (48%)	48.81 (60%)	48.37 (46%)	31.53 (33%)	29.82 (31%)
Works on Individual Land	5.67 (20%)	7.73 (17%)	9.15 (18%)	9.16 (11%)	11.92 (11%)	12.78 (14%)	13.62 (14%)
Rural Connectivity	5.03 (18%)	7.64 (17%)	9.31 (18%)	13.86 (17%)	12.83 (12%)	14.46 (15%)	12.92 (14%)
Land Development	3.98 (15%)	6.38 (14%)	7.04 (14%)	6.32 (8%)	6.61 (6%)	6.06 (7%)	5.91 (6%)
Any other activity	0.28(1%)	0.98(2%)	1.06(2%)	2.31(3%)	9.84(9%)	2.07(2%)	2.05(2%)
Bharat Nirman Rajiv Gandhi Seva Kendra	-	-	0.17 (0.33%)	0.29 (0.36%)	0.29 (0.28%)	0.34 (0.36%)	0.33 (0.34%)

Source: Government of India (2015), MGNREGA – Report to the People: 2014-15, Ministry of Rural Development, Department of Rural Development, New Delhi, p. 9; Government of India (2012), MGNREGA – Report to the People: 2011-12, Ministry of Rural Development, Department of Rural Development, New Delhi, p. 8.

1.8 Review of Literature

Since independence efforts have been made on to remove the scourge of poverty. Poverty alleviation; providing employment opportunities and basic amenities like food, housing, and drinking water; rural infrastructure like roads, education and health thus, enhancing standard of living have been the central objectives of rural planning in India. Taking into account the efforts undertaken since independence by the Government of India, a lot of scholarly analysis has been done of the various rural development policies and programmes. An attempt is made here to capture the essence of the work done covering various aspects of the rural development programmes. The literature reviewed has been presented under five headings, namely, Administrative Machinery and Procedures; People's Participation and Civil Society Organizations; Management of Human Resources and Capacities of Implementing Agencies; Transparency and Accountability. These have also been summarized in Table 1.6 as Classification and Analysis of the literature reviewed.

1.8(a) Administrative Machinery and Procedures

Chaturvedi (1977)[20] focused attention on the lack of interaction between the bureaucrats and the political leaders. He selected a sample from the district as well as the block level administrators and politicians. The project covered the three levels; individual bureaucrats, bureaucratic structure and political leaders.

Arya, Verma and Sharma (1985)[21] opined that India has made great efforts in developing and utilizing science and technology for the implementation of development programmes but imported ideas, models and technology cannot be depended upon to solve the problems. Because of poor and surplus labour, the need is to select less-expensive, more labour-oriented and employment-generating technology. The ultimate purpose of development is to provide increasing opportunities to people for a better life, income security and educational facilities. Rural development programmes need to be administered through consultative and participatory group activities of the rural people. Rural areas lack local forces that could generate ideas about rural development from below and sustain the development effort with the help of local resources. The key management problems of rural development relate to the need for clarity of policy and programmatic approaches, effectiveness and efficiency during implementation, expedition and quality in the delivery of services to the rural people. *The focus should be on the objective of the programme and entire strategy of organization, procedure, method and working of personnel.* Development process is most likely to be successful if consultation takes place at the time of goal setting and determination of priorities.

Singh (1985)[22] concluded that rural development is a multi-faceted phenomenon. Nearly thirty-two rural development programmes have been introduced after independence. The objectives of these programmes were income generation, growth, target development, area development, education and welfare. Some were successful to an extent while others faced failures. This served as an eye opener to the planners making it clear that the fruits of development are being cornered by a small section of the rural society. The governments created a number of agencies which caused confusion and overlapping of benefits. However, the planning processes for rural development have not been institutionalized beyond routine compilation of statistical data. The implementation of programmes need appropriate administrative apparatus. Proper implementation can transform the rural lives but much remains to be done in translating blueprints into reality. Full involvement of the people and the role of voluntary agencies need to be recognized in achieving the objectives of the programmes. Political leaders must constantly review the implementation of development programmes and ensure that their local-level counterparts also become sensitive to the minimum needs of the rural poor strengthening the planning machinery.

Singh (1989)[23] examined the relationship between bureaucracy and rural development. He studied the role perception and performance of public servants at the block level. He concluded that it is necessary to re-mould the old fashioned and designed bureaucracy (as described by Weber). In the present era, the role of bureaucracy should be neutral, scientifically understanding progressive, innovative, reformist and revolutionary in nature. However, it is extremely rigid especially in the field of rural development.

Maheshwari (1995)[24] viewed that the only alternative to reduce extreme pressure on bigger cities and their strained infrastructure is to develop rural areas. He described three models of rural development that India has tried since independence – first model was the community development programme initiated in 1952, a multipurpose all round rural development scheme. This scheme lost its attraction during the mid-sixties due to the serious food shortages in the country. The second model was Green Revolution started in 1966. Only landlords and big farmers were benefitted; however there was no change in condition of small and marginal farmers, rural artisans, carpenters, blacksmiths and many others. The third model was Integrated Rural Development Programme (IRDP) adopted in 1979, to which Jawahar Rozgar Yojana (JRY) was added in 1989. IRDP was prepared by scientists which was an innovation in the field of rural development in India. The idea of using science and technology in the development of rural areas sounded logical but the problem arose during implementation due to the lack of training of the scientific community. The ideal schemes could not be translated into practical schemes. Besides this, JRY failed to provide employment to the expected extent, quality of assets created was poor and maintenance of assets was unsatisfactory. Further, monitoring and supervision was generally deficient and a large part of JRY funds were wasted and leakages continued unabated. The development of alternative and separate administrative structure is needed which would exclusively deal with rural development; otherwise; the inadequacies of rural development administration would further increase with the new responsibilities.

Ghose (2004)[25] analysed that the core of employment problem in India is that of the working poor. Addressing this problem is also the most effective way of eliminating child labour and reducing gender inequality. In principle, this can be addressed either by reducing the level of under-employment, increasing the real wage rate for casual labour and facilitating the transfer of poor self-employed persons and casual labourers to regular wage paid jobs. The priority must be to generate a steady process of labour transfer, ensuring that a substantial proportion of the newly created regular wage paid jobs are for low-skilled workers.

Hirway (2004)[26] analyzed the Employment Guarantee Plan announced in the Common Minimum Programme of the UPA government. She concluded that it has been designed to protect the interests of the poor by detailing the rules of the guarantee and imposing penalties for non-compliance. It has also drawn heavily on the Maharashtra Employment Guarantee Act, which has been in operation for thirty years. However, two major drawbacks of the proposed programme are its unrealistic underlying assumptions and short-term vision. The Act should not result in the creation of a large permanent army of unskilled workers to be supported by the National Exchequer. The provisions of the Employment Guarantee Programme should be strengthened to achieve the objectives of poverty reduction, construction of productive assets and promoting main stream employment.

Papola (2005)[27] concluded that it is feasible to have an employment guarantee programme covering all rural households and offering work to all persons, on all the required days, in all districts right from the beginning at a cost lower than the one being projected for a restricted programme. A universal programme will be closer to the spirit of a guarantee and reduce the bureaucratic problems in administering a restricted programme.

Jacob and Varghese (2006)[28] analyzed the implementation of NREGA in Kerala and concluded that the socio-economic conditions in the state have a great influence on the successful implementation of the scheme. The implementation has been largely fair and corruption free, but the scheme needed to be more efficiently and effectively used so that the long-term requirements of the state and its people are met.

Louis (2006)[29] analyzed the implementation of NREGA in Bihar and observed that the state government seemed to be strong on rhetoric and weak in implementation. Out of the two hundred districts that were selected for the first phase of implementation of the scheme, twenty-three were from Bihar. He evaluated that Bihar has a tradition of non-implementation of development schemes, even those sponsored and supported by the union government.

Savale (2006)[30] compared Maharashtra's Employment Guarantee Scheme with the Sampoorna Gramin Rozgar Yojana to find whether the programme is better or worse than the SGRY. He concluded that EGS is more effective than SGRY in meeting the needs of the rural poor particularly in favouring labour versus machinery in the completion of projects and hiring local workers. Despite the features of EGS that seem to favour the poor, there is more variation in the performance among EGS than SGRY projects. The SGRY is organized in such a way that it is unlikely to generate labour mobilization ever. To the extent that the organizational framework for rural public works in Maharashtra continue to shift from one local programme to another, the prospects for the political mobilization of rural labour around public works will decrease.

Chakraborty (2007)[31] studied the state-wise employment demand-supply data and the use of funds released under the NREGA by the Central Government (2005-Aug 2006). This secondary data based study concluded that the scheme has fallen short of meeting the demand in various states. The budget analysis revealed that the fund utilization ratio to actual utilization remains low in poorer states in the country. The fund allocation is only marginally higher than what was spent by the government on various rural employment programmes in the past. The monthly data of the first few months provided on the progress of implementation of NREGA by the Ministry of Rural Development revealed that the existing institutional arrangement in poorer states is not good enough to implement NREGA in an effective manner. There is an urgent need for both vertical and horizontal coordination across levels of governments within the states.

Datar (2007)[32] explained the reasons for the failure of NREGS in Maharashtra. The scheme failed to take off because government machinery is paralyzed in the state. Political as well as bureaucratic will is absent in the new scheme. There is no enthusiasm among the political class and bureaucracy to accept the new scheme which is more decentralized, more transparent and accountable to those who need work. Organizations and unions have also not come forward to claim the benefits of the scheme. They have been moulded in the old-time politics of demanding and protesting against the state but are not used to the politics of participation of the people to over-ride the state.

Mohan (2007)[33] undertook an evaluation of the functioning of NREGA in various parts of the country. She opined that the programme requires some structural and conceptual modifications to be better able to realize its objectives. Almost all the selected districts where NREGA was implemented had not been able to utilize the financial allotment made for the purpose. None of the districts could provide hundred days of employment to the job-card holders. In some remote areas, people were not aware of their right to demand work under NREGA. Also, programme guidelines were usually not obeyed. She suggested that the material–wage ratio of forty-sixty should be hiked to fifty-fifty so that bigger and better schemes can be taken up. The concerns and problems are needed to be addressed sooner rather than later if NREGA has to be successful in realizing its objectives.

Ambasta, Shankar and Shah (2008)[34] discussed that it is not possible to realize the massive potential of NREGA if the same ossified structure of implementation that has deeply institutionalized corruption, inefficiency and non-accountability into the Indian democracy are deployed. Neither a vigilant public nor a professional system has been sufficient in guaranteeing an accountable democracy, delivering development to the poor. If the reforms suggested are put into place, NREGA holds out the prospect of transforming the livelihoods of the poorest and heralding a revolution in rural governance in India.

Hirway, Saluja and Yadav (2008)[35] undertook a study in a tribal village in Gujarat to understand the impact of NREGS works undertaken in terms of production, income and employment. Their study drew attention to the potential of NREGS in a developing economy like India. If undertaken on a large scale and implemented well, it can have a medium and long-term multiplier effect in terms of output, income and employment on the local economy. The study established the validity of NREGS as a programme that promotes labour-intensive sustainable development which can take the village economy towards full employment simultaneously engendering development processes.

Kumar (2008)[36] with his experience of workshops and studies in Jalore district of Rajasthan concluded that providing sufficient employment to the rural poor is still a challenge for the government. The government had launched a number of schemes for wage employment but none of these could fully achieve its goals. Over the years each scheme proved to be better than its predecessor because it moved towards the concept of decentralized planning and implementation and tried to introduce checks and balances to ensure transparency and accountability. He discussed that NREGA is not just a plan under a government order but a scheme governed by an Act which makes it unique and effective. NREGS will ultimately succeed in providing sufficient employment opportunities to rural households.

Mehrotra (2008)[37] examined the performance of NREG programme since its launch in mid-2005. He provided a summary of progress in certain areas and highlighted specific weaknesses. He also described the challenges that lie ahead and suggested how these can be overcome. If NREGA continued along the "business as usual" manner, the programme runs the risk of going towards the way of previous wage-employment programmes. But if the weaknesses as well as the flaws in the design of its implementation are addressed, it can serve as a beacon of light for other rural development programmes, raise the stagnating rural wages, push up productivity, stem the tide of rural-urban migration and have second and third round effects that go well beyond the policymakers' original design.

Sastry, Murthy and Kamath (2008)[38] conducted a study that throws light on the contrast between Andhra Pradesh and Karnataka in their implementation of NREGA. The two districts in Andhra Pradesh scored higher in awareness of rights under NREGA as well as the implementation of the Act. The study brought out several problems in the implementation process which could dilute the basic thrust of the Act. Having administrative processes in place for giving work and disbursing payments after work has been done should take priority over all other implementation issues like assessment of demand for work, kinds of work etc. Administrative issues like lack of field-staff have reduced the flow of funds to panchayats in the two districts of Karnataka which has resulted in average implementation of the Act. In both the states, the system for payment of wages is yet to be put into place. However, the perceived usefulness of NREGA among people is very high across all the four districts.

Singh (2008)[39] provided an assessment of the programmes under NREGA. He felt that the programmes have been encouraging and instrumental by providing seasonal jobs to those below poverty line. Regardless of the experience and learning of the past two years, NREGA will be implemented more effectively in the coming times. The scheme will continue to supplement the income of the beneficiaries, create durable assets and bring long term tangible benefits to rural India.

Administrative Staff College of India (2009)[40] conducted a study to understand MGNREGA's processes, procedures and impact. The study was oriented towards good practices that could be upscaled for strengthening the programme. Research was undertaken in six blocks of three districts of Anantpur, Adilabad and Guntur in Andhra Pradesh. The findings of the study included increase in ground-water in Anantpur as a result of the assets created, improved agricultural yields across all three districts and reduction in migration. The study also discussed the problems of delays in wage payments and poor quality of assets.

Centre for Research in Rural and Industrial Development (2009)[41] conducted an assessment of MGNREGA in three districts – Sirsa in Haryana,

Sirmaur in Himachal Pradesh and Hoshiarpur in Punjab to identify efficient management practices, procedures and processes. The study revealed that more than 62 percent of the selected panchayats in Sirsa district and nearly three-fourth panchayats in Sirmaur district had reported increased agricultural productivity due to MGNREGA activities. However, more than 87 percent panchayats of Hoshiarpur district reported that NREGA did not have any impact on agriculture and irrigation. Further, there was no change in in-migration of the workers in Sirmaur and Hoshiarpur districts while 37 percent panchayats in Sirsa district reported that in-migration had decreased due to NREGA works at their native place.

Dreze and Siddhartha (2009)[42] examined that NREGA workers had to put up with numerous infringements of their rights without being able to do much about it – lack of work, delays in wage payment, non-payment of minimum wages, absence of worksite facilities, etc. There is confusion about the operational requirements of the Act, absence of grievance redress system and lack of independent monitoring of the scheme. The Union Ministry of Rural Development does not even have a copy of each of the state schemes. With operational guidelines reduced to a "best practice" template, the NREGA is being implemented in a dangerous vacuum. Both Central and State governments have failed to put in place; any system to respond to people's complaints. Transparency and accountability rules have been drafted and discussed for months, without real performance. Further, there is lack of independent monitoring of NREGA, whether in states or at the Centre. The Central Employment Guarantee Council (CEGC) is virtually non-functional. Similarly, the condition of the State Employment Guarantee Councils is worst in most cases. The Central government bears a heavy responsibility for this state of affairs as NREGA is a National Act and about 90 per cent of the funds for works come from the Central Government.

Shah (2009)[43] observed that in the current recessionary phase, NREGA has provided money to the people in rural India. A mutual relationship between investment and income is catalysed by NREGA. Investment generates demand and income through the multiplier. Then, income stimulates investment via the accelerator. The rising incomes also improve capacity utilisation and happier expectations act as incentives for more investment. Under NREGA, farmers have come back to land they long abandoned, as increased output, in an atmosphere of renewed hope, spurs further investment. Converging NREGA with other programmes for rural livelihoods would carry this momentum forward in a positive upward spiral, which will broad-base the growth process via downstream multiplier-accelerator effects. Thus, a wage employment programme can be transformed into a source of sustainable livelihoods generating self-employment. However, NREGA has fallen short of its potential because the preparation needed for this revolutionary Act was not in place before it was launched. If a new architecture of implementation is put in place here, we could see not only the multiplier but a productivity enhancing accelerator in action that transforms livelihoods for millions of our poorest people, in a manner sustainable in both economic and ecological terms.

Maoist Regions

Banerjee and Saha (2010)[44] examined various developmental issues related to NREGA in the states of Jharkhand, Chhattisgarh and Orissa. They concluded that since these areas are under the influence of Maoists, the state intends to flush-out the anti-developmentalists by force and then proceed with the development. The field survey revealed that, the charge that the Maoists have been blocking developmental schemes, does not seem to hold much ground. Overall, NREGA is not a programme with which the Maoists in the backward areas have a tense relation as they have been encouraging the conduct of social audits, enforcement of minimum wages, etc. in these areas. The state has only to blame itself and its corrupt bureaucracy for flawed implementation of the programme.

Bhatia and Adhikari (2010)[45] discussed various hardships that NREGA workers had to face in case of banks or post offices located away from their homes. The study also highlighted the difficulties of the workers when the transactions are processed through the post offices as the post offices have poor record-keeping and are incapable of mass payments to NREGA wages.

Deininger and Liu (2010)[46] examined targeting of NREGs and its effect on welfare indicators. The data used is from 2500 households in Andhra Pradesh surveyed in 2004, i.e. before NREGS was conceived; in 2006 when NREGS was implemented in first phase and in 2008 when NREGS was implemented throughout the country. The data is combined with detailed administrative data on NREGS roll-out and work records. The findings revealed that NREGS targets the poor. However, a higher propensity of participation for households playing a leadership role in the village points towards some influence of village leaders in allocation of work. A lower participation propensity for illiterate and female-headed households also suggested that awareness of the programme or other constraints on the ability to supply labour continued to be relevant. The findings also pointed towards significant and positive impacts of NREGS participation on consumption expenditure, intake of energy and protein, and asset accumulation which suggested that the short-term effects of NREGS on participating households were positive and greater than programme cost.

Dey and Bedi (2010)[47] scrutinised selected aspects of the functioning of NREGS in Birbhum district of West Bengal. The study reported universal awareness about the NREGS. The job-cards have been made available to all those who applied for jobs and NREGS-related information is well maintained and relatively accessible. However, NREGS failed to fulfil its role of providing work when alternative employment opportunities are limited. The state of West Bengal has limited capacity to generate employment. There is a need for an innovative thinking on how to use the available resources to create jobs and construct useful rural infrastructure. Focusing, as in the case of Birbhum, only on excavation and re-excavation of ponds is unlikely to lead to the development of useful rural infrastructure or sustain job creation.

Sharma (2010)[48] critically examined the Mahatma Gandhi National Rural Employment Guarantee Act as a rights-based legal framework for guaranteeing basic livelihood security to rural households. It examined the legal design and policy innovations and the extent to which they facilitated the fulfilment of the objectives of the Act. The discussion of MGNREGA in terms of its design and key factors that constrain and facilitate the achievement of its objectives engages several questions. It suggests possibilities of reviewing some aspects of the Act as well as offers insights to similar policy exercises.

Ghosh (2011)[49] compared wage differentials between MGNREGA activities and other wage employment activities across five districts of West Bengal. The pattern of migration from rural to urban areas is also compared. The MGNREGA wage was found to be higher than the wage for agricultural workers in the state and this led to distortion of the wage labour market. The study postulated that the net effect of MGNREGA has been negligible.

Imbert and Papp (2011)[50] examined equilibrium labour market impacts of NREGA by comparing the gradual roll-out of the programme in districts where MGNREGA was implemented earlier as compared to those that received it later. The study revealed that due to the introduction of the programme, public employment increased by three days per prime-aged person per month more in early districts than in the rest of country. Casual wages increased by 4.5 percent and private sector work for low-skill workers fell by 1.6 percent. It emphasised that public sector hire people out of the private sector work and thus increase private sector wages. The welfare gains increase in private sector wages are large in comparison to the gains received solely by programme participants. The study concluded that the equilibrium labour market impacts are first-order concern when work-fare programmes are compared to other anti-poverty programmes.

Jha, Gaiha and Pandey (2011)[51] explored the issue of real income transfers and net of the opportunity cost of time under the National Rural

Employment Guarantee Scheme for three States, namely, Rajasthan, Andhra Pradesh and Maharashtra. The study also compared the per capita monthly expenditures of participants with and without alternative employment opportunities in the absence of NREGS as well as the determinants of such opportunities. The distribution of such net transfers across households as well as the distribution of benefits across villages in the three states is also discussed. In general, net transfers under the NREGS are quite modest. The study elaborated that the accurate measurement of such transfers also matters in an anti-poverty strategy.

Kajale and Shroff (2011)[52] made an assessment of MGNREGA with respect to the extent of employment generation, wage differentials, rural-urban migration, asset creation, determinants of participation and implementation in five districts of Maharashtra. The study indicated that the State has not been able to show satisfactory performance in terms of employment generated and assets created. However, in places where it was implemented well, there has been a positive impact on food security, reducing poverty and out-migration.

Khosla (2011)[53] attempted to measure the effect of caste reservation policies on the provision of public goods and services in gram panchayats in Andhra Pradesh. The study found that the effect of reservation varied tremendously in different social, political and institutional contexts, shedding light on the conflicting results of similar studies. It provided important lessons for future research and policy about the caste-political conditions in which reservation can produce positive or negative results.

Kumar and Maruthi (2011)[54] assessed the performance of MGNREGA in terms of employment generation, rural-urban migration, asset creation, determinants of participation and implementation in five districts of Karnataka. The main findings of the study were that the household size, land owned, wage rate, age of members, education and other work opportunities were the major factors determining MGNREGA participation. The wage rate has increased more than 50 percent in the agricultural sector and 75–100 percent in non-agricultural sector after the implementation of MGNREGA. Around 55 percent of the participants stated that NREGA has enhanced food security by providing employment while around 37 percent agreed that NREGA provided protection against poverty.

Morgan (2011)[55] indicated that the advent of NREGA has resulted in a significant structural break in rural wage inflation. Pre-NREGA, nominal wages in the rural economy grew at an average annual rate of 2.7 percent. However post-NREGA, average wage inflation almost quadrupled to 9.7 percent between 2006 and 2009. Between January 2010 and May 2011, annual nominal wage growth was almost 20 percent. But even these averages are misleading, because nominal wages have shown a sharp and secular acceleration over the preceding 18 months, with wage inflation reaching almost 22 percent by May 2011. While the increase in wages in 2011 is partially a result of NREGA wages being indexed, a sharp acceleration of wages was evident in 2010, even before indexation was announced or came into effect.

Mukherjee and Sinha (2011)[56] analysed the impact of NREGA on rural labour market, income of poor households and overall agricultural production. It is seen that the income from NREGA alone can be a substantial part of the target income of the poor. Thus, the poor may exhibit a backward bending supply curve of labour which may lead to an aggregate reduction in agricultural output. This adverse production-effect, can happen even when NREGA activities lead to a moderate improvement in agricultural productivity.

Sankaran (2011)[57] observed that for several decades there had been an unresolved debate about the feasibility of having a national minimum wage. However, the National Rural Employment Guarantee Act with its provision for a country-wide wage rate has placed the possibility to do so squarely on the agenda. The NREGA wage rate must logically be a need-based national minimum wage under the Minimum Wages Act. Declaring a need-based minimum wage rate under NREGA which is linked to the schedule of rates allows for sufficient flexibility to account for regional/ geographical variation. There can be no dispute that ensuring a basic minimum for a decent life is a first charge upon any government. The crisis around NREGA wage rate can be an opportunity to rationalise wages both under NREGA and the Minimum Wages Act, 1948 and bring about a true need-based minimum wage which is a necessary in the informal economy.

World Bank (2011)[58] assessed that India's urge in growth and rapid expansion in public spending in the past decade has created new possibilities for its social protection system. The report used existing and new data sources including analysis of administrative data, several rounds of the National Sample Survey data, social protection survey undertaken for the report in 2006 in the rural areas of Orissa, Madhya Pradesh and Karnataka; dedicated surveys on social pensions in Karnataka and Rajasthan in 2005 and 2006 respectively and a living standards survey conducted in Jharkhand in 2005.

Dutta, et.al., (2012)[59] analysed the data from India's National Sample Survey for 2009-10 that revealed considerable unmet demand for work in all states. The study reported that poorer families tend to have more demand for work under the scheme. Despite the unmet demand, the self-targeting mechanism allows it to reach to poor families and backward castes. However, the extent of the unmet demand is greater in the poorest states where the scheme is needed the most. Labour-market responses to the scheme are likely to be weak. The scheme is attracting poor women into the workforce, although the local-level rationing processes favour men.

Government of India (2012a)[60] set up a committee to examine the ways in which Operational Guidelines of MGNREGA could be revised. The revision was needed to expand the list of permissible works under MGNREGA in order to strengthen the synergy between MGNREGA and rural livelihoods; respond to the demands of the states for greater location-specific flexibility in permissible works; help improve the ecological balance in rural India and provide a cleaner and healthier environment to its people. The revision was also required to suggest procedural changes that would help strengthen the demand-driven character of MGNREGA; strengthen the participatory planning and implementation process under MGNREGA so that the programme could result in the creation of durable assets and an increase in farm productivity. The changes would infuse the programme with greater efficiency and help overcome the major complaints under the programme such as delays in payment of wages and develop effective mechanisms for eliminating the scope of corruption under the programme.

Verma (2012)[61] examined that MGNREGS is influenced by the rural farm and non-farm labour markets. The note summarised the lessons learnt from the field studies undertaken in 2009-10 and 2010-11 by 50 post-graduate students from the Institute of Rural Management, Anand deployed by the International Water Management Institute to understand how MGNREGA and village labour markets interact. The survey was conducted in 26 villages in 11 districts of nine states in 2009 and 13 villages in 11 districts of nine states in 2010. Further, village leaders, labourers and farmers in 75 villages were interviewed from Gujarat, Rajasthan, Bihar and Kerala.

Ravi and Engler (2013)[62] analysed the impact of Mahatma Gandhi National Rural Employment Guarantee Scheme (MGNREGS) on food security, savings and health outcomes of 1064 households from 200 villages of Medak district, Andhra Pradesh over two years. The findings indicated that NREGS increased the monthly per capita expenditure on food by Rs 25.8 (9.6 percent) and on non-food consumables by Rs 11.17 (23 per cent). The programme also improved food security by a significant reduction in the number of meals foregone by households per week. The probability of holding savings for a rural household raised by 21 percent and the per capita amount saved increased by Rs 18.60. There was a reduction of 12 percent in reported depression and improvements in mental health indicators. However, no significant changes in physical health outcomes were reported. The results showed that in the initial years, the programme predominantly attracted 78 percent of non-agricultural labour as NREGS participation was concentrated during lean agricultural season. Over the period of time, the programme attracted 55.3 percent households that would have participated in agriculture labour had NREGS not existed.

Ravallion (2014)[63] reported that the Central government's proposal to decrease mandatory share of unskilled wages in MGNREGA from 60 percent to 51 percent by allowing a greater share to skilled labour and materials is not required. Such changes may not solve the main problems relating to effective implementation of the scheme. For example, Bihar, one of the poorest states of the country, has the lowest participation in the scheme. The scheme would have a large impact on rural poverty in Bihar, bringing the poverty rate down by at least 14 percentage points in 2010 under the idealized conditions. However, in reality, the actual impact on the poverty rate was around one percentage point. The poor families are neither getting the work they want under the scheme nor getting the full wages due to them in the state. The people have to give up other income-earning activity in order to take up work under MGNREGA. However, the unmet demand for work is the single most important factor for the gap between actual performance and the scheme's potential impact on poverty. A study found very low public awareness among people about what needs to be done to obtain work. A number of constraints like poor implementation capacity, weak financial management and defective monitoring and grievance-response systems were identified. MGNREGA needs to be focused on backward areas only. Instead of bringing changes in the design, realizing the scheme's potential is required on two fronts. First, administrative capacities for implementation and monitoring should be improved. Second, there needs to be greater public awareness of the rights and rules of the scheme, more active public mobilization and better mechanisms for following up on problems.

Sampath and S. (2015)[64] asserted that critics have branded MGNREGA as wasteful and ineffective creating poor quality works. This criticism draws support from the urban middle class. However, it is not true considering the vast number of research done over the world branding the programme as pro-growth and success as an anti-poverty programme. The study reported findings from four states, namely, Uttar Pradesh, Telangana, Bihar and Chhattisgarh. It stated that the works under MGNREGA have helped in the creation of rural assets and infrastructure. The programme has boosted agricultural productivity through development of wasteland, construction of storage facilities and work sheds. It cited other research studies to quote positives of the programme like improved ground water levels, increased availability of drinking water for humans and livestock. However, inspite of innumerable pros, the programme suffers from many cons like delayed wage payments resulting in decrease in demand for work which may lead to untimely death of the programme.

World Bank (2015)[65] reported that a growing number of developing countries are investing in social safety nets to improve the lives and livelihoods of billions of poor and vulnerable people, yet around 55 percent of the world's poor or 773 million people with acute needs still lack safety net coverage especially in lower-income countries and in urban areas. It examined that more than 1.9 billion people in 136 low and middle income countries are on beneficiary rolls of social safety net programs. In Africa, the number of countries setting up social safety net programmes has doubled over the past three years. But three quarters of the poorest people in low and lower-middle income countries and more than one-third of the poorest people in middle income countries lack safety net coverage and remain at risk. These programmes include cash and in-kind transfers targeted to poor and vulnerable households with the goal of protecting families from the impact of economic shocks, natural disasters and other crises; ensuring that children grow up healthy, well-fed, and can stay in school and learn; empowering women and girls and creating jobs. MGNREGA has been ranked as the world's largest public works programme, providing social security net to almost 15 percent of the country's population. It reported that India is among the five middle-income countries running the world's largest social safety net programmes.

1.8(b) People's Participation and Civil Society Organizations

Bhatnagar and Chib (1987)[66] pleaded that unless the masses are involved through active participation, rural poverty cannot be eliminated from India. They advocated the replacement of "official centralization" by "public decentralization" and also self-reliance through local initiative, participation and mobilization of existing resources. Rural development would be meaningless if distributive justice does not reach the poor segments of rural population. Central leadership or coordination for planning purposes, decentralization and participation at the local level for implementation purposes, training of manpower resources are some of the characteristics within which rural development programmes should be designed and implemented. The limited nature of resources has forced the planners to work out some order of priorities. Further, the community is the best judge of its needs and requirements and it alone knows how these can be fulfilled. Therefore, the masses need to be trained so that they can expand their resources for a better quality of life.

Shah (2005)[67] believed that the 2004 Employment Guarantee Bill needs to be modified in order to realize its objectives. The critics and supporters of the programme should be able to reach a compromise on the identification of beneficiaries, coverage and wage rates. The Employment Guarantee Act is incomplete without the Right to Information Act. The people's organizations at the grass-root level have a critical role to play in mobilizing people to deploy the powers inherent in their right to information. The grass-root organizations need to assist gram sabhas to reflect the will of the most disadvantaged and needy sections within the village.

Joseph (2006)[68] discussed various non-political outfits involved in the introduction of Maharashtra's Employment Guarantee Scheme. These organizations understand the potentialities of Employment Guarantee Scheme as a means to address various issues relating the marginalized sections of society including dalits, women, tribals and the landless. These non-party political formations engaged with the state in defining the scope and reach of Employment Guarantee Scheme. However, over a period of time the definition of Employment Guarantee Scheme was enlarged by these groups to ensure the employment of the poor.

Patel (2006)[69] presented an analysis of the research conducted by University of Pune on the implementation of the Employment Guarantee Scheme (EGS) in Maharashtra over three decades beginning from the 1970's. The analysis of the growth and developments that emerged in the context of the programme is from the sociological and political perspective. The growth is studied in three phases. During the first phase the EGS was able to initiate radical political consciousness among the poor. During the second phase this political mobilization of the oppressed became a means to develop and organize tribal, dalit and women movements in the rural areas. These movements developed a structural critique of the state and questioned its efforts to guarantee comprehensive development for all. During the third phase, however, these movements started declining and EGS was limited to a few areas in the state (top ten districts). This secondary data based analysis concluded that by allowing and encouraging people's mobilization, EGS has the potential for generating movements that can make a critical assessment of the state, its development policies and the class interests it represents. It can turn out to be a radical instrument of social change.

Shah (2007)[70] assessed that as India celebrates sixty years of Indian democracy with millions of people hungry and insecure, the reach and quality of our political process is worrisome. People expect their representatives to work to guard their interests honestly and effectively. But most of the people's movements have resorted to violence as their voice is not heard; they believe that violence is the only language an insensitive state listens to. However, National Rural Employment Guarantee Act (NREGA) is best seen as an attempt to provide a big push in India's regions of distress. It is an employment guarantee programme that focuses on asset-creating works which are labour-intensive and could tackle problems of unemployment, poverty, environmental regeneration and agricultural growth in on stroke. He opined that for NREGA to be able to realize its potential the role of civil society organizations in the monitoring of the programme is also critical. He envisioned a society where every individual participates and benefits from the development process.

Raghavan, et. al., (2008)[71] focused on the implementation of NREGS scheme in the state of West Bengal. The aim was to find some other successful models which were being implemented by non-governmental organizations over the years that could be implemented through NREGS. The study was conducted in twenty-four villages across three districts of Purulia, Birbhum and North 24 Parganas. An NGO which has been working in these districts and has successfully developed eco-friendly, economically profitable and sustainable livelihood models as pilot projects in these villages was also involved. The study focused on the models implemented by the NGO and analysed on how these models could be integrated with NREGS. It gave a comparative study of these models vis-à-vis the models implemented through NREGS. The study gave recommendations which could be implemented in a centralized way as well as measures that can be implemented at Panchayat level to address the problems uncovered.

Central Institute of Fisheries Education (2009)[72] undertook an assessment of MGNREGA in two districts of Maharashtra, namely, Thane and Akola. The study found that women, SCs and STs have significant representation in MGNREGA works because of the increased employment opportunities available at the village level. The constraints identified in the study were unemployment allowance not paid, delay in wage payments, lack of work-site facilities and so on.

Hazarika (2009)[73] studied the impact of the National Rural Employment Guarantee Programme on women's empowerment and gender inequality and identified major constraints on their access to productive employment opportunities through the employment guarantee programme in two selected districts of Assam. The gendered distribution of assets and the resultant fallout on women substantially limits the national efforts at overcoming poverty, thus indicating the urgent need for addressing issues relating to persistent gender discrimination and factors affecting women's ownership and control of assets. The study highlighted the impact of the programme on the lives of women workers and gender relations. The benefits reported include income gain, social empowerment, more say in intra-household decision making and creation of community assets. The study concluded by identifying certain barriers to women's access to MGNREGA and important learning lessons for policy.

Ambasta (2010)[74] examined the experience of MGNREGA to reveal how the programme has fallen short of its potential because of inadequate support structures. The author suggested reforms in MGNREGA to realise its true potential in the form of adequate deployment of human resource, detailed use of Information Technology and proper mechanism for grievance redressal. He further argued that grass-root mobilisation is necessary for rural development and empowerment of the poor to take place. Hence, the role of civil society is important for grass-root mobilisation.

IIT Chennai (2010)[75] assessed MGNREGS activities with relevance to six key aspects, i.e. effective tracking of job requests, wage difference across districts, impact on agriculture, high participation of women in MGNREGS, human rights and MGNREGA, effectiveness of gram sabha in decision making and reasons for low Below Poverty Line (BPL) participation in MGNREGA. The findings revealed that MGNREGA has benefited a major section of rural people by providing 100 days of employment to the households. It also highlighted best practices including prompt wage payment, protection of the rights of rural women and provision of helpline.

IRMA (2010)[76] reported that MGNREGA has provided a supplementary source of income to families without discriminating between men and women. This is the reason for higher participation of women in the programme. The study also reported that MGNREGA has enhanced food security and employment opportunities for the rural people. However, a better mechanism for durability and sustainability of assets created under the scheme needs to be ensured.

Pankaj and Tankha (2010)[77] examined the empowerment effects of NREGS in rural areas of Bihar, Jharkhand, Rajasthan and Himachal Pradesh. They argued that women workers had gained more as individuals because of the paid employment opportunity under NREGS. As a community, they had been slow in realising the potential benefits of the scheme. Participation in the gram sabha meetings, frequent interactions with government officials and PRI representatives and access to Banks and Post-offices were accessed in a limited manner. Increased participation in procedural aspects and greater control over the types and management of assets could increase social and community benefits. Despite the difficulties and hurdles for women, prospects lie in their collective mobilisation, especially in laggard states.

Srivastava and Srivastava (2010)[78] observed that while rural women's employment has grown over the decades, they are still largely self-employed in agriculture. They are also subjected to various forms of discrimination which gives them a lower wage compared to men. Education may not positively influence a women's participation in work, but for women who are in the workforce, education is the most important determinant of better quality non-agricultural work. Women autonomy, measured in terms of control over land, mobility and a willingness to join self-help groups enables them to move into non-agricultural jobs. The paper calls for policy interventions to increase work opportunities, enhance wages for rural women workers and bridge the gaps between different classes of women hailing from different social and economic backgrounds.

Azam (2011)[79] assessed causal impacts of NREGA on public works participation, labour force participation and real wages of casual workers across Indian districts during various phases. The author found that there is a strong gender dimension to the impacts of NREGA. There is a positive impact on the labour force participation which is mainly driven by an impact on female labour force participation. NREGA also has a significant positive impact on the wages of female casual workers. The real wages of female casual workers increased 8 percent more in NREGA districts as compared to non-NREGA districts. However, the impact of NREGA on wages of casual male workers has been only one percent.

Bordoloi (2011)[80] studied the impact of MGNREGA in five districts of Assam on wage differentials and migration. The study also assessed the scheme's processes and procedures. The study concluded that MGNREGA does not have a significant impact on migration as it is unable to meet the demand from wage seekers. However, the scheme has reduced gender differentials in wages. Further, a majority of beneficiaries perceive the assets created under MGNREGA as beneficial.

Chandrashekar and Ghosh (2011)[81] reported that inspite of all its flaws, limitations and difficulties NREGS have had positive affects on women workers in rural labour markets. The study analysed NSSO's 64th Round data to show that real wages, specifically for women increased in the rural areas after implementation of NREGA. The casual wages in agriculture remained constant in comparison to 2004-05. The labour costs account for less than half and usually around one-third of the total agricultural costs. MGNREGA had positive effects on women workers in rural labour markets. It has caused gender gaps to come down. Before the scheme was implemented, these were not really anticipated as likely outcomes. But this positive impact may have longer term beneficial effects on social and economic dynamics in rural India.

Dasgupta and Sudarshan (2011)[82] examined that women's participation in NREGA has been increasing. The state-wise participation of the women in NREGA is positively correlated to women's participation in rural areas, though in NREGA it is often higher than other forms of recorded work so far. Further, women's participation is negatively correlated with the existing gender wage gap in unskilled agricultural labour. As women's actual wages in comparison to men is lower in the private sector, therefore women are flocking to work in this government programme. This may result in increased bargaining power for women, thus playing a critical role in reducing gender disparities in the labour market. The study also elaborated that the outcomes of NREGA are mediated by the intervening institutions including both the gendered nature of the labour market and the efficacy of the local government.

Holmes, Rath and Sadana (2011)[83] assessed the extent to which MGNREGA integrates a gender-sensitive approach to public works programmes in Madhya Pradesh. The study revealed that women's employment in MGNREGA has improved the economic status of women and enhanced their decision-making power to some extent. The study assessed that the MGNREGA design and implementation should be strengthened to avoid exacerbating gender inequalities. It concluded that supporting women's participation in decision-making will empower women and enhance gender equality.

Hirway and Batabyal (2012)[84] revealed that MGNREGA has been found to enhance women's empowerment in the village of Movasa, Gujarat, through guaranteed daily wage employment, equal pay, mobilisation of collective strength and active participation in gram sabha and social audit meetings. However, MGNREGA has also added to women's time burden and drudgery. A lot needs to be done to empower women to become active participants as well as real beneficiaries of the programme.

Narayanan, et.al. (2014)[85] conducted a survey of over 4100 MGNREGA works and over 4800 randomly selected users across 100 villages in 20 districts in Maharashtra. The study verified the existence of the assets and user perceptions of the problems and benefits associated with the work. Nearly 87% of the works existed and more than 75% of them were directly or indirectly related to agriculture. Other works were mainly related to rural roads that connect habitations to farms and provided access to agricultural markets. The study also found that 92% of the randomly selected users were farmers; half of them were small and marginal farmers. 90% of respondents considered the works very useful or somewhat useful; only 8% felt the works were useless. The study further reported that when people played a part in deciding the work, they were more likely to rank it as useful and well-maintained. The study concluded that the works were supportive of agriculture and of small and marginal farmers. However, there was a scope to improve the design of assets and inclusive work selection process.

Tewari (2015)[86] reported that the political parties would target rural population in the upcoming Bihar polls. An analysis of MGNREGA showed that the state has consistently performed worse than an already dismal national average in the last five years. As per the Socio Economic Caste Census of 2011, 88.82 percent households in Bihar were rural, second only to Assam. Bihar has remained below the national average in parameters such as average days of work provided to households in a year, timely wage payments and women's participation. In terms of the average person-days of work provided to each household, the state has 39, 45, 42, 34 and 28 person-days in the years 2011-12 to 2015-16 as against the corresponding national average of 43, 46, 46, 40, 29. Further, the proportion of wage payments made within 15 days from 2012-13 to 2015-16 has been 29.8, 26.8, 17.4 and 23.3 percent as compared to the corresponding national average of 50, 50, 27 and 48.5 percent. Bihar was also below the national average as far as women's participation is concerned, however, it was above the mandatory requirement of 33 percent of women workers.

1.8(c) Management of Human Resources and Capacities of Implementing Agencies

Raghava (1980)[87] concluded that the success of rural development through democratic decentralization largely depends on two basic factors – the emergence and growth of egalitarian power structure in democratic institutions at the grass root and the economically viable size of these institutions. He investigated these two issues at the level of village panchayats in Tanakur district of Karnataka and concluded that the larger panchayats having population of more than four-thousand would be economically viable to implement rural development programmes. He suggested that such a unit of four thousand persons should form the basis for a panchayat, a cooperative or any other institution dealing with rural development.

Prasad (2003)[88] stated that earlier rural development was taken to be synonymous with the agricultural development. However, it is equally concerned with the development of infrastructure. Income and employment opportunities have to be generated in the rural areas to exploit labour and generate development. "Rural prosperity will not be judged merely by link roads, electric connections, Green and White Revolutions and the like". Employment is a vital indicator of rural development, particularly in thickly populated countries like India. But the schemes like TRYSEM (Training of Rural Youth for Self Employment) and NREP (National Rural Employment Programme) failed to deliver goods. Besides the territorial overlapping of the programmes like RLEGP (Rural Landless Employment Guarantee Programme), short duration of training, insufficient incentives and their different funding patterns created considerable difficulties not only in effective monitoring but also thwarted achievements of the programmes. The beneficiaries themselves have to be activated on local resources to move forward with the aid and assistance of outside agencies in such a way that the role of the agencies decreases progressively. The local community has to be given the power and responsibility to understand its problems and work unitedly for their solutions. Also, research on rural development must not begin with a prior notion of what constitutes rural development and how it is best attained. Rather it should attempt to find out what rural people themselves desire in terms of content and goals.

Shah (2004)[89] discussed that the proposed employment guarantee programme will generate work for the poorest. It is also an opportunity to revive public investment in agriculture, tackle the prevailing environmental crisis that is gripping rural India. The proposed legislation should not put in place a weak and diluted job programme. The NREGA can become a new major instrument for galvanizing PRIs in India. The role of grass-root civil society institutions is also crucial.

Bhaduri (2005)[90] concluded it is a misfortune for both the theory and practice of economic policy in India that a coherent scheme about how to take advantage of an expanding domestic market involving the poor and the marginalized has not been worked out yet in this era of globalization. The expansion in purchasing power can come from public works financed initially, if necessary, through deficits of central and state budgets. The panchayats must have the full financial authority to design and implement these projects. Transparency and the right to information at all levels would be the mechanism through which our political democracy is brought closer to our as yet grossly distorted economic democracy.

Vaidyanathan (2005)[91] stated that the protagonists of the National Rural Employment Guarantee Scheme favour entrusting the programme to panchayats and incorporating provisions to this end in the national law. But this aspect is not articulated as strongly and emphatically in the public debate on issues relating to scale and coverage. The campaign for a wider and better funded NREGS must be combined with a campaign to generate strong public opinion and mobilize elected panchayats all over the country to bring pressure on the central and state governments to strengthen democratic panchayats and empower them to plan and implement all local development programmes.

Vaidyanathan (2005a)[92] analyzed the Standing Committee's recommendations on NREG that called for basic changes in the concept and design envisaged in the draft bill. They were essential and imperative if the programme was to be effective. However, the concurrence of the state governments and their willingness to abide by the operational implications of the legislation was essential. The gaps and weaknesses were needed to be seriously addressed, clarified and rectified in recasting the draft bill. The scheme was needed to be effective in achieving its immediate objectives of generating additional employment for the needy segment and also empowering panchayats to play an effective role in promoting local development through a democratic process.

Aiyar and Samji (2006)[93] concluded that the earlier wage employment programmes failed due to common problems of ineffective targeting, leakages and poor quality asset creation. Therefore, while developing rules and guidelines for the implementation of National Rural Employment Guarantee Act, 2005 more attention should be given to the lessons learnt from past experiences. This Act has the potential to strengthen social security and community mobilization, ensure better responsiveness of the local governments to community needs and priorities and most of all enhance governance outcomes. They attempted to articulate some key design principles that could strengthen the effectiveness of the new Act.

Hooja and Parnami (2007)[94] discussed that for a country like India, there continues to be a strong moral imperative to look after the development of rural people and rural areas. It is the rural human and physical resources, rural produce as well as demand for goods and services which are the major engines for growth. Rural hinterlands form a unified system with urban centres and neither can grow nor develop without the other. Thus, in common usage, in India, the term development administration has got linked with rural development, so that administration for rural development tends to be referred to as development administration. Rural development is very broad in terms of scope and involves changes in attitudes, customs, beliefs, values; employment patterns and magnitudes, productivity and production; living standards; policy initiatives related to land and water, forests, physical as well as social infrastructure; backward areas and deprived sections of society; food security; self-sufficiency and self-sustenance; people's involvement and participation and roles of community-based organizations. Whether we consider development administration or rural development, the focus remains primarily on the people and secondarily on the area development.

Comptroller and Auditor General of India (2008)[95] undertook an audit of MGNREGA to evaluate the effectiveness of the states in implementing MGNREGA in comparison to previous wage employment programmes. CAGI conducted audit in 26 states in the country. The audit noticed several procedural deviations by the states with the regard to the operational guidelines of the scheme like non-appointment of the functionaries, non-payment of unemployment allowance, delay in wage payments, etc. The report highlighted the need to appoint the requisite number of functionaries for the proper implementation of the programme.

Dey (2008)[96] pointed out that a big challenge to the Act is the need for adequate staff to carry out its requirements and come up with meaningful productive employment as physical space for earth-works and traditional public works gets used up. He questioned if the Act can provide an opportunity for building a pool of skilled workers and managers whose abilities get upgraded because of NREGA works. He recommended reserving three percent funds for productive employment of the physically challenged.

Dhar (2008)[97] observed that India's labour force is growing at a rate of 2.5 percent annually, but employment is growing only at 2.3 percent. The country is faced with the challenge of not only absorbing new entrants to the job market estimated at seven million people every year, but also clearing the backlog. The seventies and the eighties saw the emergence of special schemes like NREP and RLEGP to provide wage employment through public works programmes and schemes. The country would also have to meet the challenge of increasing the skilled work force from the present five percent to about fifty percent.

Rao (2008)[98] evaluated the significance of NREGA and called it a lifeline for the vulnerable sections. NREGA added a dimension of equality in the growth process. It created a rights based framework for wage employment programmes by conferring legal entitlements and made the government accountable for providing employment in a time bound manner. Also, by prioritizing natural resource management and emphasizing the creation of durable assets, it has the potential of becoming a growth engine for substantial development of an agriculture-based economy.

Action for Food Production (2009)[99] assessed 37 MGNREGA works in 28 villages and 10 gram panchayats in Chainpur block of district Gumla in Jharkhand. The MGNREGA works were randomly selected. It stressed upon the need to learn from various works carried out and their effectiveness in supporting sustainable livelihood at the community level. The study also highlighted the priority to select smaller structures for soil and water conservation, selection of need-based works, increased public ownership of infrastructure created, effective participation of villagers in the decision-making processes, orientation of functionaries and coordination among line departments.

Ambasta (2009)[100] observed that programmes like NREGS need an independent body to look after Information Technology, human resource development, evaluation, social audit and grievance redress, without which quality outcomes of the programme would remain elusive. He called for setting up of a National Authority for NREGS (NAN) as an autonomous body. According to him, NAN would be charged with the key functions of human resource development (deployment as well as capacity-building) and streamlining Information Technology systems to facilitate effective monitoring and social audit. For the flagship programme to be effective, it needs to be programmed to succeed. Therefore, a central anchoring agency such as NAN may well hold the password to such a programme, in the course of time, unlocking the gates to let the necessary changes in.

Birner, et.al., (2010)[101] conducted a study of two districts in Bihar and indicated various governance issues in the implementation of NREGA like misappropriation of funds, lack of capacity due to staff shortages and lack of training. The study also highlighted the problems of elite capture of MGNREGA works, exclusion in issuing of job-cards, lack of awareness and capacity among rural people.

Centre for Education and Research Development (2010)[102] conducted a study at Chittoor and Vizianagaram districts in Andhra Pradesh and Shahdol and Seoni districts in Madhya Pradesh to assess the benefits and challenges of MGNREGA and studied the existing management practices. It recommended empowering vulnerable groups through awareness generation and extending out-reach in participation. The study also recommended best practices for other states to follow like mobile musters and muster roll maintenance, weekly cycle of opening and closure of musters, fixed daily activity schedule in generating pay-orders/system of weekly cycle and the system of wage cum withdrawal slips. Public private partnership may be explored for enhancing awareness levels of wage seekers and the masses on the patterns of Andhra Pradesh.

Institute for Development of Youth, Women and Child (2010)[103] conducted a study in four districts of two states of Madhya Pradesh and Rajasthan. It critically evaluated development effectiveness, asset creation and livelihood sustainability through NREGS. The findings suggested that NREGS has substantially improved the livelihood scenario of rural India by providing multiple livelihood options. The average wage has increased resulting in the creation of more flexible and fair labour market in rural areas. The study also reported that the average income of the households has increased considerably. The study has evaluated nearly 580 NREGS works on varied parameters. The structures were found to be sustainable, e.g., the wells, check dams and anicuts were built with right quality and technical inputs. The study also showed a positive trend in agricultural productivity in villages.

Dreze (2011a)[104] undertook a study in Bheramgarh block of district Dantewada in Chhattisgarh. The author identified various constraints in the implementation of MGNREGA including, suspension of works in rainy season, shortage of staff, low awareness levels and hoarding of job-cards, etc. in the area of study. The essay is based on a report prepared for the Central Employment Guarantee Council (CEGC) in September 2008.

Mangatter (2011)[105] explored whether MGNREGA has strengthened rural self-employment in Bolpur subdivision (West Bengal) or not. The study assumed that additional incomes stimulate rural demand and facilitate investments and assets created during MGNREGA works can be used for remunerative activities. Only 17 percent of the sampled households could use MGNREGA assets or other incomes to run, expand or start a rural business. However, the investigations also revealed the causes for MGNREGA's limited impact on rural entrepreneurship and showed under what conditions the Act could become a catalyst for rural business initiatives. The study concluded that MGNREGA incomes must become more reliable and women self-help groups must be involved in the planning of MGNREGA works.

Bonner, et.al., (2012)[106] compared MGNREGA performance in the states of Tamil Nadu and Uttar Pradesh with regard to the influence of socio-economic characteristics of the states, political influences and organisational capacity of respective state governments. The study indicated that apart from leadership commitment, state-level politics have minimal impact on MGNREGA's implementation. Rather, it is the strength of the district, block, and gram panchayat's administrative and organisational capacity that appears to be a determining factor of success. In Tamil Nadu, MGNREGA is performing well due to effective administrative capacity. In contrast to Tamil Nadu, Uttar Pradesh has entrusted significant responsibility to staff at the gram panchayat level. However, gram panchayats are often not equipped with sufficient resources, skills or experience to effectively carry out their functions. The study also highlighted obstacles to MGNREGA's implementation in both Tamil Nadu and Uttar Pradesh like the states' reluctance to disburse unemployment allowance to workers and the questionable productivity of assets created. Further, the higher participation of women in Tamil Nadu is primarily attributed to cultural factors, effective state and local institutions, Self-Help Groups and high wage differences in private sectors. On the contrary, the low participation in Uttar Pradesh is mainly due to caste and religion.

Aiyar (2014)[107] evaluated that although the demand for work under MGNREGA in poorer states like Bihar and Uttar Pradesh was high, richer states like Andhra Pradesh and Tamil Nadu were able to provide more employment. Poorer states spend lower per-capita on MGNREGA, have higher vacancies, lower staff motivation with limited technical capacities and were therefore, unable to meet the demands of the programme. This could be resolved by building the institutional capabilities of local governments to deliver the scheme. There were also serious problems of corruption and weak implementation both in poor and non-poor states. The poor often received less than their share of wages, payment was delayed and corruption in the use of materials in MGRNEGA work-sites was on the increase. Therefore, greater use of materials would only enhance rather than reduce corruption. However, MGNREGA had witnessed a proliferation of experiments, mostly in better governed states, from creating improved financial management systems to using technology-enabled banking solutions like smart cards, social audits and building grievance redressal systems. The focus must be on evaluating these experiments and drawing lessons to improve administration in the poorly governed states.

Sharma (2015)[108] analyzed the influence of MGNREGS on agricultural operations and cultivation costs. The author revealed that focus of MGNREGS on community works could be reoriented to proactively promote improvements on the landholdings of small and marginal farmers through the creation of durable assets, which in turn, would be beneficial for agricultural productivity and income. The thrust of the MGNREGS in the past eight years has been to open up works on community lands. The proportion of works taken up on private lands in 2014 was only 11 percent. The impetus to agriculture could be triggered through greater asset creation on individual farms. This would incentivize small holders to take up works leading to restoration and revitalization of their own farmland, higher productivity and therefore, more agricultural employment. The productive value of small landholdings could be enhanced further with material and technical inputs from effective convergence with other ongoing agricultural development programmes such as the National Food Security Mission, the horticulture mission, Rashtriya Krishi Vikas Yojana, the National Rural Livelihoods Mission and the National Agro-Forestry Policy.

Khera (2016)[109] examined MGNREGA on completion of ten years of the programme. It provided evidence of assets created under the programme and their importance for the rural people. The best practices cited were related to different types of works undertaken in the villages throughout the country in the form of clearing water supply channels, de-silting and deepening of ponds, digging irrigation channels, rural connectivity works, flood protection works, fish farm ponds, plantation works, solid waste management and so on. The positive experiences demonstrated the potential of doing useful works through MGNREGA.

1.8(d) Transparency and Accountability

Singh (1999)[110] emphasized that to achieve the objectives of rural development policy efficiently, a set of appropriate instruments like institutional credit, creation of new institutions, changes in the institutional framework etc. needs to be identified. He also emphasized upon the human resource development through education, training, health care and creation of environment for the full utilization of untapped human resources. It is necessary to induct fresh, professionally trained rural managers at all levels and reorient the existing staff engaged in rural development administration through short-term training courses. While the government implemented a number of programmes to improve the socio-economic condition of the poor, but there exists a number of rural development programmes and policies with unresolved objectives and divergent approaches. The review of the failure of these programmes revealed the gaps in their implementation, monitoring and evaluation. The need is to treat rural development as a joint venture of public, corporate, cooperative and private sectors. Panchayati Raj Institutions, cooperatives, voluntary agencies, NGO's, can all play vital roles in the process of development by complementing and supplementing the functions and activities of the government.

Jain (2005)[111] examined the report of Standing Committee of Ministry of Rural Development on the Employment Guarantee Bill. The committee assigned principle role and comprehensive responsibilities to the panchayats for planning, implementation and monitoring of the Employment Guarantee Scheme. The panchayats must be given a greater role and the work under the scheme must be a part of the village area plan as outlined in the seventy-third amendment to the constitution. For the employment generating works to succeed, the existing schemes at the village should be abolished and the funds so liberated must be entrusted to the panchayats.

Khera (2008)[112] examined the implementation of NREGA in Orissa where the programme has been under the scanner due to the allegations of embezzlement of funds on a large scale. This has posed a serious doubt about the adequacy of transparency safeguards in the Act itself. The use of Management Information System needs to be implemented more seriously in terms of job-cards and muster rolls. The need is to build more pressure to ensure transparency and accountability.

Reddy (2008)[113] examined the report of Comptroller and Auditor General on NREGA. The report takes up the procedural problems that are holding up the effective implementation of the Act. If the scheme is to be carried forward, immediate rectification of the gross neglect of the staffing needs of the NREGA programme is required by the state administration. Also, non-payment of the minimum wages defeat NREGA's objectives of providing livelihood security. The process of social audits is yet to be adopted with enthusiasm. The strict enforcement of the transparency safeguards under NREGA can go a long way in preventing corruption.

Siddhartha and Vanaik (2008)[114] examined that the draft report of the Comptroller and Auditor General on the working of NREGA was used by many sections of the media to strongly criticize employment programme. The report has been widely used to dismiss the Act as a failure by presenting the findings in a biased manner. They concluded that despite falling short on a number of counts, the CAG report has highlighted many genuine problems and pointed out improvements that are required.

Dhuru and Pandey (2009)[115] evaluated the Right to Information Act and social audit provisions of NREGA. Although the audit provisions enable people to demand accountability from the government, it works differently in reality. The demand for rights by the workers has met with violence. They quoted several cases in Uttar Pradesh where people have to fight for their wages. There are a lot of problems of the underpaid workers also.

Gopal (2009)[116] evaluated the social audits conducted in Andhra Pradesh and assessed that while much has been said and written about them, in reality these audits have achieved less than advertised. NREGA stipulates that gram panchayats will undertake social audits but they have been ignored both in conducting social audits and implementation of NREGA. Interestingly, thousands of personnel engaged in the field along with the technical and computer staff for NREGA is booked as 'daily wage workers' and funds are thus being diverted from rural employment programme. NREGA data has been digitized to enable easy access to the people but the cumulative data available cannot be verified, some information is in English and other in Telugu. Most of the information is not placed on the website. The social audit exercise has seemed to falter and thus, not acted as a detterent to corruption. The social audit process has a long way to go before it can claim to have contributed to transparency, empowerment and good governance.

Posani and Aiyar (2009)[117] analytically narrated the evolution of thought and practice in public accountability. They gave an overview of the different mechanisms and instruments through which citizens scrutinize the state and the limitations in the citizen-led accountability initiatives. They argued that a number of issues remain on the substantive aspects of new citizen state engagement for accountability and any uncritical acceptance of the *status quo* would only amount to complacence. Much needs to be done to translate the gains into practical and sustainable improvements in accountability.

Rajanna and Ramesh (2009)[118] conducted a study in Karimnagar district of Andhra Pradesh by selecting five hundred beneficiaries to assess the impact of NREGA as a facet of inclusive growth. They analyzed that NREGP has contributed substantially for improved living and economic conditions by reducing the income imbalances and wage differences in various works by distributing equal wages to male and female workers. It has helped in overcoming the uncertainty in employment and reducing disguised and seasonal unemployment in the agricultural sector. The study revealed that in order to be more comprehensive, the programme needs more transparency in its implementation and effective social audit to eliminate bogus beneficiaries.

Siwach and Kumar (2009)[119] evaluated that NREGA was enacted with fanfare to bring socio-economic transformation in the lives of the rural people. Its component of social audit was no doubt a salient feature but the experience revealed that there was a wide gap between the intended aims of the Act and the cultural milieu of the villages in Haryana. The elected members of the PRI's perceive social audit as a daunting challenge to their traditional power structure. NREGA, by and large, has the potential not only to strengthen social security in India but also community mobilization to ensure better responsiveness of the local government to community's needs and priorities.

Adhikari and Bhatia (2010)[120] analyzed that the shift from cash payment of wages under MGNREGA to settlement through bank accounts has been very encouraging. This has been done in order to prevent defrauding of workers and to give them greater control over their wages. The survey conducted in two blocks each in Allahabad (Uttar Pradesh) and Ranchi (Jharkhand) districts found that it is a substantial protection against embezzlement. They suggested bringing the bank's MGNREGA related documents in the public domain and proactive disclosure of the gram panchayat's bank account details.

Aiyar, Mehta and Samji (2011)[121] examined the accountability effects of regular, reliable institutionalized social audits in the state of Andhra Pradesh. The mandatory provision for social audits has acted as a catalyst for conducting audits in MGNREGA by the gram sabha at least once every six months. Andhra Pradesh is the only state to take steps to institutionalize the social audit process for MGNREGA and undertake regular social audits through the government machinery. Social audits have been conducted by a government led team of social auditors. The beneficiaries of MGNREGA have responded enthusiastically to the social audit process and attended social audit public hearings in large numbers. The Andhra Pradesh experiment provided an opportunity to examine the process of conducting social audits at scale and evaluate the effects of these audits on accountability. However, while social audits have been effective in ensuring answerability, they have been less effective in ensuring enforcement despite a well-defined institutional structure for grievance redressal. The effective enforcement on social audit findings was constrained by the administrative system characterized by complex hierarchies and overlapping lines of reporting, which makes it difficult for a single agency to effectively enforce decisions.

Dreze (2011)[122] evaluated the effectiveness of transparency safeguards under MGNREGA. During the initial stages of implementation of the scheme claims were made that MGNREGA funds were not reaching the poor based on misleading accounts of a Comptroller and Auditor General report. However, the field studies undertaken indicated positive findings and showed improvement. There were fewer incidences of corruption and leakages of funds under MGNREGA as compared to other programmes like National Food for Work.

Khera (2011)[123] conducted field visits to the states of Chhattisgarh, Gujarat, Jharkhand, Madhya Pradesh, Rajasthan, Uttar Pradesh and West Bengal and discussed the issue of delay in MGNREGA wage payments and the reasons for this delay. The study also recommended that the payment process should be streamlined as in the case of Andhra Pradesh and Tamil Nadu. Regularly updating records, issuing job-cards, maintenance of muster rolls, etc. would go a long way in speeding up the wage payment process.

Pani and Iyer (2011)[124] evaluated the effectiveness of MGNREGA in Karnataka and recommended specific steps that could improve them. The issues related to the processes involved in the worker seeking work, the process of providing that work, the consequences of that work for the rural economy and society and the processes involved in enabling and monitoring the scheme.

Ravallion (2012)[125] assessed that undoubtedly there is corruption in the Mahatma Gandhi National Rural Employment Guarantee Scheme. However, the simple indices that claim to measure corruption and make an assessment of inter-state levels of corruption can offer a wrong understanding.

Sukhtankar (2012)[126] surveyed Koraput, Rayagada and Gajapati districts in Orissa. The data was collected from three thousand households. The study recommended conducting careful evaluations before implementing big policy changes. Technological solutions, like electronic benefit transfers connected to biometrically-authenticated IDs such as Aadhar were suggested to improve the effectiveness of MGNREGA wage payments.

Pande and Mann (2014)[127] asserted that the contribution of MGNREGA to the rural revival in the last decade cannot be dismissed. MGNREGA has been a strong pillar of rural prosperity in the last decade. One in four rural households have benefited from it with at least 50 percent beneficiaries being women, scheduled castes and scheduled tribes. MGNREGA has been able to increase rural wages. After implementation of MGNREGA in 2005-06 to 2010-11, the growth rate of agricultural wages has increased to 2.7 percent per annum for men and 3.7 percent for women. Raising agricultural productivity is one of the fundamental objectives of MGNREGA. For this, works such as land levelling, making of embankments, drought-proofing, etc., have been undertaken on lands of lakhs of small and marginal farmers. It has also been claimed that MGNREGA has "contributed more to inflation than to rural wealth." However, there is no direct evidence linking MGNREGA to inflation. In fact, the scheme has given the poorest households the ability to withstand economic shocks and deal with inflation. Almost 65 percent of the total expenditure on MGNREGA since its inception has been credited directly into the accounts of the MGNREGA workers through banks and post offices. Although MGNREGA have issues such as delays in wage payments, asset, quality, leakages and other weaknesses, therefore; there is need to identify the problems through concurrent evaluations and feedback and addressing them. To constantly improve and check leakages, streamline money flows, institute more transparency, etc. the detailed management information systems have been put in place to track every work undertaken in MGNREGA.

The Indian Express (2016)[128] examined that the revival of MGNREGA in the times of agrarian crisis due to droughts in 2014 and 2015 has signaled that some respite has reached the poor in the rural areas. This has happened due to better implementation and release of funds in time. The revival of the programme has shown that the programme is no longer a victim of political differences. However, there is a strong need of creating awareness as well as instituting effective grievance redressal mechanisms for the programme.

Table 1.6: Classification and Analysis of the Literature Reviewed

S.No.	Theme	Gist of Analysis	Reference and Surname (Year)
1.	Administrative machinery and procedures	The literature reviewed highlighted that there is lack of coordination among implementing agencies, duplication of functions, lack of clarity of role, inadequate infrastructural facilities, lack of political and administrative will, administrative delays, work overload, harassment of contractual employees by permanent employees, corruption prevailing in administrative machinery for development programmes. In order to overcome above mentioned inadequacies, there is need for structural modifications and use of Management Information Systems for record keeping in implementation of programmes, clearly defined roles, need for clarity of policies and programmatic approaches.	Chaturvedi (1977), Arya, Verma and Sharma (1985), Singh (1985), Singh (1989), Maheshwari (1995), Krishan (2000), Ghose (2004), Hirway (2004), Papola (2005), Jacob and Varghese (2006), Louis (2006), Savale (2006), Chakraborty (2007), Datar (2007), Mohan (2007), Ambasta, Shankar and Shah (2008), Hirway, Saluja and Yadav (2008), Kumar (2008), Mehrotra (2008), Sastry, Murthy and Kamath (2008), Singh (2008), ASCI (2009), CRRID (2009), Dreze and Siddhartha (2009), Shah (2009), Banerjee and Saha (2010), Bhatia and Adhikari (2010), Deininger and Liu (2010), Dey and Bedi (2010), Sharma (2010), Ghosh (2011), Imbert and Papp (2011), Jha, Gaiha and Pandey (2011), Kajale and Shroff (2011), Khosla (2011), Kumar and Maruthi (2011), Morgan (2011), Mukherjee and Sinha (2011), Sankaran (2011), World Bank (2011), Dutta, et. al., (2012), Government of India (2012), Verma (2012), Ravi and Engler (2013), Ravallion (2014), Sampath and S. (2015), World Bank (2015).

2.	People's Participation and civil society organizations	Lack of people's participation, non-involvement of civil society organizations, low awareness among people regarding importance of participation in gram sabhas are the serious lacunae hampering people's participation. Studies suggest that there is need for people's participation at different levels of designing and implementation of projects, social mobilization through involvement of civil society organizations, generating awareness, etc.	Bhatnagar and Chib (1987), Shah (2005), Joseph (2006), Patel (2006), Shah (2007), Raghavan, et. al., (2008), CIFE (2009), Hazarika (2009), Ambasta (2010), IIT Chennai (2010), IRMA (2010), Pankaj and Tankha (2010), Srivastava and Srivastava (2010), Azam (2011), Bordoloi (2011), Chandrashekar and Ghosh (2011), Dasgupta and Sudarshan (2011), Holmes, Rath and Sadana (2011), Hirway and Batabyal (2012), Narayanan, et. al., (2014), Tewari (2015).
3.	Management of human resources and capacity of implementing authorities	Review of literature suggests that inadequate support staff at village and block levels, lack of capacity to plan and implement works among the implementing authorities, neglect of staffing needs, no incentive system to reward good performance, low remuneration, delay in salaries of employees has hampered effective implementation of development programmes. Thus, in order to effectively implement development programmes there is need to provide adequate staff, need to organize regular training programmes and impart training through scientific methods, development of quality content for training programmes.	Raghava (1980), Prasad (2003), Shah (2004), Bhaduri (2005), Vaidyanathan (2005a), Vaidyanathan (2005b), Aiyar and Samji (2006), Hooja and Parnami (2007), CAGI (2008), Dey (2008), Dhar (2008), Rao (2008), AFPRO (2009), Ambasta (2009), Birner, et. al., (2010), CERD (2010), IDYWC (2010), Dreze (2011), Mangatter (2011), Bonner, et. al., (2012), Aiyar (2014), Sharma (2015), Khera (2016).
4.	Transparency and Accountability	Lack of organized monitoring and evaluation mechanisms, defunct transparency and accountability mechanisms like social audit, grievance redressal committees, Ombudsman, etc., lack of awareness of these mechanisms has led to lack of transparency and unaccountability in the working of MGNREGA. Thus, in order to ensure transparency and accountability there is need for active monitoring of the development programmes for achieving better outcomes, to do away with completing formalities only.	Singh (1999), Jain (2005), Khera (2008), Reddy (2008), Siddhartha and Vanaik (2008), Dhuru and Pandey (2009), Gopal (2009), Posani and Aiyar (2009), Rajanna and Ramesh (2009), Siwach and Kumar (2009), Adhikari and Bhatia (2010), Aiyar, Mehta and Samji (2011), Dreze (2011), Khera (2011), Pani and Iyer (2011), Ravallion (2012), Sukhtankar (2012), Pande and Mann (2014), The Indian Express (2016).

1.9 Inferences Drawn from the Review of Literature

A classification of the literature reviewed in terms of the level of analysis, nature and issues addressed has been provided in Table 1.6. Most of the studies focus on the planning and implementation machinery. The studies conclude that the planning and implementation machinery is not constituted to meet the objectives of the programme. The implementation process is yet to go beyond the routine compilation of the statistical data. The implementation of MGNREGA has suffered on accounts of inadequate manpower and overburdening of the existing authorities and agencies. The studies have also highlighted the practice of allotting MGNREGA work as an additional duty to the permanent staff at many places. No timely monitoring, supervision and evaluation of the programmes is done to check hindrances and accelerate the process of development.

The literature revealed that women participation in MGNREGA has increased over the years. The women specific provisions in the programme, such as, one third of the workers be women, work-site facilities like availability of crèche and equal wages for men and women has helped in this regard.

The literature reviewed also highlighted that in wake of decentralization, there is need to develop the capacities of the rural local bodies for undertaking the delegated functions and roles. Various studies reported the lack of adequate capacities among the functionaries of local bodies as the sole reason for the unsuccessful delivery of services and in the process proper implementation of development programmes has suffered. The lack of capacity among the local officials for planning and executing MGNREGA has turned the bottom-up decision making process into top-down process thereby alienating local voice.

The literature suggested that the social mobilization and involvement of civil society organizations is important for designing and implementation of the programmes. Civil Society Organizations needs to be involved in assisting gram sabhas and creating awareness among the rural people. In various cases cited in the literature, the continuous involvement of the Non-Government Organizations has played an important role in the successful implementation of the programmes and making people aware regarding their entitlements.

The literature also suggested that the use of Information Technology (IT) in the form of Management Information System has helped in ensuring transparency and accountability. Further, the use of other transparency and accountability techniques such as social audit, grievance redressal committees, Ombudsman, vigilance and monitoring committees also needs to be strengthened. The literature revealed that in most of the cases, the mechanisms for ensuring accountability and transparency are defunct. In lieu of this, only formalities are completed by the officials for submitting the reports and thus the mechanisms are rendered meaningless.

1.10 Scope and Significance of Study

The literature reviewed shows that a fair amount of work has been done on MGNREGA. There is literature related to planning, structural problems in terms of implementation of the governmental schemes, decentralization, coordination among various implementing agencies, transparency and accountability mechanisms. However, MGNREGA is an ongoing effort and it is important that its monitoring continues in light of the feedback received from time to time. Further, as we proceed to narrow down our focus of MGNREGA in district Patiala in Punjab, the literature available is very limited and most of the literature available is in the form of newspaper articles and reports. The survey of literature also reveals that the people's perspective, by and large, has been ignored.

This study has taken into account the perspective of the beneficiary households i.e. the people's perception of the scheme and also the perspective of the rural local bodies. The study also explored the role of implementing agencies of MGNREGA. Moreover, the studies in Punjab have mainly been done either in the Phase I or Phase II districts of the implementation of the Act. Being a district of Phase III, no known implementation studies of MGNREGA had been conducted in Patiala district.

1.11 Period of the Study

As stated earlier, MGNREGA had universal implementation in three phases in the country. In Punjab, the programme was implemented in Hoshiarpur district in the first phase in 2006 on pilot basis. Subsequently, in second phase, the programme was implemented in three more districts of Amritsar, Nawanshahar and Jalandhar in 2007-08. In the third phase, the programme was implemented in all the districts of Punjab from April 2008. Since MGNREGA was implemented in the district of Patiala in the third phase of implementation i.e. in April, 2008, the period of study commenced in 2008 to study as much of the implementation as possible, the field work continues until December, 2015. Thus, the time period of the study corresponds with the launch of Phase III of MGNREGA in the district i.e. 2008 till 2015.

1.12 Objectives of the Study

The objective of study is to examine the implementation of MGNREGA with reference to the administrative machinery set up for implementation of MGNREGA, awareness generated among the job-card holders with the outreach of the programme, change in the socio-economic conditions of the women workers post-MGNREGA, capacity of the local bodies to draw plan and implement MGNREGA works and working of transparency and accountability mechanisms available under MGNREGA in the locale of study. Specifically the objectives of the study were to:

1. study the administrative machinery for implementation of MGNREGA in Punjab.
2. comprehend the outreach of the programme to the beneficiaries.
3. study the impact of the programme on the socio-economic conditions of the women workers.
4. evaluate the capacity building of the local bodies under MGNREGA.
5. study the working of transparency and accountability mechanisms provided under MGNREGA.
6. prescribe suggestions for improving the implementation of MGNREGA in the district.

1.13 Hypotheses

Keeping in view the objectives of the study, the following hypotheses were formulated:

1. The administrative machinery for the implementation of MGNREGA does not fulfil the provisions of the Act.
2. The outreach of MGNREGA has generated awareness of its key provisions among the job-card holders in the rural areas.
3. MGNREGA has been instrumental in improving the socio-economic conditions of women workers.
4. The local bodies have the capacity to plan and implement MGNREGA works at the village level.
   - (i) Adequate human resource is available with the local bodies to undertake MGNREGA works.
   - (ii) The elected and appointed officials have the capacity to plan and implement MGNREGA works.
   - (iii) Regular training programmes are conducted for the officials to build their capacities for the implementation of MGNREGA.
5. The mechanisms to ensure transparency and accountability under MGNREGA are functional.
   - (i) The mechanisms of information disclosure under MGNREGA are working to ensure transparency.
   - (ii) Regular social audit of the works is conducted under MGNREGA.

(iii) Vigilance and Monitoring committees are actively involved in the monitoring of MGNREGA works.

(iv) Grievance redressal mechanisms are functional under MGNREGA.

1.14 Research Methodology

The study is based on both primary and secondary data. The primary data was collected from the three blocks of district Patiala in the state of Punjab. Patiala is divided into eight administrative blocks out of which three were selected on the basis of MGNREGA funds utilized till 2010-11 (Annexure I). In terms of their percentage of utilization of funds, Samana block with highest utilization, Nabha block with medium utilization and Sanour block with lowest utilization were selected (Table 1.7).

Table 1.7: Selection of the Blocks

S.No.	Status of the block in terms of %age of funds utilized	Selected Blocks	%age Of MGNREGA funds utilized till 2010-11 (2nd May, 2011)
1.	Highest utilization	Samana	90.71%
2.	Medium utilization	Nabha	82.27%
3.	Lowest utilization	Sanour	73.08%

Source: MGNREGA website www.nrega.nic.in

In order to make a detailed study of the various aspects of the implementation of MGNREGA , four villages per block were selected on the base of status of works, i.e., villages with ongoing work, villages with completed work, villages with the completed and ongoing work, and villages with no MGNREGA work (Figure 1.1).

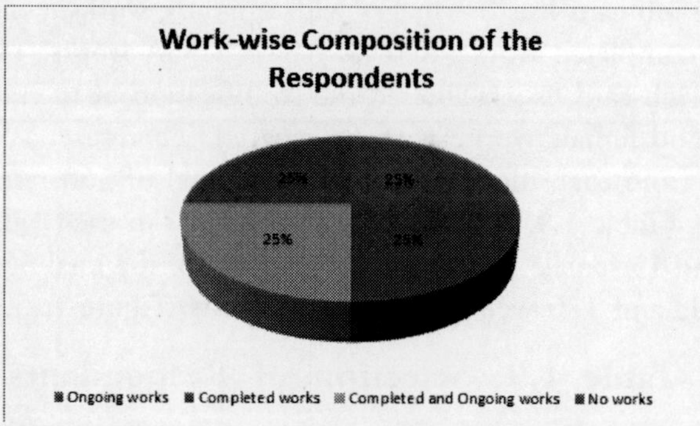

Figure 1.1: Work-wise Composition of the Respondents

The villages were selected in consultation with the block level officials. Table 1.8 lists the selected villages in the blocks of Samana, Nabha and Sanour.

Table 1.8: Selected Villages in Block Samana, Nabha and Sanour

Name of Block	Status of Work	Villages Selected	Types of Works
Samana	Ongoing work	Majri	Bharat Nirman Rajiv Gandhi Sewa kendra
	Completed work	Dhenthal	Renovation of traditional water body
	Completed and Ongoing work	Kakra	Renovation of traditional water body (completed and ongoing)
	No work	Fatehpur	Nil
Nabha	Ongoing work	Bina-Heri	Bharat Nirman Rajiv Gandhi Sewa kendra
	Completed work	Rohti-Mouran	Renovation of traditional water body
	Completed and Ongoing work	Rohti-Khaas	Renovation of traditional water body (completed), Tree plantation (Ongoing)
	No work	Kot-Khurd	Nil
Sanour	Ongoing work	Bolri	Rural Connectivity
	Completed work	Shermajra	Renovation of traditional water body
	Completed and Ongoing work	Devinagar	Renovation of traditional water body (Completed and Ongoing)
	No work	Rawas Barahmana	Nil

A stratified sample of 30 respondents per village was selected with a random start from the job-card lists in villages with ongoing works; completed works; ongoing and completed works; and no MGNREGA works. The mention of gender in the job-card lists facilitated the stratification of the sample; separate lists of male and female workers were prepared. Therefore, 120 respondents were selected from each block, thus making a total of 360 respondents from twelve villages (Table 1.9). Further, 30 respondents in each village comprised of 15 male and 15 female respondents. Thus, out of the total 360 respondents, 180 were male and 180 were female respondents (Figure 1.2).

Table 1.9: Selection of Respondents

S. No.	Blocks	Number of villages selected	Number of respondents per block
1.	Samana	4	120
2.	Nabha	4	120
3.	Sanour	4	120
Total		12	360

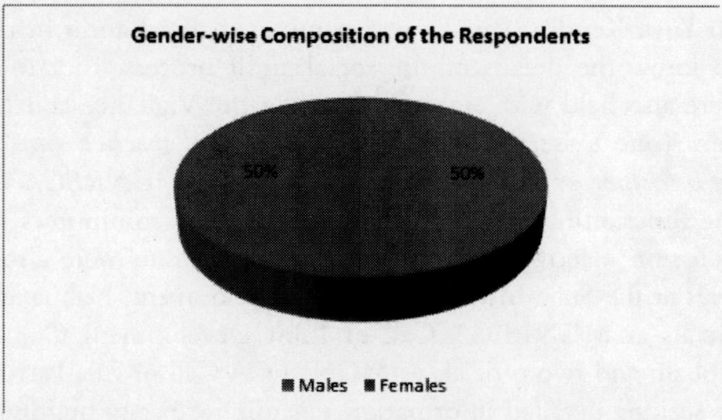

Figure 1.2: Gender-wise Composition of the Respondents

The primary data was collected through questionnaires to comprehend the outreach of the programme to the job-card holders and assess the socio-economic conditions of the women workers. As most workers were illiterate, the responses to the questionnaire were recorded by the researcher. Check-list and observation method was used to observe working conditions and the facilities provided at the work-sites. Apart from this, focus group discussions were held with the women job-card holders to fathom the detailed impacts of the programme on their lives.

Two different questionnaires were administered in the villages. A questionnaire was administered to the job-card holders in the villages with the ongoing works; completed works; and completed and ongoing works (Annexure II). Since the questionnaire administered to these three categories of villages was irrelevant in villages with no MGNREGA work, another questionnaire was administered to the job-card holders in these villages (Annexure III).

Interview schedule was used to collect information regarding the various aspects of the programme. Interviews were held with twelve Sarpanches (Panchayat Heads) and thirty panchayat members at the village level; 9 Sarpanches and 26 panchayat members of villages with ongoing work, completed work; and completed and ongoing works were asked different set of questions (Annexure IV) from 3 Sarpanches and 4 panchayat members of no MGNREGA work villages (Annexure V). Three Assistant Programme Officers (APO's) at the block level were also interviewed (Annexure VI). Face-to-face and telephonic interactions were held from time to time over the course of research with officials concerned with the implementation of MGNREGA, namely, eight Panchayat Secretaries, three Junior Engineers, three Computer Operators-cum-Accounts Clerks, eight Gram Rozgar Sahayaks (GRS) and three mates (work-site supervisors) in order to investigate the detailed aspects of implementation. Discussion meetings were also held with five volunteers of the Nehru Yuva Kendra, Patiala who conducted social audit in the selected villages to know the details of the social audit process. Face-to-face interactions were also held with eight members of the Vigilance and Monitoring Committees (*one ex-serviceman, one local school teacher, one anganwadi worker, two former panchayat members and three MGNREGA workers*) to analyze the functioning of vigilance and monitoring committees at the local level. Discussion meetings and face-to-face interactions were also held with four officials at the State Institute of Rural Development, Nabha and Mohali; seven officials at MGNREGA Cell of Joint Development Commissioner's Office, Mohali; and two officials at MGNREGA Cell of Zila Parishad Office, Patiala for seeking detailed information regarding capacity building measures and training programmes organized, grievance redressal mechanisms and vigilance and monitoring mechanisms at the state and district levels. Further, observation was used to supplement the data (Table 1.10).

Table 1.10: Officials Interviewed

S.No.	Designation of the respondents	Number of respondents	Tool of data collection
1.	Sarpanches	12	Interviews, face-to-face and telephonic interactions, discussion meetings
2.	Panchayat member	30	
3.	Additional Programme Officer	3	
4.	Gram Rozgar Sahayak	8	
5.	Mates	3	
6.	Panchayat Secretary	8	
7.	Junior Engineer	3	
8.	Computer Operator-cum-Accounts Clerk	3	
9.	Volunteer of Nehru Yuva Kendra	5	
10.	Members of the Vigilance and Monitoring Committees in the villages (one ex-serviceman, one local school teacher, one anganwadi worker, two former panchayat members and three MGNREGA workers)	8	
11.	Officials of State Institute of Rural Development	4	
12.	Officials at MGNREGA Cell, Zila Parishad	2	
13.	Officials at the Joint Development Commissioner's Office, Mohali	7	

Secondary data was collected from MGNREGA website, annual reports of the Ministry of Rural Development, MGNREGA annual reports, Reports of the working groups of the Central Employment Guarantee Council, monthly and annual reports of the district administration, Department of

Rural Development, Punjab, Five-Year plan documents, performance audit reports of the Comptroller and Auditor General of India and other government documents, various journals/ periodicals, newspaper articles, books and other published material, reports of study groups appointed by the Government of India. Internet was a valuable resource in accessing data sources.

The data has been presented in tabular and graphic forms. Along with this, qualitative discussion has been used to describe the impacts of the scheme on the respondents as well as officials and also to present the detailed results of the interviews and the focus group discussions held.

Endnotes

1 B.K. Prasad (2003), Rural Development: Concepts, Approach and Strategy, Sarup and Sons, New Delhi, p. 32.

2. Ibid, p. 43.

3. Ibid, p. 46.

4. Ibid, p. 51.

5. Government of India (1992), Eighth Five Year Plan, 1992-1997, Volume II, Planning Commission, New Delhi, p. 27.

6. Prasad, op. cit., p. 57.

7. James H. Copp (1972), "Rural Sociology and Rural Development", Rural Sociology, Volume 37, Number 4, pp. 515-523.

8. A.P.J. Abdul Kalam (2008), "PURA: A Road Map for New Rural India", in P. Jegadish Gandhi (ed.), Dr. Kalam's PURA Model and Societal Transformation: Providing Urban Amenities in Rural Areas, Deep and Deep Publications Pvt. Ltd., New Delhi, pp. 23-37.

9. Ruddar Datt (2008), "PURA: A Road Map for New Rural India", in P. Jegadish Gandhi (ed.), Dr. Kalam's PURA Model and Societal Transformation: Providing Urban Amenities in Rural Areas, Deep and Deep Publications Pvt. Ltd., New Delhi, pp. 59-65.

10. S.S. Chib (1987), "Dimensions of Rural Poverty and Rural Development in India: An Evaluation of Concepts and Approaches", in Satyavan Bhatnagar and Sukhdev Singh Chib (eds.), Rural Development in India: A Strategy for Socio-economic Change, Ess Ess Publications, New Delhi, p. 40.

11. Government of India (2006), Unlocking Human Capital: Entitlements and Governance – A Case Study, Second Administrative Reforms Commission, Ministry of Personnel, Public Grievances and Pensions, Department of Administrative Reforms and Public Grievances, New Delhi, p. 1.

12. Chib, op. cit., p. 39.

13. Ibid, p. 41.

14. Government of India (2006), op. cit., p. 7.

15. Government of India (2013), Mahatma Gandhi National Rural Employment Guarantee Act (MGNREGA) (Annual Report, 2012-13), Ministry of Rural Development, Department of Rural Development, New Delhi, pp. 12-13.

16. Government of India (2009), National Rural Employment Guarantee Act, 2005: Report to the People 2008-09, Ministry of Rural Development, Department of Rural Development, New Delhi, pp. 4-5.

17. Government of India (2013), op.cit., pp. 14-15.

18. Government of India (2007), National Rural Employment Guarantee Act (NREGA): Some Reports from the Field, 2006-07, Ministry of Rural Development, Department of Rural Development, New Delhi, p. 2.

19. Ibid, p. 4.

20. H.R. Chaturvedi (1977), Bureaucracy and Local Community: Dynamics of Rural Development, Allied Publishers, Bombay.

21. K.S. Arya, J.C. Verma and K.K. Sharma (1986), Rural Development in India: Some Facets, D.A.V. College, Chandigarh.

22. Hoshiar Singh (1985), Rural Development in India, Print well Publishers, Jaipur.

23. Shivraj Singh (1989), Bureaucracy and Rural Development, Mittal Publications, New Delhi.

24. S.R. Maheshwari (1995), Rural Development in India: A Public Policy Approach, Sage Publications, New Delhi.

25. Ajit K. Ghose (2004), "The Employment Challenge in India", Economic and Political Weekly, Volume 39, Number 48, pp. 5106-5116.

26. Indira Hirway (2004), "Providing Employment Guarantee in India: Some Critical Issues", Economic and Political Weekly, Volume 39, Number 48, pp. 5117-5124.

27. T.S. Papola (2005), "A Universal Programme is Feasible", Economic and Political Weekly, Volume 40, Number 7, pp. 594-597.

28. Arun Jacob and Richard Verghese (2006), "NREGA Implementation-1: Reasonable Beginning in Palakkad, Kerala", Economic and Political Weekly, Volume 41, Number 48, pp. 4943-4945.

29. Prakash Louis (2006), "NREGA Implementation II: Birth Pangs in Bihar", Economic and Political Weekly, Volume 41, Number 48, pp. 4946-4947.

30. Sanjay Savale (2006), "Is Local Really Better? Comparing EGS and Local–Managed Rural Work Programmes in Nasik District", Economic and Political Weekly, Volume 41, Number 50, pp. 5133-5139.

31. Pinaki Chakraborty (2007), "Implementation of Employment Guarantee: A Preliminary Appraisal", Economic and Political Weekly, Volume 42, Number 7, pp. 548-551.

32. Chhaya Datar (2007), "Failure of National Rural Employment Guarantee Scheme in Maharashtra", Economic and Political Weekly, Volume 43, Number 34, pp. 3454-3457.

33. Saumitra Mohan (2007), "National Rural Employment Guarantee Programme: How Effective?", The Administrator, Volume 50, Number 1, pp. 15-20.

34. Pramathesh Ambasta, P.S. Vijay Shankar and Mihir Shah (2008), "Two Years of NREGA: The Road Ahead", Economic and Political Weekly, Volume 43, Number 7, pp. 41-50.

35. Indira Hirway, M.R.Saluja and Bhupesh Yadav (2009), "Assessing Impact of NREGA works in a village based on village SAM", in The National Rural Employment Guarantee Act (NREGA): Design, Process and Impact, UNDP, New Delhi, pp. 31-52.

36. Rohit Kumar (2009), "NREGS: Not just supplementing employment opportunity in Jalore district, Rajasthan", in The National Rural Employment Guarantee Act (NREGA): Design, Process and Impact, UNDP, New Delhi, 2009, pp. 53–57.

37. Santosh Mehrotra (2008), "NREG: Two Years On: Where Do We Go from Here?", Economic and Political Weekly, Volume 43, Number 31, pp. 27-35.

38. Trilochan Sastry, Rajluxmi V. Murthy and Rajalaxmi Kamath (2009), "NREGA Implementation: Comparative Studies for Karnataka and Andhra Pradesh", in The National Rural Employment Guarantee Act (NREGA): Design, Process and Impact, UNDP, New Delhi, 2009, pp. 61–71.

39. Raghuvansh Prasad Singh (2008), "Two Years of NREGA", Yojana, Volume 52, pp. 12-16.

40. Administrative Staff College of India (2009), Quick Appraisal of NREGA in Andhra Pradesh, Report submitted to the Ministry of Rural Development / UNDP, Administrative Staff College of India, Hyderabad.

41. Centre for Research in Rural and Industrial Development (2009), Appraisal/ Impact Assessment of NREGS in Selected Districts of Himachal Pradesh, Punjab and Haryana, Report submitted to the Ministry of Rural Development/UNDP, CRRID, Chandigarh.

42. Jean Dreze and Siddhartha (2009), "Flaws in the System", Frontline, Volume 26, Issue 01, pp. 5-7.

43. Mihir Shah (2009), "Multiplier accelerator synergy in NREGA", The Hindu, April 30, New Delhi, p. 7.

44. Kaustav Banerjee and Partha Saha (2010), "The NREGA, the Maoists and the Developmental Woes of the Indian State", Economic and Political Weekly, Volume 45, Number 28, pp. 42-47.

45. K. Bhatia and A. Adhikari (2010), "NREGA Wage Payments: Can We Bank on the Banks", Economic and Political Weekly, Volume 65, Number 1, pp. 30-37.

46. K. Deininger and Y. Liu (2010), "Poverty Impacts of India's National Rural Employment Guarantee Scheme: Evidence from Andhra Pradesh", Paper prepared for presentation at the Agricultural and Applied Economics Association, Colorado, July 25-27, Colorado.

47. Subhashish Dey and Arjun S Bedi (2010), "The National Rural Employment Guarantee Scheme in Birbhum", Economic and Political Weekly, Volume 45, Number 41, pp. 19-23.

48. Amita Sharma (2010), "Rights-based Legal Guarantee as Development Policy: Mahatma Gandhi National Rural Employment Guarantee Act", A Discussion Paper, UNDP, India, pp. 5-78.

49. J.K. Ghosh (2011), Impact of NREGA on Wage Rates, Food Security and Rural Urban Migration in West Bengal, Report submitted to the Ministry of Agriculture, Agro-Economic Research Centre, Visva-Bharati Santiniketan, Birbhum.

50. C. Imbert and J. Papp (2011), "Equilibrium Distributional Impacts of Government Employment Programs: Evidence from India's Employment Guarantee", PSE Working Papers n2012-14, Paris School of Economics, Paris, pp. 3-65.

51. R. Jha, R. Gaiha and M.K. Pandey (2011), "Net Transfer Benefits under India's Rural Employment Guarantee Scheme", Journal of Policy Modelling, Volume 34, Number 2, pp. 296-311.

52. J. Kajale and S. Shroff (2011), Impact of NREGA on Wage Rates, Food Security, and Rural Urban Migration in Maharashtra, Report Submitted to the Ministry of Agriculture, Gokhale Institute of Politics and Economics, Agro-economic Research Centre, Pune.

53. R. Khosla (2011), "Caste, Politics and Public Goods Distribution in India: Evidence from NREGS in Andhra Pradesh", Economic and Political Weekly, Volume 45, Number 12, pp. 63-69.

54. P. Kumar and I. Maruthi (2011), Impact of NREGA on Wage Rate, Food Security and Rural Urban Migration in Karnataka, Report submitted to the Ministry of Agriculture, Agriculture Development and Rural Transformation Centre, Institute for Social and Economic Change, Bangalore.

55. J. P. Morgan (2011), "Wages in Rural India Accelerated Sharply Post-NREGA", [Online] Available from http://indiaer.blogspot.in/2011/10/india-rural-wages-surge-to-support.html, [Accessed on 15th April, 2015].

56. D. Mukherjee and U.B. Sinha (2011), Understanding NREGA: A Simple Theory and Some Facts, Centre for Development Economics, Delhi School of Economics, New Delhi, pp. 1-29.

57. Kamala Sankaran (2011), "NREGA Wages: Ensuring Decent Work", Economic and Political Weekly, Volume 46, Number 7, pp. 23-25.

58. World Bank (2011), Social Protection for a Changing India, World Bank, Washington DC.

59. P. Dutta, R. Murgai, M. Ravallion, and W.V. Dominique (2012), "Does India's Employment Guarantee Scheme Guarantee Employment?", Policy Research Working Paper 6003, World Bank, Washington DC, pp. 1-13.

60. Government of India (2012a), Report of the Committee on Revision of MGNREGA Operational Guidelines, Report submitted to the Ministry of Rural Development, New Delhi.

61. S. Verma (2012), Labour Markets Dynamics in Post-MGNREGS Rural India, Unpublished note shared with the Ministry of Rural Development, New Delhi, pp. 1-8.

62. S. Ravi and M. Engler (2013), "Workfare as an Effective Way to Fight Poverty: The Case of India's NREGS", [Online] Available from: http://ssrn.com/paper=1336837, [Accessed on 12th July, 2015].

63. Martin Ravallion (2014), 'MGNREGA is unwell', The Indian Express, October 24, New Delhi, p. 7.

64. G. Sampath and Rukmini S. (2015), "Is the MGNREGA being set up for failure?", The Hindu, May 31, New Delhi, p. 6.
65. World Bank (2015), "The state of social safety nets 2015", World Bank Group, Washington DC, [Online] Available from: http://documents.worldbank.org/curated/en/2015/07/24741765/state-social-safety-nets-2015, [Accessed on 21st September, 2015].
66. S. Bhatnagar and S.S. Chib (1987), Rural Development in India: A Strategy for Socio–Economic Change, Ess Ess Publications, New Delhi.
67. Mihir Shah (2005), "Saving the Employment Guarantee Act", Economic and Political Weekly, Volume 40, Number 7, pp. 559-602.
68. Shaji Joseph (2006), "Power of the People: Political Mobilisation and Guaranteed Employment", Economic and Political Weekly, Volume 41, Number 50, pp. 5149-5156.
69. Sujata Patel (2006), "Empowerment, Co-option and Domination: Politics of Maharashtra's Employment Guarantee Scheme", Economic and Political Weekly, Volume 41, Number 50, pp. 5126-5132.
70. Mihir Shah (2007), "Employment Guarantee, Civil Society and Indian Democracy", Economic and Political Weekly, Volume 42, Number 45 and 46, pp. 43-51.
71. Karthik Raghavan, Niki Singh, Saswata Das, Shardul Bist, Subhamoy Das, Unnati Gajjar, Veena Singh, Vibha Singh and Development of Research and Communication Service Centre (2008), The National Rural Employment Guarantee Scheme (NREGS) West Bengal: A Study of Sustainable Livelihood Models, Mudra Institute of Communications, Entrepreneurship Development Cell (MICA – EDC), Ahmedabad, pp. 4-29.
72. Central Institute of Fisheries Education (2009), A Study Report on Appraisal on MGNREGA Programme in Thane and Akola Districts of Maharashtra, Report submitted to the Ministry of Rural Development/UNDP, Central Institute of Fisheries Education, Mumbai.
73. P.G. Hazarika (2009), Promoting Women Empowerment and Gender Equality through the Right to Decent Work: Implementation of National Rural Employment Guarantee Program (NREGP) in Assam State (India)— A Case Study, Institute of Social Studies, The Hague, pp. 3-24.
74. P. Ambasta (2010), "MGNREGA and Rural Governance Reform: Growth and Inclusion through Panchayats", Paper presented at International Conference on Dynamics of Rural Transformation in Emerging Economies, Planning Commission, Government of India and Institute for Human Development, New Delhi, on 14-16 April.
75. IIT Chennai (2010), NREGA in Districts of Dharmapuri, Erode, Nagapattinam, Perambalur, Thanjavur, Theni, Thoothukudi, Tiruvallur, Vellore, Villupuram of Tamil Nadu, Report submitted to Ministry of Rural Development/UNDP, Indian Institute of Technology, Chennai.
76. Institute of Rural Management Anand (2010), An Impact Assessment Study of the Usefulness and Sustainability of the Assets Created under Mahatma Gandhi Rural Employment Guarantee Act in Sikkim, IRMA, Anand, pp. 2-17.

77. Ashok Pankaj and Rukmini Tankha (2010), "Empowerment Effects of the NREGS on Women Workers: A Study in Four States", Economic and Political Weekly, Volume 45, Number 30, pp. 45-55.

78. Nisha Srivastava and Ravi Srivastava (2010), "Women, Work, and Employment Outcomes in Rural India", Economic and Political Weekly, Volume 45, Number 28, pp. 49-63.

79. M. Azam (2011), "The Impact of Indian Job Guarantee Scheme on Labour Market Outcomes: Evidence from A Natural Experiment", [Online] Available from: http://ssrn.com/abstract=1941959, [Accessed on 20th January, 2012].

80. J. Bordoloi (2011), Impact of NREGA on Wage Returns, Food Security and Rural-Urban Migration – Assam, Report submitted to the Ministry of Agriculture, Agro-Economic Centre for North-East India, Assam Agricultural University, Jorhat.

81. C. Chandrashekar and J. Ghosh (2011), "Public Works and Wages in Rural India", [Online] Available from: http://www.macroscan.org/fet/jan11/fet110111Public_Works.htm, [Accessed on 11th January, 2011].

82. S. Dasgupta and S. Sudarshan (2011), 'Issues in Labour Market Inequality and Women's Participation in India's National Rural Employment Guarantee Act', *Working Paper Number 98*, International Labour Organization, Geneva, pp. 1-32.

83. R. Holmes, S. Rath and N. Sadana (2011), An Opportunity for Change? Gender Analysis of the Mahatma Gandhi National Rural Employment Guarantee Act, Overseas Development Institute and Indian Institute of Dalit Studies, London, pp. 1-4.

84. I. Hirway and S. Batabyal (2012), MGNREGA and Women's Empowerment, United Nation Women South Asia, New Delhi, pp. 2-6.

85. Sudha Narayanan, Krushna Ranaware, Upasak Das and Ashwini Kulkarni (2014), MGNREGA works and their Impacts: A Rapid Assessment in Maharashtra, Indira Gandhi Institute of Development Research, Mumbai, pp. 2-54.

86. Ruhi Tewari (2015), "In MNREGA, Bihar slower than rest", The Indian Express, September 10, New Delhi, p. 7.

87. D.V. Rao Raghava (1980), Panchayats and Rural Development, Ashish Publishing House, New Delhi.

88. B.K. Prasad (2003), op. cit.

89. Mihir Shah (2004), "National Rural Employment Guarantee Act: A Historical Opportunity", Economic and Political Weekly, Volume 39, Number 50, pp. 5287-5291.

90. Amit Bhaduri (2005), "First Priority: Guarantee Employment and the Right to Information", Economic and Political Weekly, Volume 40, Number 4, pp. 267-269.

91. A. Vaidyanathan (2005), "Employment Guarantee and Decentralization", Economic and Political Weekly, Volume 40, Number 16, pp. 1582-1587.

92. A. Vaidyanathan (2005a), "Need for Involvement of States", Economic and Political Weekly, Volume 40, Number 33, pp. 3646-3649.

93. Yamini Aiyar and Salimah Samji (2006), "Improving the Effectiveness of National Rural Employment Guarantee Act", Economic and Political Weekly, Volume 41, Number 4, pp. 320-326.

94. Rakesh Hooja and K.K. Parnami (2007), Development Administration and Rural Development, Aalekh Publishers, Jaipur.

95. Comptroller and Auditor General of India (2008), Performance Audit of Implementation of National Rural Employment Guarantee Act (NREGA), Performance Audit Report No. 11, CAG, New Delhi, pp. 1-57.

96. Nikhil Dey (2009), "Introduction: The NREGA Full Salient Features and Programme Outcomes", in The National Rural Employment Guarantee Act (NREGA): Design, Process and Impact, UNDP, New Delhi, pp. 9-30.

97. M.L. Dhar (2008), "Employment Scenario in India", Kurukshetra, Volume 56, Number 4, pp. 13-17.

98. V. Mohan Rao (2008), "Employment Guarantee Scheme is a Lifeline for the Vulnerable Sections", Kurukshetra, Volume 56, Number 8, pp. 3-7.

99. Action for Food Production (2009), Infrastructure Development and Beyond: Exploring the Scope for Sustainable Livelihood Support under NREGA, Report submitted to the Ministry of Rural Development/UNDP, New Delhi, pp. 3-37.

100. Pramathesh Ambasta (2009), "Programming NREGS to succeed", The Hindu, October 31, New Delhi, p. 5.

101. R. Birner, K. Gayathridevi, K.G. Raabe, E. Schiffer and M. Sekhar (2010), "How to Overcome the Governance Challenges of Implementing NREGA", Discussion Paper 00963, International Food Policy Research Institute (IFPRI), US, 2010, pp. 5-36.

102. Centre for Education and Research Development (2010), NREGA Processes in Andhra Pradesh and Madhya Pradesh: Appraisal and Research Study, Report submitted to the Ministry of Rural Development/UNDP, Centre for Education and Research Development, New Delhi.

103. Institute for Development of Youth, Women and Child (2010), Impact Assessment of Mahatma Gandhi National Rural Employment Guarantee Scheme on Sustainable Asset Creation and Livelihood, Report submitted to Ministry of Rural Development/ UNDP, IDYWC, Chhindwara.

104. J. Dreze (2011a), "Dantewada: Guarantee Withdrawn", in R. Khera, (ed.), The Battle for Employment Guarantee, Oxford University Press, New Delhi, pp. 220-33.

105. S. Mangatter (2011), Does the Mahatma Gandhi National Rural Employment Guarantee Act (MGNREGA) Strengthen Rural Self-employment in Bolpur subdivision (West Bengal, India)?, Master's Thesis, Philipps-Universität Marburg, Germany, pp. 5-132.

106. Kim Bonner, Jennifer Daum, Jessie Duncan, Ellen Dinsmore, Kari Fuglesten, Leslie Lai, Julian Lee, Katherine Manchester, Feker Tadesse, Robert Quinn (2012), "MGNREGA Implementation: A Cross-State Comparison", Paper for The Woodrow Wilson School's Graduate Policy Workshop, Woodrow Wilson School of Public and International Affairs, Princeton University, New Jersey, pp. 1-60.

107. Yamini Aiyar (2014), "Re-framing the MGNREGA debate", The Hindu, November 8, New Delhi, p. 7.

108. Rita Sharma (2015), "For a better MGNREGA", The Indian Express, July 5, New Delhi, p. 5.

109. Reetika Khera (2016), "Digging holes, filling them up", The Indian Express, February 3, New Delhi, p. 11.

110. Katar Singh (1999), Rural Development: Principles, Policies and Management, Sage Publication India, New Delhi.

111. L.C. Jain (2005), "Putting Panchayats in Charge", Economic and Political Weekly, Volume 40, Number 33, pp. 3649-3650.

112. Reetika Khera (2008), "The Black Hole of NREGA Records", Yojana, Volume 52, pp. 5-9.

113. C. Rammanohar Reddy (2008), "Wake up Call on Rural Employment Guarantee", Economic and Political Weekly, Volume 43, Number 4, pp. 5-6.

114. Siddhartha and Anish Vanaik (2008), "CAG Report on NREGA: Fact and Fiction", Economic and Political Weekly, Volume 43, Number 25, pp. 39-45.

115. Arundhate Dhuru and Sandeep Pandey (2009), "The Wages of Protest", The Hindu, April 5, New Delhi, p. 7.

116. K.S. Gopal (2009), "NREGA Social Audit: Myths and Reality", Economic and Political Weekly, Volume 44, Number 3, pp. 70-71.

117. Bala Posani and Yamini Aiyar (2009), "State of Accountability: Evolution, Practice and Emerging Questions in Public Accountability in India", Accountability Initiative, Working Paper Number 2, Centre for Policy Research, New Delhi, pp. 2-28.

118. Mamidipally Rajanna and Gundeti Ramesh (2009), "NREGP–Facet of Inclusive Growth: A Study of Karimnagar district in Andhra Pradesh", Kurukshetra, Volume 57, Number 4, pp. 4-7.

119. Raj Kumar Siwach and Sunil Kumar (2009), "Implementing NREGS in Haryana: A Study of Social Audit", Kurukshetra, Volume 57, Number 6, pp. 8-12.

120. Anindita Adhikari and Karthika Bhatia (2010), "NREGA Wage Payments: Can We Bank on Banks?", Economic and Political Weekly, Volume 45, Number 1, pp. 30-37.

121. Yamini Aiyar, Soumya Kapoor Mehta and Salimah Samji (2011), "Strengthening Public Accountability: Lessons from Implementing Social Audits in Andhra Pradesh", Accountability Initiative, Working Paper Series, Centre for Policy Research, New Delhi, pp. 8-54.

122. J. Dreze (2011), "Breaking the Nexus of Corruption", in R. Khera, (ed.), The Battle for Employment Guarantee, Oxford University Press, New Delhi, pp. 241–250.

123. R. Khera (2011), "Wage Payments: Live without Pay?", in R. Khera, (ed.), The Battle for Employment Guarantee, Oxford University Press, New Delhi, pp. 132-157.

124. N. Pani and C. Iyer (2011), Evaluation of the Impact of Processes in the Mahatma Gandhi National Rural Employment Guarantee Scheme in Karnataka, National Institute of Advanced Studies (NIAS), Bangalore, pp. 5-36.

125. M. Ravallion (2012), "Corruption in the MGNREGS: Assessing an Index", Economic and Political Weekly, Volume 47, Number 8, pp. 1374- 1392.

126. S. Sukhtankar (2012), What Determines MGNREGA Wages?: Some Evidence on Voice and Exit from Orissa, University of Pennsylvania, USA, pp. 8-47.

127. Varad Pande and Neelakshi Mann (2014), "MGNREGA: A tale of rural revival", [Online] Available from: http://www.livemint.com/Opinion/tdKbJga16hmXmKs42zHeuK/MGNREGA-A-tale-of-rural-revival.html, [Accessed on 23rd September, 2015].

128. The Indian Express (2016), "MGNREGA Message", Editorial, January 7, New Delhi, p. 10.

2

Organizational Structure of MGNREGA

21 Introduction

"Organizations are defined as collectivities that have been established for the pursuit of relatively specific objectives on a more or less continuous basis. Organizations have more or less fixed boundaries, a normative order, authority, rank, a communication system and an incentive system which enables various types of participants to work together in the pursuit of common goals."[1] In the words of Amitai Etzioni, "modern civilization depends largely on organization as the most rational and efficient form of social groupings. By coordinating a large number of human actions, the organization creates a powerful social tool. It combines its personnel with its resources, weaving together leaders, experts, workers, machines and raw materials. At the same time, it continuously evaluates how well it is performing and tries to adjust itself accordingly in order to achieve its goal.....".[2] The study of organization has enabled us to study how formal organizations are structured, governed, maintained and changes over time.

Organizations are designed and structured in order to ensure efficiency and effectiveness of activities in accordance with the organization's stated objectives. It divides and allocates work, authority and responsibility and indicates areas of responsibility, authority and accountability. It establishes working relationships and the means by which work is to be controlled. It also provides the basis of fair and equitable reward system.[3]

Organization structure refers to the formal configuration between individuals and the group with respect to the allocation of tasks, responsibilities and authority within organizations. It depicts the authority and responsibility relationships between various positions in the organization by showing who reports to whom. Since these positions are held by various persons, the structure is the relationship among people in the organization. The framework of an organization is the structure, wherein the job of each and every person is defined, described and coordinated to achieve the organizational goals.[4]

This chapter aims at discussing the existing organizational structure for the implementation of Mahatma Gandhi National Rural Employment Guarantee Act (MGNREGA), 2005, at the central, state and local level (Figure 2.1).

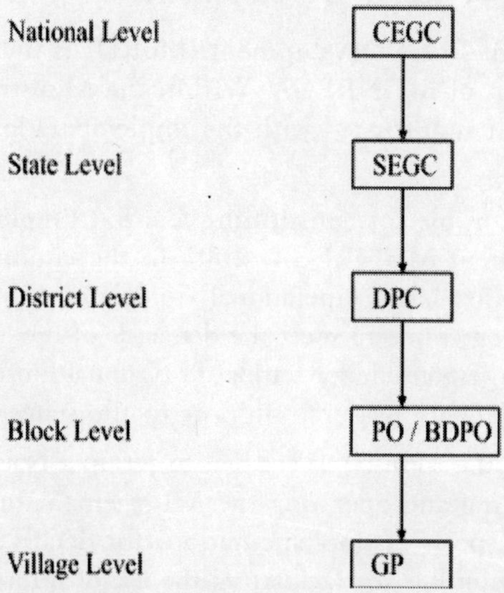

Figure 2.1: Administrative Agencies/Authorities for MGNREGA

Expended form of Abbreviations

Key CEGC – Central Employment Guarantee Council
SEGC – State Employment Guarantee Council
DPC – District Programme Coordinator
PO – Programme Officer
BDPO – Block Development and Panchayat Officer
GP – Gram Panchayat

It was hypothesized that "The administrative machinery for the implementation of MGNREGA does not fulfil the provisions of the Act." In this regard, the appointment, functions and working of the implementing agencies involved at the centre, state and local levels have been detailed. Also, an effort was made to look into the coordination between various agencies at these levels.

2.2 Implementing Agencies for MGNREGA at the Central Level

The Central government is entrusted with the responsibility of implementing MGNREGA in the country. The following sub-sections discuss the role of the Ministry of Rural Development, other agencies and divisions required to be appointed for implementing MGNREGA namely Central Employment Guarantee Council, National Management Team and its various divisions like Programme Management; Human Resource and Capacity Building; Monitoring and Evaluation; Information Technology; Social Audit, Vigilance and Grievance Redressal Division.

2.2(a) Ministry of Rural Development

The Ministry of Rural Development (MoRD) is the nodal agency for the implementation of MGNREGA. Within the Ministry, Department of Rural Development is entrusted with the implementation of MGNREGA (Annexure VI).

MoRD is responsible for constituting Central Employment Guarantee Council to implement MGNREGA, 2005 in the country (for details see page 71). The Ministry issues Operational Guidelines and review permissible works under the programme to meet the demands of the State Governments. The Ministry is also responsible for setting up National Employment Guarantee Fund to ensure adequate resource support to the states.

As per the Act, the Ministry is entitled to set up a National Management Team for maintaining and operating the Management Information System (MIS) on critical aspects of implementation (for details see page 73). The Ministry is also responsible for facilitating the use of information technology to increase efficiency and transparency in the implementation of the Act. Facilitating the technical support and capacity building to improve outcomes of the programme also comes under the Ministry's purview. Further, the Ministry is responsible for monitoring, evaluation and research on the performance of MGNREGA.[5]

2.2(b) Central Employment Guarantee Council

Section 10 of the MGNREGA Act, 2005 provides for the appointment of the Central Employment Guarantee Council (CEGC) as the national level implementing and monitoring agency. The Council is prescribed to advise the Central government on all matters concerning the implementation of the Act. It is required to establish a central evaluation and monitoring system; review the monitoring and grievance redressal mechanism and recommend the required measures to the government. CEGC is also responsible for preparing the annual reports to be laid before the Parliament.[6]

As per the mandate, CEGC is consisted of representatives from different Central level Ministries such as Ministry of Women and Child Development, Ministry of Agriculture, Ministry of Environment and Forest, Ministry of Statistics and Programme Implementation, Ministry of Panchayati Raj, Ministry of Tribal Affairs and Ministry of Social Justice and Empowerment. Apart from these, the Council is also required to include members from Planning Commission, Rural Development Departments of the State Governments, Panchayati Raj Institutions like District Panchayats and Minority Communities. Further, the Act prescribes that not less than one-third of the total number of non-official members of the Central Council must be women. The experts from various fields like social audit, wage employment, water conservation, land development, afforestation, rural engineering and so on has to be included in the Council.[7] The Union Rural Development Minister is the ex-officio Chairman of the Council.[8] A detailed composition of the CEGC has been discussed in Table 2.1.

Table 2.1: Composition of Central Employment Guarantee Council

S.No.	Designation	Member
1.	Union Minister for Rural Development	Chairperson (ex – officio)
2.	Secretary to the Government of India, *Department of Rural Development*	Member (ex–officio)
3.	A nominee of the *Ministry of Women and Child Development* not below the rank of Joint Secretary to the Government of India	Member
4.	A nominee of the *Ministry of Agriculture* not below the rank of Joint Secretary to the Government of India	Member
5.	A nominee of the *Ministry of Environment and Forest* not below the rank of Joint Secretary to the Government of India	Member
6.	A nominee of the *Ministry of Statistics and Programme Implementation* not below the rank of Joint Secretary to the Government of India	Member
7.	A nominee of the *Ministry of Panchayat Raj* not below the rank of Joint Secretary to the Government of India	Member
8.	A nominee of the *Ministry of Tribal Affairs* not below the rank of Joint Secretary to the Government of India	Member
9.	A nominee of the *Ministry of Social Justice and Empowerment* not below the rank of Joint Secretary to the Government of India	Member
10.	A representative of *Planning Commission* not below the rank of Advisor in the Planning Commission	Member
11.	Six representatives of the *Department of Rural Development* of the State Governments who shall not be below the rank of Secretary to the concerned State Government to be nominated by the Central government	Members

12.	Twelve members to be nominated by the Central Government from *Panchayati Raj Institutions*, organizations of workers and disadvantaged groups of whom, four must be women and include – (i) two representatives to be nominated from the *Scheduled Caste*, one representative each from *Scheduled Tribes*, *Other Backward Classes* and *minorities* for the period of one year; (ii) Chairpersons of two *District Panchayats* nominated by the Central Government by rotation for the period of one year	Members
13.	Three experts representing states to be nominated by the Central Government for the period of two years – in the areas of works, such as water conservation, land development, afforestation and plantation and rural engineering, etc; an expert in social audit; and an expert on wage employment	Members
14.	Joint Secretary to the Government of India in the *Ministry of Rural Development* in charge of the Mahatma Gandhi National Rural Employment Guarantee Act, 2005	Member Secretary

Source: The Mahatma Gandhi National Rural Employment Guarantee Act, 2005 (2012), Universal Law Publishing Co. Pvt. Ltd., New Delhi, pp. 37-38.

The Council is mandated to constitute an Executive Committee to give effect to its decisions. The Executive Committee is authorized to manage the administrative and financial affairs and sanction expenditure related to the Council. It is also required to appoint expert groups for technical support and advice to improve the quality of implementation of the Act. The Act stipulates that the Committee meets at least once in three months.[9] The detailed composition of the Committee has been shown in Table 2.2.

Table 2.2: Composition of Executive Committee of CEGC

S.No.	Designation	Member
1.	Secretary to the Government of India, *Department of Rural Development*	President
2.	The Financial Advisor, *Ministry of Rural Development*	Member
3.	Representative of the *Ministry of Panchayati Raj* and two members who are Secretaries of State Governments nominated by the Chairperson of the Executive Committee	Members
4.	Four non-official members of the Central Council to be nominated by the Chairperson of the Central Council	Members
5.	Member-Secretary of Central Council	Member-Secretary

Source: The Mahatma Gandhi National Rural Employment Guarantee Act, 2005 (2012), Universal Law Publishing Co. Pvt. Ltd., New Delhi, p. 40.

Technical Secretariat

The Technical Secretariat is supposed to assist the CEGC and the Executive Committee for providing logistic and technical support for the implementation of the Act. Member-Secretary heads the Technical Secretariat.

2.2(c)National Management Team

The guidelines prescribe a National Management Team (NMT) to be set up within the Department of Rural Development to perform the national-level functions under MGNREGA. NMT is to be headed by the Additional Secretary / Joint Secretary (MGNREGA). NMT has five divisions namely Programme Management; Human Resource Development and Capacity Building; Monitoring and Evaluation; Information Technology; Social Audit, Vigilance and Grievance Redressal Division (Figure 2.2). Each Division has to be comprised of one senior and two junior programme persons.[10]

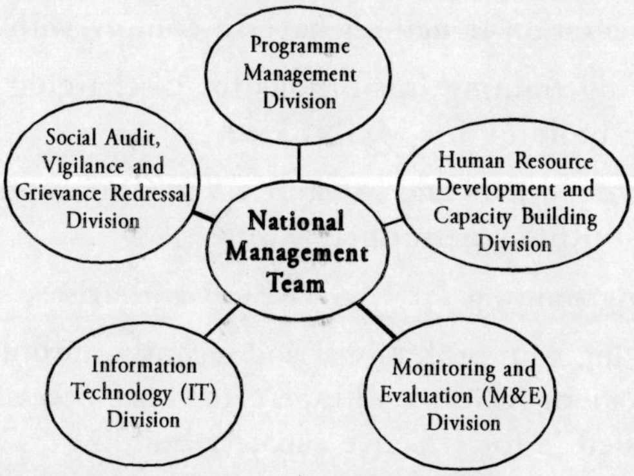

Figure 2.2: Divisions of National Management Team

2.2 (c) (i) Programme Management Division

Programme Management Division is mandated to extend need based technical assistance to states. Specifically, the division has to –

(i) follow up on advisories issued by Ministry and coordinate with states

(ii) follow up with State Governments

(iii) coordinate with different Ministries to establish linkages with MGNREGA outcomes

(iv) coordinate with state team and district team;

(v) share good practice models;

(vi) assess the wage employment requirement of each state.[11]

2.2 (c) (ii) Human Resource Development & Capacity Building Division

The Human Resource Development and Capacity Building Division's primary responsibilities include –

(i) determining standards for human resources recruited for MGNREGA implementation

(ii) formulating recruitment processes, human resource policies and performance evaluation criteria

(iii) assessing gaps, (including region-specific gaps) in human resource deployment and ensuring a steady source of human resources for MGNREGA

(iv) promoting a gender-sensitive, pro-poor and pro-active work culture

(v) working out a system of certification for human resources which all implementation structures have to comply with

(vi) identifying training institutions for discharging responsibilities of capacity building for MGNREGA

(vii) working out syllabi and structure for training courses and certification for MGNREGA personnel

(viii) arranging training for MGNREGA authorities

(ix) networking with professional and technical institutions, Civil Society Organizations (CSOs) and experts to create necessary human resource infrastructure for effective capacity building

(x) assessing training material and ensuring its dissemination across the country

(xi) promoting production and dissemination of high quality resource material (print and electronic) for MGNREGA.[12]

2.2 (c) (iii) Monitoring and Evaluation Division

The Monitoring and Evaluation Division is responsible for establishing and refining systems of monitoring the work under MGNREGA. It is also responsible for commissioning independent evaluations through a carefully selected panel of experts and consultants from across the country.[13]

2.2 (c) (iv) Information Technology Division

The Information Technology (IT) Division is responsible for –

(i) Assessing IT needs, both hardware and software for implementation of MGNREGA

(ii) Deploying the best possible expertise to advise it on effective IT deployments

(iii) Ensuring that states are complying with the IT requirements of data returns and updation and assisting states for achieving IT requirements under MGNREGA.

(iv) Ensuring that latest developments in IT are screened, piloted, developed further and disseminated for use in implementation of MGNREGA.

(vi) Pro-actively setting up a coordination mechanism with other major IT-centred initiatives of the government such as the UIDAI.

(vii) Facilitating the training of MGNREGA personnel in the use of IT.[14]

2.2 (c) (v) Social Audit, Vigilance and Grievance Redressal Division

The Social Audit, Vigilance and Grievance Redressal Division are primarily responsible for –

(i) ensuring that states follow the provisions of Audit of Schemes Rules 2011 in the conduct of social audit.

(ii) providing support in preparation of social audit reporting formats, resource materials, guidelines and manuals for the social audit process.

(iii) monitoring the outcomes of social audit and following up with states for Action Taken Report on issues raised during the social audit.

(iv) monitoring the actions taken by Vigilance Cells at the state, district and local level.

(v) providing technical support to State Government in addressing irregularities and malfeasance including those identified during social audit.

(vi) providing necessary support to State Governments for effective grievance redressal.[15]

2.2(d) A Commentary on the working of CEGC and NMT

The official MGNREGA website was last updated regarding CEGC in December 2011. A newspaper reported that the term of the previous CEGC expired in mid-2012 and since then the Council had not been notified. The previous CEGC was notified in June, 2011 and term of the non-official members expired one year later.[16] Further, the Council is required to meet at least twice a year; however as per the information available on the website, the last CEGC meeting was held in December, 2011.

The official website contains no information regarding NMT or any of its five divisions. The Annual Reports of MGNREGA are also silent about NMT. During interaction with the state officials at Mohali, it came to light that they also did not have any information regarding the establishment and composition of CEGC and NMT.

It is thus apparent that while the structure has been systematically planned, it does not exist and therefore not perform in the way it was conceived.

2.3 Implementing Agencies for MGNREGA at the State Level

The State Government is the nodal agency for the implementation of MGNREGA in the state. It is entrusted with the responsibility of constituting State Employment Guarantee Council (SEGC) and establishing State Employment Guarantee Mission (SEGM) for the effective implementation and monitoring of the scheme in the state. The role of the state government and other agencies and authorities involved in the implementation of MGNREGA in the state has been discussed in the subsequent sub-sections (Figure 2.3).

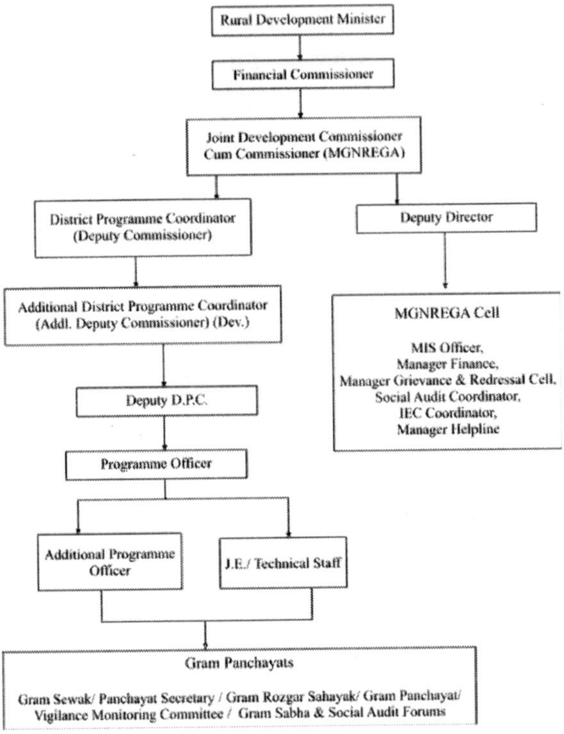

Figure 2.3: Administrative Structure of MGNREGA in Punjab

2.3(a) State Government

State government is authorized to make rules on matters pertaining to state responsibilities under section 32 of the Act and develop and notify the Rural Employment Guarantee Scheme for the state. It is responsible for constituting various agencies in the state for the implementation of the scheme. Foremost, it is responsible for setting up State Employment Guarantee Council as the implementing and monitoring agency in the state.[17] In Punjab, the State Employment Guarantee Council was first set up in 2006. For details, see page 80.

The state government is also responsible for constituting a state level MGNREGS implementation agency/mission with adequate number of high caliber professionals.[18] In Punjab, the state government has established State Employment Guarantee Mission and State Management Team with experts from varied fields such as MIS officer, Finance Manager, Grievance Redressal Cell Manager, Social Audit Coordinator, IEC Coordinator and Manager Helpline. For details see page 81.

Apart from constituting implementing agencies, the state government also has to ensure that full time dedicated personnel are in place for implementing MGNREGA in the state.[19] In Punjab, the government has appointed Additional Programme Officers, Computer Operators-cum-Accounts Clerks, Employment Guarantee Assistants or Gram Rozgar Sahayaks and the staff at the block and village levels. The state government has also delegated financial and administrative powers to the District Programme Coordinator in the district and the Programme Officer at the block level for the effective implementation of the scheme in the state.

The state government is supposed to ensure accountability and transparency in the scheme at all levels. It has to review, research, monitor and evaluate MGNREGA processes and outcomes regularly.[20] In Punjab, social audits are reported to be conducted every six months. For a detailed discussion on social audit in MGNREGA, see page 191.

The state government is also supposed to generate awareness about MGNREGA across the state. In Punjab, various mechanisms were adopted to generate awareness and impart information to the masses such as information display boards at the work-sites, gram sabha meetings, pro-active disclosures, social audits, etc. For a detailed discussion on information disclosure mechanisms, *see page 184.*

2.3(b) State Employment Guarantee Council

Section 12 of the MGNREGA, 2005 provides for the appointment of the State Employment Guarantee Council (SEGC) or 'State Council' as the implementing and monitoring agency at the state level. The Act mandates that SEGC is to be consisted of a Chairperson and such number of official members as may be determined by the State Government. The state government has to nominate 15 non-official members from the Panchayati Raj Institutions, organizations of workers and disadvantaged groups and not less than one-third of the nominated non-official members have to be women. Further, not less than one third of the non-official members must be from amongst the Scheduled Castes (SCs), Scheduled Tribes (STs), Other Backward Classes (OBCs) and minorities.[21]

The State Council is required to advise the state government on all matters concerning the implementation of the scheme in the state. It is authorized to evaluate and monitor the scheme within the state. It has to review the monitoring and redressal mechanisms from time to time and recommend improvements. The State Council is also entitled to recommend the work proposals to be submitted to the Central Government and prompt the widest possible information dissemination about the scheme in the state. It is also expected to prepare annual reports to be laid before the State Legislature by the State Government.[22]

2.3 (b) (i) Working of SEGC in Punjab

During the field survey, the officials informed that SEGC was first constituted in 2006. It consisted of 16 official members and 6 non-official members at the time of its formulation. However, the number of non-official members was increased from 6 to 15 on 5th October, 2010 as the scheme was expanded to the whole of the state in 2008. The non-official members were nominated from amongst the Panchayati Raj Institutions, Labour Organizations and weaker sections (SC's, BC's & women) by the Rural Development Minister, Punjab. One-third of the non-official members were women. Also one-third of the non-official members were SC's, ST's and OBC's.

Further, it was learnt that the Punjab State Employment Guarantee Council has not been constituted since 2013 after expiry of term of the previous SEGC. The officials at the Joint Development Commissioner's office, Mohali reported that the Council would be constituted within a month's time. However, when the researcher checked three months after, it was found that it has not been constituted.

2.3(c) State Employment Guarantee Mission and State Management Team

The Act stipulates that a State Employment Guarantee Mission (SEGM) must be established with adequate operational flexibility and autonomy to support the Panchayati Raj Institutions and other implementing agencies in the states. SEGM is to be headed by a senior Indian Administrative Service officer (Secretary/Commissioner MGNREGS), who is the Chief Executive Officer of the Mission. SEGM is also prescribed to have a Chief Operating Officer to be recruited from the open market.

SEGM's mandate is to formulate a sensitive and impartial human resource policy to recruit a team of committed experts (See Box 2.1) and establish a professional State Management Team (SMT).[23]

Box 2.1: List of Fields of the Matic Experts

Box 2.1

List of fields of thematic experts

The thematic experts build capacity, resolve problems, monitor quality of programme implementation and provide oversight at the district and gram panchayat level. The following is an indicative list of fields where thematic experts may be required –

(a) Rights and entitlements;

(b) Participatory planning process for livelihoods and convergence;

(c) Natural Resource Management (NRM), livelihoods, Quality Standardization and Assurance;

(d) Technical Works & Measurement;

(e) Wage payment;

(f) Information and Communication Technology (ICT);

(g) MIS;

(h) Strategy & Planning;

(i) Monitoring & Evaluation;

(j) Social Inclusion;

(k) Capacity building – Training of field staff at the block, cluster and GP;

(l) Human resource management – Developing a sensitive human resource management policy for contract staff and/or permanent staff;

(m) Social audit and grievance redressal;

(n) Vigilance;

(o) Knowledge Management and learning including research;

(p) External communication

Source: Government of India, (2013a), Mahatma Gandhi National Rural Employment Guarantee Act, 2005, Operational Guidelines, 2013, 4th Edition, Ministry of Rural Development, Department of Rural Development, New Delhi, p. 35.

2.2 (c) (i) Working of SEGM and SMT in Punjab

During the field survey, it was reported that the state government has appointed Joint Development Commissioner as the State Rural Employment Guarantee Commissioner for MGNREGA in the state; thus this is an additional charge. The State Rural Employment Guarantee Commissioner has to ensure that all the activities required to fulfill the objectives of

MGNREGA are carried out. The Commissioner functions as the Member Secretary of the SEGC and is authorized to hear appeals against the decisions or actions of the DPC. He is also responsible for ensuring that the grievance redressal system, social audit, applications for right to information and other measures of public accountability and transparency are effective as well as responsive to the demands of MGNREGA workers and the community.

The field survey further revealed that MGNREGA Cell has been established in the Joint Development Commissioner's Office at Mohali. Under MGNREGA cell, different personnel have been employed to look after the various implementation aspects of the scheme in the state. These personnel have been employed on annual contract basis. The various designations are MIS officer cum IT Manager; Manager Finance; Manager Grievance Redressal cell; Social Audit Coordinator; Information, Education and Communication Coordinator and Manager Helpline. Specifically the officials of the MGNREGA Cell perform the following functions –

(a) **MIS officer cum IT Manager :** The MIS officer cum IT Manager is primarily concerned with technical and software related issues of MGNREGA. His role is to develop and manage the software and also build capacity of other IT officials.

(b) **Manager Finance:** The Finance Manager has responsibility with regard to the management of central and state's share of funds in SEGF. He is also involved in preparing labour budget of MGNREGA and maintaining records regarding disbursal of MGNREGA wages. The audit reports and utilization certificates of all the districts are also compiled by him.

(c) **Manager Grievance Redressal Cell:** Grievance redressal is a significant feature of the programmes engaged in public service delivery. Similarly MGNREGA has imbibed this feature by appointing Manager Grievance Redressal Cell. The Manager is concerned with addressal of written grievances of beneficiaries and complaints of officials. The appointment of Ombudsman and its periodic appraisal is also undertaken by him. The court cases related to MGNREGA are also handled by him. He also establishes grievance helpline and ensures that demand charts related to number of person days, wages, etc. are maintained.

(d) **Coordinator Social Audit:** With a view to maintain transparency, mandatory social audit is undertaken for all MGNREGA works. In this regard, the Coordinator social audit is responsible for compiling and submitting social audit reports to the State Council.

(e) **IEC Coordinator:** Information dissemination is important in public service delivery programmes. It is the responsibility of the state to impart information and generate awareness amongst the masses so that they can claim benefits and transparency can be ensured. The IEC Coordinator is entrusted with this responsibility in the state. He is responsible for activities related to information, education and communication and preparing prospective plans in this regard. He compiles and maintains record of MGNREGA related news and takes action on such news. He is also involved in arranging MGNREGA *melas* for disseminating information.

(f) **Helpline :** The Ministry of Rural Development has established a National toll free helpline for grievance redressal where complaints can be received and sent to the states for remedial action. In Punjab, toll free helpline has been established which receive complaints and forward them to the respective districts and blocks. During interaction, the officials revealed that mostly grievances are received through helpline numbers.

2.4 Implementing Authorities at the District Level

District is the third tier of administration responsible for the implementation of MGNREGA. It is noteworthy to mention that it is also the first tier in local administration responsible for implementation of the programme. For MGNREGA, the district level is administered by District Programme Coordinator who further delegates his authority to the Additional District Programme Coordinator. The roles and duties of District Programme Coordinator and Additional District Programme Coordinator are discussed in detail in the subsequent sections.

2.4(a) District Programme Coordinator

The Act mandates that District Collector or the Chief Executive Officer, Zila Parisahd be designated as the District Programme Coordinator (DPC). The overall coordination and implementation of the scheme at the district level is the responsibility of the DPC.[24]

The DPC is responsible for assisting the district panchayat in discharging its functions, consolidating the block plans along with the district plan and prioritizing the projects for according administrative sanction for implementation. He is also expected to ensure timely release and utilization of funds and provision of work to the wage-seekers. He is responsible for reviewing, monitoring and supervising the performance of the Programme Officers and all implementing agencies of MGNREGA. He is also responsible for conducting periodic inspection of MGNREGA works and verification of muster rolls at the work-sites. He is authorized to be the coordinator of Information Education and Communication (IEC) campaign for MGNREGA within the district and develop annual plans for training and capacity building of various stakeholders in the district. He is also required to submit periodic progress of the works to the state government. He has to ensure that social audits are conducted every six months and follow up action is taken on social audit reports. He also has to ensure that all entries relating to works such as details of the shelf of works, status of implementation, photographs of works at three different stages are entered in NREGAsoft at every required stage.[25]

In Punjab, Deputy Commissioner has been designated as the District Programme Coordinator for MGNREGA. He is the overall incharge at the district level and also the signatory authority for the programme; however, he has delegated his authority to the Additional District Programme Coordinator. The officials reported that the DPC calls meetings once in two months only if the works are not progressing as per the plan.

2.4(b) Additional District Programme Coordinator

The Act mandates that a full-time Additional District Programme Coordinator (ADPC) be exclusively appointed for MGNREGS to look into its day-to-day operations at the district level. The ADPC reports to the DPC and State Employment Guarantee Mission (SEGM). He is to be supported by specialists in Agriculture engineering / Civil engineering, Agriculture / horticulture, MIS, capacity building and social mobilization. The ADPC is also entitled to head the District Employment Guarantee Scheme Unit comprising of functional wings such as Works, Finance and Accounts, Quality Control and Vigilance, Social Audit, Management and Information System, Horticulture, Natural Resource Management, Capacity Building etc.[26]

The ADPC is responsible for preparing District Labour budget and managing MGNREGS Funds, Finance and Accounts. He is also responsible for preparing the shelf of works for the district. He has to ensure opening of works to meet the labour demand, maintaining quality of works and proper management of muster rolls. He is responsible for ensuring timely payments and redressal of grievances; monitoring and inspecting works at the work sites regularly. He is also expected to be involved in conducting training & capacity building of all MGNREGS field staff in the district. He is responsible for conducting social audit and ensuring follow-up actions for maintaining transparency and accountability.[27]

During the field survey, it came to light that the Additional Deputy Commissioner (ADC) has been designated as the ADPC for MGNREGA. He looks after all the MGNREGA related work in the district and reports to the District Programme Coordinator (Deputy Commissioner) of the district. The officials at the block level corroborated that they had frequent interactions regarding MGNREGA with the ADPC. The ADPC directs them regarding utilization of grants received from the state government and undertaking various types of works in the villages. Thus, it could be said that the ADPC set the targets, to be met from time to time, for the block level officials.

2.5 Implementing Authorities at the Block Level

The block level is the second tier in local administration responsible for implementing MGNREGA. For implementing and coordinating the works in the villages, the block level administration is provided with various officials, namely, Programme Officer, Additional Programme Officer, Computer Operators-cum-Accounts Clerk, Junior Engineer. Along with the availability of these officials, it is also essential to build capacity of the officials to discharge their functions effectively. Thus, in this regard, provision of Block Resource Centre has been made. The following discussion sheds light on the roles and responsibilities of the Block Resource Centre and these officials.

2.5(a) Programme Officer

The Programme Officer (PO) is the overall in-charge of all MGNREGA works in the block and acts as a coordinator for MGNREGA at his block. The Act mandates the State Government to appoint a person not below the rank of Block Development Officer as Programme Officer at the block level. He is accountable to the DPC.[28]

The PO viz (B.B.O.) is authorized to consolidate all project proposals received from gram panchayats into the block plan and submit it to the district panchayat. He has to monitor and supervise works within the block and ensure fair payment of wages to the labourers. He is responsible for payment of unemployment allowance in case employment is not provided on time. He is also entitled to maintain proper accounts of the resources received, released and utilized and ensure completion of records like job-card register, work register, gram sabha resolution, work estimates, receipt register, muster rolls, wage payment, bills and vouchers for materials procured for each work, measurement books, asset register, etc. related to MGNREGA works. He has to ensure undertaking of social audits and following up on required actions, availability of documents required by the Social Audit Unit (SAU) to conduct social audit. He is also responsible for redressing grievances within the block and facilitating technical support to gram panchayats.[29]

During the field survey, it was reported that the Block Development and Panchayat Officers (BDPO) had been designated as the Programme

Officers at the block level. However, the BDPO's were only the signatory authority for MGNREGA; the MGNREGA related works were delegated to the Additional Programme Officers (APOs) hired specifically for MGNREGA on contractual basis. It was found that APOs were actively involved in implementing MGNREGA works. They were the link between villages and the block. As stated earlier, the targets given by ADPC were realized in the field by APOs with the help of village level officials like Gram Rozgar Sahayaks and gram panchayat members. The APOs office was placed in MGNREGA Cell in the BDPOs office.

2.5(b) Computer Operators-cum-Accounts Clerk

The state has to ensure that at least three Computer Operators-cum-Accounts Clerk are deployed at the Block Computer Centre (one per cluster). The Act mandates that the Computer Operator-cum-Accounts Clerk can operate at GP level or block level depending on the location of Computer Centre. He is prescribed to assist the GP or PO exclusively in data entry work and maintenance of MGNREGS accounts.[30] Specifically, he is responsible for performing the following duties –

(a) Data entry and generation of job-cards, work demand (registered), technical estimates, work commencement letters, etc.

(b) Generation of pay orders and preparing necessary cheques.

(c) Maintenance of Accounts, registers, files and other MGNREGS related documents.

(d) Generation of MIS and other review reports for Programme Officer.[31]

During the field survey, it was found that one Computer Operator-cum-Accounts Clerk was appointed per block. He maintained and upgraded all the MGNREGA related records at the block level. The interactions with the Computer Operators revealed that although the record maintenance of over 100 gram panchayats was a tedious job, they did not complain as they were on a contractual basis and feared losing their job. They received a remuneration of Rs. 9300 per month.

2.5(c) Junior Engineer

To ensure adequate human and technical support at sub-district levels in the implementation of MGNREGA, the Central Government has proposed to create a district cadre of staff to be deployed for ensuring engineering and other technical assistance in implementing MGNREGA.[32]

For this purpose Junior Engineers (JEs) – Panchayati Raj have been assigned additional charge for implementing MGNREGA works in the block. The JE is responsible for preparing work estimates and giving layout of works for construction / civil works under MGNREGA, obtaining necessary technical and administrative approval, monitoring execution of works as per the prescribed procedure and providing technical supervision.[33]

During the field survey it was found that two JEs were available per block i.e. for more than 100 gram panchayats. During interactions with the JEs and block officials, it was found that JEs were providing technical expertise for various MGNREGA works. However, they complained of work overload. In this regard they had also submitted a memorandum to ADPC stating that either more JEs be appointed by the government or they should be provided extra remuneration for MGNREGA works.

2.5(d) Block Resource Centre

The Operational Guidelines prescribe that a Block Resource Centre (BRC) must be set up for knowledge inputs, capacity building and convergence of MGNREGA works. BRC is required to provide technical inputs for planning; maintain data base on local natural resource endowment (viz. groundwater, rainfall, soils, etc.) needed for planning; effect convergence between MGNREGS and other production-oriented schemes of government for gap filling and value addition so that assets created under MGNREGS are productively used by the poor to enhance their incomes.[34]

During the field survey, it was reported that BRCs had not been set up anywhere in the state. Currently, State Institute for Rural Development (SIRD) is undertaking capacity building programmes of MGNREGA officials such as Sarpanches and other panchayat members, GRS, APOs, etc. The officials at the block level reported that no training had been imparted to any of MGNREGA officials for the last three years. It was learnt that the state government had sanctioned an amount of Rs. 2 crore and ten lakhs in August, 2015 for the construction of BRCs in one block of every district in the state under Rajiv Gandhi Panchayat Sashaktikaran Abhiyan (RGPSA) scheme. In district Patiala, the Sanour block has been identified as the location for BRC. However, it is too early to comment on its implementation.

2.6 Implementing Authorities at The Village Level!

The village is the lowest tier for execution of MGNREGA works. The assets created under MGNREGA are for public utilization in the villages. The village is the actual field of action for MGNREGA as the type of works to be undertaken in the village, number of households to be provided employment and other planning and execution activities are undertaken here. Further, gram sabha (assembly of all eligible voters of the village) is the main planning and executing body. The decisions of gram sabha meetings are converted into plan proposals by the gram panchayat. The gram panchayat consisting of elected village head (Sarpanch) and other elected members is assisted by Gram Rozgar Sahayak, work-site supervisor and Cluster Facilitation Team experts. The roles and responsibilities of all these functionaries have been discussed in detail below.

2.6(a) Gram Panchayat

The Gram Panchayat (GP) is the pivotal body for implementation of MGNREGA works at the village level. At least 50 percent of the works in terms of cost have to be allotted to the GPs for implementation. The GP is responsible for receiving applications for registration of the households; verifying the applications; registering households and issuing job-cards. It is also responsible for receiving applications for work; issuing dated receipts for work applications and allocating work within fifteen days of the application or from the date when work is sought in the case of an advance application, whichever is later. GP is required to conduct periodic surveys to assess demand for work. It is expected to identify and plan works and develop a shelf of projects including determination of the order of their priority; these are to be forwarded to the PO for scrutiny and preliminary approval. It is responsible for executing works and maintaining accounts and providing utilization certificates in formats prescribed by Central/State government. It is required to prepare an annual report containing the facts and figures and achievements relating to the implementation of the Scheme.[35]

The GP is responsible for generating awareness and social mobilization through pro-active disclosure of the details of works at the work-site and the GP office. It is also responsible for convening gram sabha meetings for planning and social audit of MGNREGA works. It has to ensure availability of all relevant documents including the muster rolls, bills, vouchers, measurement books, copies of sanction orders and other connected books of account and papers to the gram sabha and the SAU for the purpose of conducting social audit.[36]

During the field survey, it was found that GPs were actively involved in undertaking MGNREGA works such as renovation of traditional water bodies, tree plantation and micro-irrigation works. In all 'with-work' villages, the GPs had provided work to households by preparing their job-cards. The muster rolls were available on demand at the work-sites while other records were maintained.

However, the GPs did not perform well on account of social mobilization and conducting social audit in letter and spirit. Very few GPs had maintained display boards relating to MGNREGA works in the villages. The members of GPs reported that villagers were not interested in participating in gram sabha activities for planning of MGNREGA works; rather they were more concerned about job and wages. Also GPs had not disbursed unemployment allowance to anyone who demanded employment but could not be provided work.

2.6(b) Gram Sabha

MGNREGA follows bottom-up planning process for implementation. In this regard Gram Sabha (GS) is entrusted with the task of planning and executing MGNREGA works. It is prescribed to recommend works to be taken up and determine the order of priority in which works will be initiated under MGNREGA. It is entitled to monitor the execution of works within the GP. It is the primary forum to conduct social audit providing a platform to all residents to obtain relevant information from all the implementing agencies including GPs in relation to MGNREGA works. The GS is the principal forum for wage seekers to raise their voices and make demands. [37]

During the field survey, it was found that GSs were defunct in the locale of study. The process of planning and executing MGNREGA works was done by the GPs and the formality of gram sabha meetings was fulfilled by obtaining signature and thumb impressions of few villagers. Moreover, Sarpanches were of the view that gram sabha meetings were avoidable as invariably due to different political affiliations in the villages, the gram sabha meetings became fractious and ended without any resolution being approved. For detailed discussions, see page 185-186 and 194.

2.6(c) Gram Rozgar Sahayak /Employment Guarantee Assistant

Gram Rozgar Sahayak (GRS) is mandated to assist the GP in executing MGNREGA works in the village. The Operational Guidelines mandate that at least one GRS is deployed in every GP except in GPs where demand for work under MGNREGA is almost non-existent. Also, more than one GRS can be deployed in GPs that have high labour potential and GPs with scattered habitations and tribal areas. The GRS needs to be adequately trained in work-site management and measurement of works.[38]

The GRS is responsible for overseeing the process of registration, distributing job-cards, providing dated receipts against job applications and allocating work to the applicants. He is expected to record attendance of labour every day, either himself or through the mate at the worksite and ensure that all mates attend worksites on time and marks attendance in the prescribed muster roll at work-site only. He also has to ensure that *group mark-outs*[39] are given to the labourers and work-site facilities are provided at the work-sites. He is responsible for regularly updating job-cards of the workers and maintaining all MGNREGS-related registers at the gram panchayat level, assisting the Panchayat Secretary or any other official responsible for maintenance of MGNREGA accounts and ensuring that these documents were conveniently available for public scrutiny. He also has to facilitate gram sabha meetings and social audit. [40]

In Punjab, the GRSs have been appointed on contractual basis. The office of ADPC advertised the post in the local newspapers. The minimum qualification was senior secondary along with a diploma in Computer Applications. The office averred that interviews were conducted and applicants had been appointed on merit basis.

In district Patiala, the number of GRSs varied from block to block. In block Nabha, nine GRSs had been appointed to cover 171 GPs, while in Samana, seven GRSs had been appointed for 96 GPs. In block Sanour, the number of GRSs was six while the number of GPs in the block was 107. The GRSs were paid a fixed sum of Rs.6000 per month. There was no incentive system for their performance. However, as they belonged to that area, it was considered a big advantage not to suffer dislocation. Also, extra expense on accommodation, travel, time was saved and these factors were incentivizing the locals employed as GRS. When interviewed about the motivation for commitment on a rather low salary and absence of incentive system, the overwhelming response was the commitment arising from the GRS' belonging to those areas and identifying with the target group and the need to reach the programmes' benefits to the community.

GRSs were actively engaged with GPs in performing the task of providing job-cards to the workers, providing work-site facilities, recording attendance and maintaining all the records at the village level related to MGNREGA. But GRSs were unable to conduct social audit meetings in letter and spirit of the Act as gram sabhas were defunct in the area of study. For detailed discussion, ***see page 158, 162 and 165-166.***

2.6(d) Mates or Worksite Supervisors

A mate or worksite supervisor is required for each work-site. The guidelines prescribe that at least one mate should be appointed for every fifty workers. A mate should be literate and have worked in MGNREGS for a reasonable period of time. While selecting mates, priority is to be given to women and the differently-abled. The guidelines further prescribe that a mate should not be a worker on the same MGNREGS work site at the same point of time. Their remuneration should be equal to that of a semi-skilled labour.[41]

The mate is mandated to supervise the work-sites and capture daily attendance in the muster rolls. He is entitled to provide daily mark-outs to groups of labourers and record initial weekly measurements. He is also responsible for facilitating applications for job-cards and submitting them to the GP; facilitating demand for work from individual workers or groups of labourers, submitting them to GP and obtaining a duly dated receipt as acknowledgement. He is also responsible for submitting muster rolls with attendance duly marked to the GRS. He is responsible for creating awareness about rights and entitlements under MGNREGA and helping illiterate labourers to learn to sign and to calculate wages earned. He is also expected to ensure there is no free-riding among the workers. The availability of a first aid box with adequate materials for emergency treatment of minor injuries and other health hazards connected with the work being executed is also the mates' responsibility.[42]

In a number of states, the worksite supervision has been assigned to women Self-Help Groups (SHGs) to facilitate women participation in MGNREGA and at the same time to support SHGs financially.[43]

During the field survey it was found that when the number of workers was small, the GRSs handled the responsibilities of the mates. In case the number of workers was large, the mates were appointed from the village or near-by villages. One of the mates revealed that workers did not perform the tasks properly and when asked to do so they argued with him on the grounds that he was also one of them so he should not be telling them to do work. Further, no women worker was found to be appointed as mate in the locale of study.

It was also observed that mates were equally ignorant about the various provisions of the scheme and hence were unable to create awareness about the rights and entitlements amongst the workers. It was found that mates had not been trained ever to carry out their responsibilities. The researcher also observed that no provision for emergency treatment was available for minor injuries at the work-sites. In case of emergency, local doctors were consulted.

2.6(e) Technical Assistant

The Technical Assistant (TA) is entitled to assist the GPs in identifying and conducting measurement of works. He is to be appointed for a cluster of villages depending on the potential labour demand. He is prescribed to be trained in estimating and measuring works pertaining to watershed development, natural resource management, agriculture, horticulture and so on. He has to report to the GP and PO.[44]

The TA is responsible for identifying works as per the gram sabha resolution and preparing estimates for works. He is entitled to capture measurements on weekly basis for all the works taken up within three days of the closing of muster rolls and maintain measurement books. He is expected to maintain the quality of works and mentor mates and GRSs regarding it. He is also responsible for building technical capacities of mates and Gram Rozgar Sahayaks.[45]

During the field survey, it was learnt that there were no TAs in district Patiala while in other districts of the state TAs were appointed. The officials were unable to provide any reasons for the non-appointment of TAs in district Patiala. They reported that in the absence of TAs, JEs were doubling up as TAs. However, they were already overburdened, therefore, only some duties of TAs were performed by them. The major part of the responsibilities of TAs like weekly measurement of works, mentoring the mates and GRSs on measurement and quality of works were ignored. Thus, the unavailability of TAs has hampered the quality and timely measurement of works to great extent.

2.6(f) Cluster Facilitation Teams

The MGNREGA Operational Guidelines mandate the states to establish Cluster Facilitation Teams (CFTs) for a cluster of GPs; these are supposed to be comprised of four specialists, one each for community mobilization, soil and moisture conservation, agriculture and allied activities and MIS & ICT (Table 2.3).[46] The guidelines prescribe that initially, the CFTs could be established in the blocks which require an intensive approach for meeting the objectives of the programme. These areas would basically be where the population of landless agriculture labourers, SCs, STs and other vulnerable groups is very high.

Table 2.3: Qualifications of CFT Members

Community Mobilization	A Graduate in any discipline with at least three years of experience in rural development / rural management, Or
	An MSW or Post Graduate in Rural Development / Rural Management with atleast two years of experience in rural development
Soil and Moisture conservation	A Graduate in agriculture engineering or soil and water conservation or geologyor civil engineering with at least two years of experience in rural development, Or
	A Diploma in agriculture engineering or soil and water conservation or geology or civil engineering with at least three years of experience in rural development
Agriculture and Allied	A Graduate in agriculture engineering or soil and water conservation or geology or civil engineering with at least two years of experience in rural development Or
	A Diploma in agriculture engineering or soil and water conservation or geologyor civil engineering with at least three years of experience in rural development,
MIS and ICT	A Post Graduate Diploma in Computers with at least one year of experience in rural development Or
	A Diploma in Computers with at least two year of experience in rural development

Source: Government of India (2013a), Mahatma Gandhi National Rural Employment Guarantee Act, 2005, Operational Guidelines, 2013, 4th Edition, Ministry of Rural Development, Department of Rural Development, New Delhi, p. 31.

The states need to identify blocks for intensive interventions based on an objective criterion decided by the Ministry. Each identified block must have at least three CFTs each of which will serve a cluster of GPs, being accountable to each GP within their own cluster. A cluster will cover around 15,000 job-cards or an area of about 15,000 hectares, broadly corresponding to the boundaries of a milli-watershed and local aquifer.[47]

The CFTs are operationalized under convergence of MGNREGA with National Rural Livelihood Mission (NRLM) and with support of CSOs.[48]

The CFTs are supposed to be working with the gram panchayats and mobilizing and creating awareness among potential job seekers about their entitlements and procedures under MGNREGA. They are responsible for facilitating preparation of the Annual Plan for every GP within the cluster, shelf of works and annual labour and material budget; ensuring GS approval for such perspective plans. CFTs are also mandated to work with elected representatives and functionaries on all aspects of planning and implementation of MGNREGA including asset verification, measurement, payment, monitoring and evaluation, MIS maintenance and social audit. They are also responsible for providing training and technical guidance to elected representatives and functionaries such as Community Resource Persons (barefoot professionals), GRS, GP members and Panchayat Secretaries. They are also supposed to conduct random checks of the measurements taken by the Technical Assistants; do resource mapping i.e., an assessment of quantitative and qualitative status of natural resources (topography, soil depth and quality, rainfall, water bodies, groundwater, vegetation). They are also responsible for assessing the additional resources required.[49]

The CFT project was planned to be piloted in 250 most backward blocks of the country identified on the basis of Planning Commission Backward Index in 2014-15. The project was supposed to be a three-way convergence between MGNREGA, NRLM and CSOs. However, the project took off in only 30 blocks selected by the states for the CFT project. The states focused on areas with the presence of civil society organizations rather than on poor human development indicators.[50]

CFTs assisted in participatory planning of the allocated GPs, initiated capacity building of technical staff, Self-Help Groups, MGNREGA workers and PRI representatives on MGNREGA processes in its first year in the block. Even though these achievements are significant for participatory planning in the programme implementation, the CFT project needs to be extended in the remaining 220 blocks irrespective of the good/bad situation regarding civil society organizations presence.[51]

In Punjab, no block has been listed in the 250 backward blocks identified Planning Commission Backward Index. Thus, no CFTs have been constituted in the state.

2.7 Conclusion

The mandated administrative machinery responsible for implementing MGNREGA at the Central, State, district, block and village level has been discussed. Correspondingly, the researcher evaluated the role and duties of the existing MGNREGA agencies and authorities in the field. It was observed that the requisite agencies at Central level (CEGC and NMT) and the State level (SEGC) had not been constituted. Non-existence of these agencies has hampered the implementation of the programme to a large extent. The officials at the state level were also found to be unaware about the existence of central level agencies, even when they existed prior to 2012.

SEGM had recruited only six types of experts out of the prescribed sixteen for the State Management Team. Some important areas requiring expertise were completely ignored such as wage payment, Human Resource Management, Knowledge Management and Learning including research, social inclusion, etc. The District Programme Coordinator and Programme Officer being overburdened had delegated their authorities to the Additional District Programme Coordinator and Additional Programme Officer at the district and block levels respectively.

An acute shortage of technical manpower in the form of Junior Engineers and Technical Assistants was found in the locale of the study. The JEs (Panchayati Raj) were assigned additional charge for MGNREGA while no TAs were appointed in the district. This has led to a vicious cycle of delay in measurement of MGNREGA works, wage payments to the workers and preparation of work proposals. The shortage of other staff like data entry operators and GRS has also resulted in the overburdening of the existing staff.

The **additional responsibilities** allotted to the permanent staff and overburdening of the permanent and contractual staff has been imposed without any incentive being paid to either. To make the situation worse, MGNREGA staff has complained of delay in payment of salaries. Further, the additional charge to the permanent staff and non-appointment of the mandated MGNREGA staff has resulted in compromising the quality of works in the villages. The quality of works has also suffered as the staff has not been imparted any form of training in the last three years. Thus, a lot needs to be done including recruitment of adequate staff, doing away with the 'additional charge' practice, imparting training to the staff, timely remuneration and so on.

Hence, the hypothesis namely, "The administrative machinery for the implementation of MGNREGA does not fulfil the provisions of the Act", stands all approved.

Endnotes

1. W.R. Scott (2008), Institutions and Organizations: Ideas and Interests, Sage Publications, Los Angeles, pp. 26-45.
2. Amitai Etzioni (1964), Modern Organizations, Prentice-Hall, New Jersey, p.1.
3. Ibid, p. 3.
4. Nilanjan Sengupta, Mousumi S. Bhattacharya and R.N. Sengupta (2012), Managing Change in Organizations, PHI Learning Private Limited, New Delhi, p. 19.
5. Government of India (2013a), Mahatma Gandhi National Rural Employment Guarantee Act, 2005, Operational Guidelines, 2013, 4th Edition, Ministry of Rural Development, Department of Rural Development, New Delhi, p. 11.
6. The Mahatma Gandhi National Rural Employment Guarantee Act, 2005 (2012), Universal Law Publishing Co. Pvt. Ltd., New Delhi, p. 40.
7. Ibid, pp. 37-38.
8. Ibid, p. 13.
9. Ibid, p. 40.
10. Government of India (2013a), op. cit., p. 35.
11. Ibid, pp. 35-36.
12. Ibid, p. 36.
13. Ibid.
14. Ibid, pp. 36-37.
15. Ibid, p. 37.
16. Tewari, op. cit., p. 7.
17. Government of India (2013a), op. cit., p.10.
18. Ibid.
19. Ibid.
20. Ibid.
21. The Mahatma Gandhi National Rural Employment Guarantee Act, 2005, op. cit., p. 15.
22. Ibid, p. 15.
23. Government of India (2013a) op. cit., pp. 34-35.
24. Ibid, p. 33.
25. Ibid, pp. 8-9.
26. Ibid, p. 33.
27. Ibid.
28. Ibid, p. 32.
29. Ibid, p. 7.
30. Ibid, pp. 29-30.
31. Ibid, p. 30.

32. Ibid, p. 32.
33. Ibid.
34. Ibid.
35. Ibid, pp. 6-7.
36. Ibid.
37. Ibid, p. 6.
38. Ibid, p. 27.
39. The minimum output required to be given to every group of workers so as to earn daily wage rate.
40. Government of India (2013a) op. cit., pp. 27-28.
41. Ibid, p. 28.
42. Ibid.
43. Ibid, pp. 28-29.
44. Ibid, p. 29.
45. Ibid.
46. Ibid, pp. 30-31.
47. Ibid, p. 30.
48. [Online] Available from http://nrega.nic.in/nrega/writeraddata/circulars/nrega_doc_faqs.pdf, [Accessed online on 28th may, 2015].
49. Government of India (2013a), op. cit., p. 31.
50. [Online] Available from: http://nrega.nic.in/Netnrega/WriteReaddata/Circulars/1072Letter_ CFT_02_07_2015.pdf, [Accessed on 15th January, 2016].
51. Ibid.

3

Outreach of Mahatma Gandhi National Rural Employment Guarantee Act (MGNREGA)

3.1 Introduction

Governments design and implement development programmes for ensuring social and economic upliftment of the people. The programmes are aimed at delivering the entitlements on a universal scale. The outreach of these programmes should be maximum for the targeted population so that they can get most of the benefits. For this, the institutional arrangements are made to deliver the services efficiently and effectively. There are many instances when the policies and programmes, particularly those intended to benefit the poor and weaker sections have performed relatively ineffectively on account of weak administration, under-staffing, lack of motivation, large scale leakages and so on. The access to services is also restricted due to assymetrical information dissemination and lack of awareness regarding the services. This lack of awareness hampers the capacity of citizens to make claims for access and to demand effective service delivery.[1] Thus government, apart from implementing the programmes also needs to enhance awareness amongst the people regarding their claims and rights under the programmes. One such approach that aims at enhancing awareness is social guarantee approach.

3.2 Social Guarantee Approach

"Social guarantees are sets of legal or administrative mechanisms that determine specific entitlements and obligations related to certain rights and ensure the fulfilment of those obligations on the part of the state".[2] "These are the minimums that society provides to all its members, ensuring their access to essential opportunities and well-being. Social guarantees serve as tools for social policy design and service delivery that can advance the protection and fulfilment of social and economic rights".[3] Thus, these contribute towards bridging structural gaps that exists between legally declared norms and their effective implementation.[4] Therefore, social guarantee framework provides an innovative approach to integrate a rights-based perspective into social policy. The social guarantee approach moves beyond a purely normative framework to give concrete meaning to economic, social, and cultural rights and hence allows for their operationalization into policies and programmes.[5]

Social guarantee approach seeks to strengthen delivery and monitoring of the social programmes. It implies an institutional design that emphasizes synergy and coordination among agencies and providers to achieve full potential of the social programmes. It also helps in reducing gaps in the opportunities for citizens by promoting universal access and quality standard for the essential services. It can also strengthen democratic governance by facilitating a non-discriminatory agreement among members of society for providing basic entitlements to every individual. In other words, social guarantees are safeguards that every member of a society must be provided.[6]

Social Guarantee Approach requires specific institutional arrangements to design the programmes, implement and monitor the policies that will lead to the realization of the rights.[7] It emphasizes upon the participation of rights-holders in the design, implementation and evaluation of the social guarantees and their associated entitlements.[8] Also, the institution responsible for providing benefits must inform rights holders of the ways in which they can solicit access or claim their benefits. "Without awareness and information, possibilities to exercise rights or claim the guarantees that are rightfully theirs are significantly reduced".[9]

Further, channels for information dissemination are important so that the right-holders are aware of what can be expected from the realization of guarantees. A rights-based approach to social policy comprises of –

(i) the definition and widespread communication of rights, entitlements and standards which enable citizens to hold public policy makers and providers accountable for the delivery of the programmes.

(ii) the availability of redressal mechanisms which can be utilized by the citizens if they are unable to claim specified entitlements or social minimums.

(iii) a commitment to the equitable delivery of the specified rights, entitlements and standards to all on universal basis.[10]

A key element of all rights-based approaches is the intent to empower people to act as "rights-holding citizens" in relation to the state rather than merely as beneficiaries of services. Thus, social guarantee helps in conceptualizing the operational side of a rights-based social policy i.e.

conceptualizing a set of policy mechanisms that allow for the widespread definition and communication of rights and commitment to equitable service delivery.[11]

The approach recognizes that most of the countries have not designed social programmes on the basis of explicit guarantees. In most of the states, social programmes are at a level of pre-guarantee i.e. they ensure only partial protection and fulfilment of social rights. In some cases, the rights are legally stipulated but lack institutional and financial support while in others the rights are incorporated in programmatic and institutional operations but are not bound by law to concrete performance standards. Even if these are integrated both in law and policy, citizens cannot use services due to lack of information and awareness.[12]

The term "guarantee" is used in two different categories in relation to social policy – "implicit" and "explicit." Implicit guarantees can be taken as the sum of a set of policy measures and programmatic arrangements by the state to provide a given service; while the "explicit" offer of guaranteed delivery of a given service or benefit by a political actor to citizens does not happen. The implicit content of social protection policy in Indonesia has been described in the aftermath of the financial crisis of the late 1990s in terms of two different kinds of guarantees. The "safety net" is a guarantee of support for those falling into absolute poverty as a result of the crisis while the "safety rope" provides a guarantee of not falling more than a limit. The "safety rope" applies to both the middle class as well as the poor. This comparative metaphor has been used to distinguish between different programmes. First, the programmes which primarily work as a safety net e.g. subsidized sales of rice targeted at the poor. Second, the programmes which functioned during the crisis to help workers with different incomes to sustain their livelihood e.g. a specific job creation scheme.[13]

Explicit guarantees differ in as much as the offer to citizens of a specific guarantee by an administration creates a firmer basis for implementation and bottom-up claims. If the framework of institutions is strong enough for the guarantee, it will create pressure on the executive to keep adjusting policies and resource allocations until the guarantee is met in practice. Codification of the guarantee into law provides a legal basis that encourages both citizens and officials to adjust their strategies and behaviours to realize the benefits e.g., employment guarantee programmes, legal instruments and practices in India. This has grown into a national programme, backed up by national legislation and operational in every state of India. By 2010, the various state-level programmes operating under the umbrella framework of the Mahatma Gandhi National Rural Employment Guarantee Act (MGNREGA) of 2005 reached 52 million households across the country making it the largest social protection programme in the world.[14]

3.3 Employment Guarantees in India

Employment guarantees in India have their origin in the Maharashtra Employment Guarantee Scheme (MEGS) of the 1970s. The original Maharashtra programme offered employment on public works schemes as a right given under certain specific conditions. The scheme guaranteed employment within 15 days of the demand being made to all adults (above 18 years) in rural areas and willing to do manual unskilled work on a piece-rate basis. If the site of work was more than 8 kilometres from the workers' residence, the administration was also obliged to provide temporary shelter.[15]

Adoption of "guarantees" in context of the state's delivery of policy undertakings creates an explicit connection to "rights-approach" of the social policy as it captures the side of a right which is about the state's obligation to deliver.[16] The original MEGS, contained a number of features which encouraged expectations from the public institutions. Firstly, there was a legal framework underpinning the programme. Secondly, the funding patterns established for funding MEGS such as inclusion of specific taxes and obligation of state government to match the amounts raised in tax. Thirdly, coordination between Revenue Department that oversaw the scheme and various line agencies that plan and implement the works such as Departments of Irrigation, Forestry, Agriculture, etc. The articulation of political environment and a solid basis in the legal, fiscal and programmatic domains provided certainty, credibility and predictability to the programme.[17]

The programme illustrated that a potential benefit translate economic and social rights into concrete entitlements or guarantees. This relates to their role in the transition from a clientelist mode of politics to one where claims can be made on the basis of citizenship, rather than patron-client or other particularistic relationships. In other words, people may be encouraged to mobilize as citizens – with equal rights and obligations – in their dealings with the state, rather than seeking benefits through particularistic relations. In practice, this is likely to be a gradual and incremental change and will build on the political dynamics which make it feasible. Nonetheless, the notion that a rights-based mode of delivery of social policy can facilitate the evolution of a political culture towards greater equity and voice is persuasive. In a study of the political process which generated the National Rural Guarantee Scheme established by the national legal instrument of 2005, it was observed that a broad range of civil society groups perceived guaranteed employment as the most important instrument through which rural distress could be addressed.[18] This was because "it was felt that a demand-based system (where applicants must apply for work) would strengthen civil action".[19] The groups had different interests and foci, including women's empowerment, local-level democratization, workers' rights etc.

The success of MEGS encouraged the development of the national framework for employment guarantees to a great extent. The national legislation, National Rural Employment Guarantee Act (NREGA) was passed in 2005. Some significant chages were made while developing framework of the national legislation e.g., the requirement of 50 people in MEGS to initiate works has been reduced to ten in the national legislation. The gram panchayat and gram sabhas has also been assigned more role in the new scheme for registering households and issuing job cards at the panchayat level; preparing shelf of works like water conservation, drought-proofing, irrigation, land development, flood control and rural connectivity. The national legislation is also more explicit than the Maharashtra programme on many matters; for example, wage levels are pinned to the national official minimum wage; the use of contractors is prohibited which were heavily utilized in MEGS. However, its key features clearly derive from the Maharashtra experience. These are notably the guarantee of 100 days of work every year to all those who request it; 15 days time period within which the administration must respond to requests and the codification of the guarantee through detailed legal instruments.[20]

This chapter aims to view the awareness amongst the primary stakeholders to claim the guarantees imbibed in law. The chapter is drafted in order to test the outreach of MGNREGA among the workers with respect to the level of awareness. It was hypothesised that "The outreach of MGNREGA has generated awareness of its key provisions among the job-card holders in the rural areas".

3.4 Mechanisms of Awareness Generation in MGNREGA

Awareness generation has been considered a significant factor for accessing the entitlements and guarantees under MGNREGA. The rights based approach of MGNREGA is premised on the expectation that poor delivery can be overcome by the people themselves if they demand their rights and pressurize the delivery system to be more efficient and accountable.[21] Specific actions have been prescribed by various stakeholders for creating awareness among the people. These have been discussed in detail in the following paragraphs.

(i) Information, Education and Communication plan : The MGNREGA Operational Guidelines, 2013 mandate that states need to develop an Information, Education and Communication (IEC) plan to reach out to the masses. The IEC activities are aimed at facilitating dissemination of right based provisions of the Act to ensure that the workers know their right to demand wage employment and exercise the right of applying for jobs according to their need. The guidelines further mandate that the IEC plan must clearly indicate state, district, block and local level activities. For preparing the

IEC plan, workshops can be held to clearly delineate timelines and target audience for each activity.[22]

(ii) Interpersonal communication methods : The guidelines prescribe that a combination of interpersonal communication (IPC) methods and mass media can be adopted to disseminate information. Special strategies like puppet shows, folk dances and songs, street plays, focused group discussions, participatory games, wall writings, posters, notice boards, etc. can be used to target women, small and marginal farmers, below poverty line families, SCs, STs and other extremely disadvantaged groups to ensure their greater participation in MGNREGA works.[23]

(iii) Role of Youth : The youth needs to be involved in awareness generation campaigns like Bharat Nirman Volunteers (BNV)[24] at the grass root level. The volunteers of Bharat Nirman and Nehru Yuva Kendra, SHGs can be engaged for mobilizing gram sabhas and Panchayati Raj Institutions.[25]

(iv) Civil Society Organisations: The Act also prescribe that Civil Society Organisations (CSOs) must be involved in information dissemination as they can play a major role in supporting and strengthening IEC activities. These are to be engaged in mobilizing workers so that the wage seekers are able to secure their rights, entitlements, demand work and wage payments on time.[26]

(v) Involvement of other departments in the state: The State Public Relations Department as well as publicity and extension units of various departments like Agriculture, Social Welfare, Education, Health and Family Welfare of both State and Central Government should be actively involved in planning and implementation stages to achieve maximum information dissemination. State units of Press Information Bureau, Directorate of Audio Video Publicity, Field Publicity Bureau, Song and Drama Division etc can be involved for wider coverage.[27]

Apart from these, a number of MGNREGA agencies and authorities have also been entrusted with the responsibility for creating awareness among people. These agencies and authorities are namely:

(i) Central Employment Guarantee Council,

(ii) State Government,

(iii) State Employment Guarantee Council,

(iv) District Programme Coordinator,

(v) Gram Panchayat,

(vi) Mates or Work site Supervisors,

(vii) Community Based Organisations (CBOs) involved in grass-roots work like Self-Help Groups (SHGs), watershed committees, water user groups, etc.

The guidelines also prescribe the State Governments to prepare best practices related to MGNREGA and share it with Ministry of Rural Development (MoRD) for bringing in necessary changes within the system to replicate such successful initiatives.[28] Other methods prescribed are –

(i) Project initiation meetings to discuss details of work and explain entitlements to the workers and the expected benefits of the work.

(ii) Use of help lines and rural common service centres for communication with various target groups.

(iii) Wall paintings related to MGNREGA at common places in the village e.g. offices of panchayats, aanganwadis and schools, fair price shops, etc.

(iv) Door to door contact method to create social mobilization.

(v) Involvement of schools and colleges for activities like interactive sessions on MGNREGS and quiz competitions.

(vi) Village libraries to be provided with copies of MGNREGA guidelines, local labour budgets and performance data from time to time.

(vii) Prompt grievance redressal mechanisms.

(viii) Vigilant social audits by the Gram Sabhas.[29]

3.5 Awareness of Key Provisions of MGNREGA among the Job-Card Holders

During the field survey, the awareness among the job-card holders has been tested on the basis of their perceptions regarding various provisions of the Act such as mandatory person-days of employment, job-cards, unemployment allowance, wages, travelling allowance, social security, selection of works in gram sabha meetings, work site facilities, etc. in villages where works have been completed or on-going (with-work villages) and villages where no work have been undertaken (no-work villages) under MGNREGA. These provisions are the basic rights of the beneficiaries under MGNREGA. Awareness regarding these help the beneficiaries in availaing hassle free entitlements under the programme.

(i) Mandatory Person-days of Wage Employment : The Act mandate 100 days guaranteed wage employment in a financial year to every household whose members volunteer to do unskilled manual labour.[30] The awareness regarding this basic entitlement is essential to avail the benefits under the programme.

The field survey results revealed that out of 360 respondents, only 40.5 percent of the respondents were aware of 100 days guaranteed wage employment. 40 percent of the respondents in with-work villages and 42.3

percent respondents in no-work villages were aware of 100 days of mandatory wage employment (Table 3.1).

Table 3.1: Awareness Regarding Wage Employment

Are you aware regarding 100 days Wage employment?	With-work Villages	No-work Villages	Total
Yes	108 (40)	38 (42.3)	146 (40.5)
No	162 (60)	52 (57.7)	214 (59.5)
Total	270 (100)	90 (100)	360 (100)

***Note:** Percentages in parenthesis.

Therefore, the awareness about the mandatory person-days of wage employment was found to be more or less the same. It was also observed during the survey that people knew only about the employment opportunity under MGNERGA and not the number of days for which employment could be demanded.

The Sarpanches stated that generally people had knowledge of only those aspects of the programme which were availed by them. As far as 100 days of employment was concerned; the authorities were unable to provide 100 days of employment to any household in the village. The Sarpanches further stated that the shorter duration works like tree plantation were unable to generate 100 days of employment; while in the longer duration works like de-silting of ponds, as the number of people with job-cards was high, rotation basis was adopted to cover as many people as they could. Thus, long duration works also could not generate 100 days of employment for all job-card holders. As no household in the village or near-by villages had received 100 days of employment, this obligation of MGNREGA was not known to the people.

(ii) Job-cards: The job-card is a key document that records workers' entitlements under MGNREGA. It legally empowers the registered household to apply for work. The job-card contains information regarding the number of work-days and description of work done, amount of wages paid, thus ensuring transparency and protecting the workers against fraud. The Act mandate the issue of job-cards to every household in the gram panchayat area for availing employment under the scheme.[31]

The field survey results revealed that majority of the respondents were aware about job-cards (68.1 per cent). Not many variations have been observed in with-work and no-work villages. For example 69.3 percent respondents in with-work villages and 64.4 percent respondents no-work villages were aware about job-cards (Table 3.2).

Table 3.2: Awareness Regarding Job-cards

Are you aware about Job-cards?	With-work Villages	No-work Villages	Total
Yes	187 (69.3)	58 (64.4)	245 (68.1)
No	83 (30.7)	32 (35.6)	115 (31.9)
Total	270 (100)	90 (100)	360 (100)

Note: Percentages in parenthesis

Replying to why people were unaware about job-cards, the Sarpanches stated that they had imparted information regarding the job-cards for a number of times but they had failed to understand why people were unaware about it.

The guidelines also prescribe that the job-cards must be in the possession of the worker to whom it belongs. If the job-cards are taken by any implementing authority for the updating of records, it should be returned to the job-card holder on the same day. The possession of the job-card with any official without any valid reason is an offence punishable under section 25 of the Act.[32]

During the field survey, out of the total respondents, 76.7 percent of the respondents had job-cards in their possession. Around 90 percent of the respondents in with-work villages while 36.7 percent in the no-work villages had the possession of their job-cards (Table 3.3). However, in case of non-possession in with-work villages, the job-cards were found in the possession of the Sarpanch of the village while in no-work villages, majority of the respondents had not collected their job-cards from the authorities at the village or block level because of non-initiation of work. There were some cases where the job-cards were submitted to the block office for rectification of the data.

Table 3.3: Possession of Job-cards

Is your job-card in your possession?	With-work Villages	No-work Villages	Total
Yes	243 (90)	33 (36.7)	276 (76.7)
No	27 (10)	57 (63.3)	84 (23.3)
Total	270 (100)	90 (100)	360 (100)

Note: Percentages in parenthesis

The Act further prescribe that the job-card should contain the following information regarding the household –

(a) Job-card number
(b) Household member-wise work demand and allocation
(c) Description of the work done
(d) Muster roll numbers by which wages have been paid
(e) Amount of wages paid
(f) Unemployment allowance, if any paid
(g) Postal/Bank account number
(h) Insurance Policy number
(i) Photographs of adult member applicants

The entries in the job-card must be authenticated by signature of an authorised officer.[33]

During the field survey, the researcher checked 100 job-cards and found that only 86 job-cards had complete information regarding the household to which it belonged.

The guidelines state that the job-cards must be given free of cost.[34] However, in the area of study, out of the total respondents, 6.4 percent respondents said that they paid money for getting their job-cards prepared. Around 5.6 percent respondents in with-work villages and 8.9 percent respondents in no-work villages paid money to get their job-cards prepared (Table 3.4).

Table 3.4: Paid Money for Preparing Job-Card

Whether paid money for job-card preparation?	With-work Villages	No-work Villages	Total
Yes	15 (5.6)	8 (8.9)	23 (6.4)
No	255 (94.4)	82 (91.1)	337 (93.6)
Total	270 (100)	90 (100)	360 (100)

***Note:** *Percentages in parenthesis*

On inquiring from the block office, it came to light that some people from the worker unions of MGNREGA had charged money from the people under the pretext that they would get their job-cards prepared. The block officials stated that from then onwards they directed gram panchayats to send people directly to the block office to get their job-card prepared or ask only the Gram Rozgar Sahayak for it.

(iii) Unemployment Allowance: Section 7 of the Act provide for the payment of unemployment allowance under the scheme in case of non-provision of employment within fifteen days of receipt of application seeking employment. The payment of unemployment allowance is the responsibility of the State Government under Section 7 of the Act.[35]

In the area of study, it was found that out of the total respondents, only 11.7 percent of the respondents were aware of unemployment allowance. Around 14.4 percent respondents in with-work villages and 3.3 percent respondents in no-work villages were aware of the unemployment allowance (Table 3.5).

Table 3.5: Awareness Regarding Unemployment Allowance

Are you aware regarding Unemployment allowance under MGNREGA?	With-work Villages	No-work Villages	Total
Yes	39 (14.4)	3 (3.3)	42 (11.7)
No	231 (85.6)	87 (96.7)	318 (88.3)
Total	270 (100)	90 (100)	360 (100)

Note: *Percentages in parenthesis*

When further asked from the 42 aware respondents whether they were able to claim unemployment allowance under any condition, seven replied that they were provided employment whenever they needed and asked for it, so they were not eligible to claim unemployment allowance. However, the remaining 35 responded that they demanded unemployment allowance but did not get it.

Many Sarpanches were also found to be unaware about unemployment allowance. Others stated that unemployment allowance had never been sanctioned. The sanctioning process being cumbersome, they had never encouraged people to go for the claim. In few cases the Sarpanches had sent applicants to the block and district levels, however, they also did not receive any amount. Further, the Act clearly states that the payment of unemployment allowance is the sole responsibility of the state government if it fails to provide employment within 15 days. It came to light that the information regarding unemployment allowance was deliberately concealed by few officials. Apparently, the apathetic attitude of the higher officials is the main factor hampering information dissemination and disbursal of unemployment allowance.

(iv) Wages: The workers working under the scheme are entitled to wages at the wage rate notified by the Central Government under section 6 (1) of the Act. State governments and the programme authorities shall make all efforts to publicize the notified wages and displaying them prominently at the worksites.[36] In the area of study, out of the total respondents, 51.7 percent respondents were aware about the prevailing wage rate. Around 51.9 percent of the respondents in with-work villages and 51.1 percent of the respondents in no-work villages were aware about the prevailing wage rate (Table 3.6). However, the researcher did not find any display of information about the notified wage rate at any of the work sites visited. But it was found that the sanctioned wages were being paid.

Table 3.6: Awareness Regarding Wage Rate

Are you aware about the current wage rate under MGNREGA?	With-work Villages	No-work Villages	Total
Yes	140 (51.9)	46 (51.1)	186 (51.7)
No	130 (48.1)	44 (48.9)	174 (48.3)
Total	270 (100)	90 (100)	360 (100)

Note: Percentages in parenthesis

The guidelines also prescribe that in order to ensure timely payment of wages to the workers for the work done, State shall fix maximum limits for every process so that the wage seeker gets the wage payments by the end of the subsequent week.[37] During the field survey, it was found that out of the total respondents, only 22.5 percent of the respondents were aware about it. Around 23 percent of the respondents in with-work villages and 21.1 percent respondents in no-work villages were found to be aware about it. Further, the researcher found that around 57 percent of the respondents were paid wages within 14 days (Table 3.7).

Table 3.7: Awareness Regarding Wages to be Paid Within 14 Days

Are you aware about provision of wages within a fortnight?	With-work Villages	No-work Villages	Total
Yes	62 (23)	19 (21.1)	81 (22.5)
No	208 (77)	71 (78.9)	279 (77.5)
Total	270 (100)	90 (100)	360 (100)

Note: Percentages in parenthesis

Delay in wage payments was found to be a major problem faced by the workers. The Sarpanches revealed that the payments were being delayed for more than six months and the situation had worsened in wake of online system of payments. For a detailed discussion, see page 197 and 206.

The guidelines also provide for compensation to the workers in case of wages delayed beyond 15 days of work done under provisions of Payment of Wages Act along with wages.[38] During the field survey, out of the total respondents, only 2.5 percent of the respondents were aware about the compensation. Around 2.6 percent of the respondents in with-work villages and 2.2 percent in no-work villages were aware of it (Table 3.8).

Table 3.8: Awareness Regarding Compensation for Delayed Wage Payment

Are you aware regarding provision of compensation in delay of wages?	With-work Villages	No-work Villages	Total
Yes	7 (2.6)	2 (2.2)	9 (2.5)
No	263 (97.4)	88 (97.8)	351 (97.5)
Total	270 (100)	90 (100)	360 (100)

Note: Percentages in parenthesis

The officials stated that when wages were not being paid, how could compensation for delayed payments be expected? Keeping this in mind, the officials deliberately did not impart information regarding compensation to the workers; they believed that raising the issue of compensation would be futile and create unresolvable complications.

(v) Travelling Allowance: The Act mandate that if a worker is provided employment beyond five kilometres from his/her residence, then he is entitled to a travelling and subsistence allowance i.e. ten per cent of the wage rate as extra wages to meet additional transportation and living expenses.[39] During the field survey, out of the total respondents, only 6.1 percent respondents were aware about travelling allowance under MGNREGA. Around 6.3 percent of the respondents in with-work villages and 5.6 percent respondents in no-work villages were aware of it (Table 3.9). The researcher could not find any worker who had worked at the work-site beyond five kilometres from his residence. However, some of the women respondents stated that they were asked by the gram panchayat officials to work in the adjoining villages when work was not initiated in their own village but they refused to join work because of the distance they had to travel. The women respondents revealed that they were not told about the provision of travelling allowance by the GP officials.

Table 3.9: Awareness Regarding Travelling allowance

Are you aware about provision of traveling allowance?	With-work Villages	No-work Villages	Total
Yes	17 (6.3)	5 (5.6)	22 (6.1)
No	253 (93.7)	85 (94.4)	338 (93.9)
Total	270 (100)	90 (100)	360 (100)

Note: Percentages in parenthesis

The Sarpanches reported that whenever the job-card holders had sought to work under MGNREGA, they were either told that the work would start in the village soon or they were provided employment in the nearest village where MGNREGA work was going on. Therefore, the workers had been employed at locations where the authorities did not have to pay travelling allowance. Though the sample did not have any respondent who had worked beyond 5 kilometers from his residence, awareness regarding travelling allowance was found to be poor (6.1 percent respondents).

(vi) Insurance

MGNREGA workers are covered under the Janashree Bima Yojana (JBY) implemented by the Ministry of Finance. JBY provides life coverage and disability benefits to rural people. Further, Rashtriya Swasthya Bima Yojana (RSBY) has been extended to all MGNREGA workers who have worked for more than 15 days in the preceding financial year. The District Programme Coordinators and Programme Officers are responsible to make workers aware of these schemes. They should also help in enrollment for RSBY whenever enrollment takes place in respective district or block.[40] During the field survey, out of the total respondents, only 3.9 percent respondents were aware of insurance under MGNREGA. Around 4.1 percent of the respondents in with-work villages and 3.3 percent respondents in no-work villages were aware about it (Table 3.10). Further, the researcher did not find the insurance policy number mentioned in any of the job-cards.

Table 3.10: Awareness Regarding Insurance

Are you aware regarding insurance under MGNREGA?	With-work Villages	No-work Villages	Total
Yes	11 (4.1)	3 (3.3)	14 (3.9)
No	259 (95.9)	87 (96.7)	346 (96.1)
Total	270 (100)	90 (100)	360 (100)

Note: Percentages in Parenthesis

(vii) Gram Sabha as a primary forum for selection of works: The Gram Sabha is the principal forum for MGNREGA workers to raise their voices and make demands. The Act prescribe that gram sabha shall recommend works to be taken up and is the final authority to determine the order of priority of the initiation of works.[41] During the field survey, out of the total respondents, only 17.5 percent respondents were aware about the gram sabha as the primary forum for selection of MGNREGA works. Around 18.1 percent of the respondents in with-work villages and 15.6 percent respondents in no-work villages were aware of it (Table 3.11).

Table 3.11: Awareness Regarding Gram Sabha Meetings for Selection of Works

Are you aware about Gram Sabha meetings for the selection of MGNREGA works?	With-work Villages	No-work Villages	Total
Yes	49 (18.1)	14 (15.6)	63 (17.5)
No	221 (81.9)	76 (84.4)	297 (82.5)
Total	270 (100)	90 (100)	360 (100)

Note: Percentages in Parenthesis

Further, out of 63 respondents who were aware of gram sabha as a primary forum for the selection of works, only 26.9 percent respondents participated in the selection of works. Around 28.6 percent of the respondents in with-work villages and 21.4 percent respondents in no-work villages participated in the selection of works (Table 3.12).

Table 3.12: Participation in Selection of works

Did you participate in the selection of works?	With-work Villages	No-work Villages	Total
Yes	14 (28.6)	3 (21.4)	17 (26.9)
No	35 (71.4)	11 (78.6)	46 (73.1)
Total	49 (100)	14 (100)	63 (100)

Note: Percentages in parenthesis

The Sarpanches stated that people were less aware about gram sabha as the primary body for selection of MGNREGA works because gram sabha meetings were not held regularly. The officials revealed that local level politics dominate the agenda of the meetings and in the process local groups often clashed. In order to avoid such situations, the gram panchayats started preparing work proposals in consultation with the GP officials like Panchayat Secretary and Gram Rozgar Sahayaks and gram sabha meetings remained only in paper; it was also the practice to have them ratified by getting the thumb impressions of members at their residences (see page 194 for detailed discussion). Therefore, as the meetings were not held regularly, the awareness and participation of people was low.

(viii) Work site facilities: The awareness among the respondents regarding the worksite facilities has been measured with regard to muster roll, daily attendance, availability of shaded area for rest, drinking water, crèche facility, crèche incharge and wage-material ratio. These have been discussed in detail in the following sub-sections.

(a) Muster Roll : Before starting a work, the gram panchayat shall inform the PO, so that the PO can issue the required muster rolls. The muster rolls should be authorized by the PO and issued to GPs within three days from the date they declare their intent to start works. Only those muster rolls that are certified by PO are considered authentic. The numbered muster rolls must be maintained at the work-site. Muster roll is used to record the attendance of the workers working at the work-site. No kachha muster roll (a document which is not authorized or issued by the PO) can be used at the work-site for recording attendance.[42] During the field survey, out of the total respondents, 65.3 percent were aware about the muster roll. Around 75.2 percent in with-work villages and 35.6 percent in no-work villages were aware of it (Table 3.13).

The guidelines provide that any person desirous of seeing the current muster roll will be provided access to it at the work-site during working hours on all working days.[43] However, out of the six work-sites visited, muster rolls were available at only two work-sites. At the remaining four work-sites, the muster rolls were not made available.

Table 3.13: Awareness Regarding Muster Roll

Are you aware about muster roll?	With-work Villages	No-work Villages	Total
Yes	203 (75.2)	32 (35.6)	235 (65.3)
No	67 (24.8)	58 (64.4)	125 (34.7)
Total	270 (100)	90 (100)	360 (100)

Note: Percentages in Parenthesis

Regarding the low awareness in no-work villages, the officials stated that as no work had been initiated in the villages, therefore, people had no knowledge about the muster-rolls. However, they failed to respond to the lack of awareness about the muster-rolls among the respondents in the villages where MGNREGA works were running.

(b) Daily Attendance: The guidelines prescribe that the workers attendance should be recorded in the muster roll authorized by the PO.[44] During the field survey, out of the total respondents, 54.2 percent were aware of the mandatory record of daily attendance. Around 61.9 percent in with-work villages and 31.1 percent in no-work villages were aware of it (Table 3.14). However, the researcher was able to check the recorded daily attendance of the workers in the muster rolls at only two of the six work-sites visited which was found to be satisfactory.

Table 3.14: Awareness Regarding Daily Attendance

Are you aware about marking of daily attendance at the work site?	With-work Villages	No-work Villages	Total
Yes	167 (61.9)	28 (31.1)	195 (54.2)
No	103 (38.1)	62 (68.9)	165 (45.8)
Total	270 (100)	90 (100)	360 (100)

Note: Percentages in Parenthesis

(c) Availability of Shaded Rest Area: MGNREGA guidelines also provide for the availability of shaded area to the workers for taking rest during the rest period.[45] In the area of study, out of the total respondents, 54.2 percent respondents were aware of it. Around 60.4 percent in with-work villages and 35.6 percent in no-work villages were aware of it (Table 3.15). Further, the researcher found that shade facility was available to the workers at the six work-sites visited. The workers were found to be taking rest under the trees during the rest hours.

Table 3.15: Awareness Regarding Shaded Rest Area

Are you aware about provision of shade at the worksite?	With-work Villages	No-work Villages	Total
Yes	163 (60.4)	32 (35.6)	195 (54.2)
No	107 (39.6)	58 (64.4)	165 (45.8)
Total	270 (100)	90 (100)	360 (100)

Note: Percentages in Parenthesis

(d) Drinking Water: MGNREGA guidelines provide for the availability of drinking water to the workers at the worksites during the working hours.[46] During the field survey, out of the total respondents, 65 percent were aware of it. Around 69.3 percent in with-work villages and 52.2 percent in no-work villages were aware of it (Table 3.16). At the six worksites visited, the drinking water stored in earthen pots was available to the workers.

Table 3.16: Awareness Regarding drinking water facility

Are you aware about provision of drinking water at the work site?	With-work Villages	No-work Villages	Total
Yes	187 (69.3)	47 (52.2)	234 (65)
No	83 (30.7)	43 (47.8)	126 (35)
Total	270 (100)	90 (100)	360 (100)

Note: Percentages in parenthesis

(e) Creche Facility: The Act mandate the provision of crèche facility at the work-site in case the number of children below six years of age accompanying the women workers are five or more.[47] During the field survey, out of the total respondents, 19.4 percent of the respondents were aware of it. Around 24.4 percent in with-work villages and 4.4 percent in no-work villages were aware about it (Table 3.17).

Table 3.17: Awareness Regarding Crèche Facility

Are you aware about provision of crèche facility to children below six years of age?	With-work Villages	No-work Villages	Total
Yes	66 (24.4)	4 (4.4)	70 (19.4)
No	204 (75.6)	86 (95.6)	290 (80.6)
Total	270 (100)	90 (100)	360 (100)

Note: Percentages in parenthesis

However, inspite of the presence of children below six years of age accompanying the female workers at the work-sites, the creche facility was not available at any of the work-sites. The officials stated that in the rural areas most of the families are joint families, so the women workers usually leave children at home with the old people and come for work. One of the officials stated that thay used to provide the crèche facility to the female workers with children. However, subsequently the women workers started quarrelling over the appointment of crèche incharge as everyone wanted to be crèche incharge instead of working at the work-site. When the issue blew out of proportion, the authorities decided to do away with the crèche facility and ordered the women workers to leave the small children at home in case they wish to work.

(f) Crèche Incharge: The Act mandate that a woman shall be deputed to look after the children below six years of age of the women workers working at the work-site. She must be paid wages equal to wage rate paid to other unskilled workers.[48] In the area of study, out of the total respondents, 10 percent of the respondents were aware of this facility. Around 12.2 percent of the respondents in with-work villages and 3.3 percent in no-work villages were aware of it (Table 3.18). However, during the field survey, it was found that because no creche was maintained at the work-sites, therefore there was no appointment of the creche incharge also.

Table 3.18: Awareness Regarding Crèche Incharge

Are you aware regarding appointment of crèche incharge?	With-work Villages	No-work Villages	Total
Yes	33 (12.2)	3 (3.3)	36 (10)
No	237 (87.8)	87 (96.7)	324 (90)
Total	270 (100)	90 (100)	360 (100)

Note: Percentages in Parenthesis

(g) Wage-material Ratio : The Act prescribe that the ratio of wage costs to material costs should be no less than the minimum norm of 60:40. The cost of material component including the wages of skilled and semi-skilled workers shall not exceed forty percent of the total cost of the project.[49] It means that sixty percent of the total cost of the project to be spent on the wages shall be spent on the wages of unskilled workers only. During the field study, out of the total respondents, 9.2 percent were aware of it. 10 percent of the respondents in with-work villages and 6.7 percent in no-work villages were aware of this fact (Table 3.19).

Table 3.19: Awareness Regarding wage-material Ratio

Are you aware about Wage-material ratio?	With-work Villages	No-work Villages	Total
Yes	27 (10)	6 (6.7)	33 (9.2)
No	243 (90)	84 (93.3)	327 (90.8)
Total	270 (100)	90 (100)	360 (100)

Note: Percentages in Parenthesis

Majority of the officials were unable to provide reasons for the low awareness regarding wage-material ratio among the workers. However, one of the Sarpanches stated that workers were more concerned about their own wages rather than the wage-material ratio; hence their disinterest could be the reason behind their low awarenss about wage-material ratio.

3.6 Summary of Hypothesis

The field survey revealed that the job-card holders were not aware of 8 out of 14 key provisions of MGNREGA; the percentage of unaware respondents being over 55 percent. The findings related to this has been summarised in Table 3.20. Therefore, this clearly showed that the hypothesis, "The outreach of MGNREGA has generated awareness of its key provisions among the job-card holders in the rural areas" stands partially validated.

Table 3.20: Summary of Findings

S. No.	Parameters of Awareness	Findings
1.	100 days wage employment	Majority (59.5%) of the respondents were **not** aware of it.
2.	Job-cards	Majority (68.1%) of the respondents were aware of it.
3.	Unemployment Allowance	Majority (88.3%) of the respondents were **not** aware of it.
4.	Wages	Majority (51.7%) of the respondents were aware of it.
5.	Travelling Allowance	Majority (93.9%) of the respondents were **not** aware of it.
6.	Insurance	Majority (96.1%) of the respondents were **not** aware of it.
7.	Selection of works in Gram Sabha meetings	Majority (82.5%) of the respondents were **not** aware of it.
8.	Muster roll	Majority (65.3%) of the respondents were aware of it.
9.	Daily attendance	Majority (54.2%) of the respondents were aware of it.
10.	Shade availability	Majority (54.2%) of the respondents were aware of it.
11.	Drinking water	Majority (65%) of the respondents were aware of it.
12.	Crèche facility	Majority (80.6%) of the respondents were **not** aware of it.
13.	Crèche Incharge	Majority (90%) of the respondents were not aware of it.
14.	Wage-material ratio	Majority (90.8%) of the respondents were not aware of it.

3.7 Conclusion

The discussion revealed that the awarenesss level among the job-card holders regarding the various entitlements under MGNREGA was poor. Majority of the respondents were unaware about the mandatory 100 person-days of wage employment, possession of job-cards with themselves, unemployment allowance, payment of wages within a fortnight, compensation in case of delay in payment of wages, travelling allowance, insurance, gram sabha meetings for selection of MGNREGA works, provision of crèche facility at the work-site, appointment of creche incharge and wage material ratio (Table 3.20). Thus inspite of the rights and guarantees being legally stipulated, job-card holders were unable to access them due to lack of information and awareness. This information asymmetry among the respondents was due to various reasons.

Firstly, although the information dissemination mechanisms were incorporated through institutions like gram sabha, but they were largely defunct; while those which were functional could not perform their functions effectively, e.g. gram panchayats. Secondly, it was observed that the authorities deliberately avoided information dissemination to the job-card holders. Thirdly, some of the officials out-rightly shrugged off their responsibility of awareness generation. Therefore, the authorities responsible for providing benefits did not inform the right-holders (job-card holders) deliberately of the ways in which they could access or claim their benefits. Thus, the possibilities of exercising their rights and claiming the guarantees that rightfully belonged to the people (job-card holders) were significantly reduced by the attitude and approach of the authorities.

Endnotes

1. Anthony Hall and James Midgley (2004), Social Policy for Development, Sage Publications, London, p. 3; Ravi Kanbur (2006), "What's social policy got to do with economic growth?", [Online] Available from http://www.arts.cornell.edu/poverty/kanbur/SocPolEconGrowth.pdf., [Accessed on 2nd April, 2015].
2. Luigi Ferrajoli (2001), The Basis of Fundamental Rights, Editorial Trotta, Madrid, p. 25.
3. World Bank (2008), Realizing Rights Through Social Guarantees: An Analysis of New Approaches to Social Policy in Latin America and South Africa, World Bank, Washington DC, p. 1.
4. *Ibid*, p. 8.
5. *Ibid.*
6. *Ibid*, p. 9.
7. *Ibid*, p. 7.
8. *Ibid*, p. 10.
9. *Ibid.*

10. *Ibid,* p. 5.
11. *Ibid,* p. 2.
12. *Ibid,* p. 10.
13. Andrew Norton (2011), "Social Guarantees – Rights as Smart Politics", in Maximillan Ashwill and Andrew Norton (eds.), Building Citizenship through Social Policy in the East Caribbean: The Role of Social Guarantees, The World Bank and Overseas Development Institute, Latin America and Caribbean Region, p. 9; Sudarno Sumarto and Asep Suryahadi (2001), "Principles and Approaches to Targetting: With Reference to the Indonesian Social Safety Net Programs", MPRA Paper Number 58670, The SMERU Research Institute, Indonesia, 2001, pp. 4-19.
14. Norton, ibid, pp. 9-10; Nidhi Vij (2011), "Building Capacities for Empowerment: the Missing link between Social Protection and Social Justice-Case of Social Audits in Mahatma Gandhi National Rural Employment Guarantee Act", Paper for the International Conference Social Protection for Social Justice, Institute of Development Studies, UK, 13-15 April, 2011, pp. 1-26.
15. Norton, ibid, p. 10; Anuradha Joshi and Mick Moore (2000), "The mobilising potential of anti-poverty programs", IDS Working Paper Number 374, Institute of Development Studies, UK, 2000, pp. 1- 29; Anuradha Joshi (2009), "Do Rights Work? Law, Activism and the Employment Guarantee Scheme", World Development Report 38, Volume 4, 2009, pp. 620-630.
16. Norton, ibid; Parr Fakuda, Sakiko, Remer Lawson, Terra and Susan Randolph (2009), "An Index of Social Rights Fulfillment: Concept and Methodology", Journal of Human Rights, Volume 8, Number 3, pp. 1-120.
17. Norton, ibid; Joshi and Moore, op. cit., p. 27.
18. Norton, ibid; Ian Macauslan (2008), India's National Rural Employment Guarantee Act: A Case Study for How Change Happens, Oxfam, UK, pp. 5-45.
19. Norton, ibid.
20. Ibid, pp. 10-11.
21. Government of India (2010a), Report of the Working Group on Transparency and Accountability of Central Employment Guarantee Council, Submitted to Ministry of Rural Development, Government of India, New Delhi, p. 3.
22. Government of India (2013a), op. cit., p. 45.
23. Ibid, p. 46.
24. A Bharat Nirman Volunteer (BNV) is an individual who comes voluntarily from a rural household to act as an organic link between rural families and various line departments to ensure the unreached households to access benefits under various government sponsored progarmmes. In order to provide connectivity with the rural households, the potential youth in the name of Bharat Nirman Volunteers (BNVs) is used to create awareness about all welfare and development programmes among rural households for better planning and quality implementation of programmes.
25. Government of India (2013a), op. cit., p. 46.
26. Ibid, p. 46.
27. Ibid.
28. *Ibid,* pp. 46-47.

29. *Ibid.*
30. The Mahatma Gandhi National Rural Employment Guarantee Act, 2005, op. cit., p. 10.
31. Government of India (2013a), op.cit., p. 13.
32. *Ibid*, pp. 17-18.
33. Ibid, p. 18.
34. Ibid, p. 21.
35. *Ibid*, p. 23.
36. *Ibid*, p. 69.
37. *Ibid*, p. 76.
38. *Ibid.*
39 *Ibid*, p. 16.
40. *Ibid*, p. 76.
41. *Ibid*, p. 6.
42. *Ibid*, pp. 63-64.
43. *Ibid*, p. 65.
44. *Ibid.*
45. *Ibid*, p. 66.
46. *Ibid.*
47. Ibid.
48. *Ibid*, p. 66.
49. *Ibid*, p. 59.

4

Women Empowerment through Employment Generation in MGNREGA

4.1 Introduction

The role of women in working population is increasing rapidly over the years.[1] But in developing countries the contribution of women in economic activities is not fully recognized due to existing social, economic and political disparities in terms of gender. Although gender equality has been a significant focus of development, a large number of women are at a disadvantage in terms of wages and legal and social protection. In 2012, out of total 1.2 billion working women, around 650 million women workers worked in vulnerability and poverty or engaged in unpaid family work.[2] Women across the globe face discrimination in terms of access to education, skill development and lower income/wages.

Gender gap is not limited to developing countries only; women in developed countries also face gender disparity. The World Bank Report, 2012 stated that "gender disparities remain salient even among the richest countries". Although in the developing countries, a large number women have entered the labour force, in the past quarter century but the increased participation has not provided them equal employment opportunities or earnings equal to men. Women and men tend to work in very different parts of the 'economic space', with little change over time, even in high-income countries.[3] Therefore, it is important to acknowledge that "gender equality, across numerous dimensions, will not occur automatically as countries get richer".[4]

Creating employment and income generation opportunities and enhancing access to social protection are two key measures to address the issues of gender disparity, women's poverty and vulnerability. Many technical co-operation programmes and projects involving women's economic empowerment and extending social protection through innovative approaches have proven that such developmental programmes and projects are effective in increasing their income, improving poor women's well-being and health, enhancing their self-esteem and often even enhancing their community and political participation, i.e., ultimate women empowerment and improved gender equality.[5]

Despite the efforts being made by international communities in the form of Millennium Development Goals, Beijing Platform for Action for gender main-streaming, gender gap persists. Historically, with the beginning of the United Nations Decade for Women (1976), gender issues gained centre stage at policy-making institutions and new bureaucratic structures were set up for streamlining women's interests into the policy-making process. With gender themes being centre-stage and pressure exerted by international and national women's movements, a large number of development agencies began to include gender specific provisions at the programme level. Governments also started incorporating gender considerations in their national development plans and strategic economic policies.[6] However, activists faced a lot of challenges and road blocks from within the power structures to include gender into development issues.

Focus of Very Treatise

This research attempts to study MGNREGA's comprehensive poverty alleviation strategy of providing work against wages and increasing capacities and choices of women involved in the programme with the aim to empower marginalised women. The key to poverty alleviation inherently manifests the strategy to women's empowerment.[7] This framework is neither new nor an imposition of the global north but was adopted in the mid-1980s in the context of contentious development discourse, as a result of the debates generated by feminist movement.[8] The lexicon of women's empowerment signifies a transformative strategy to poverty alleviation based primarily on the principles of public participation, self-help, micro-credit and reservation of women within local self-governments.[9] Beteille discussed empowerment as power distribution without having clear power. According to him, "the main point behind empowerment is that it seeks to change society through a rearrangement of power".[10]

Before analyzing the impact of MGNREGA on women empowerment, it is essential to discuss the discourses of women empowerment and understand the graduation of the concept of Women in Development (WID) discourse to Gender and Development (GAD) discourse.

4.2 Discourses of Women Empowerment

The relationship between development and women became the dominant theme of the development discourse in the second half of the 20th century. The discourse on women empowerment underwent a substantial shift from Women in Development (WID) to Gender and Development (GAD). Both the discourses – WID and GAD have been discussed in detail in the following paragraphs.

4.2(a) Women in Development

The Women in Development approach was the first contemporary movement to specifically integrate women in the development agenda.[11] WID originated during the 1975 World Conference of the International Women's Year at Mexico City and the United Nations Decade for Women (1976-1985), which emphasized social justice and equity for women.

Protagonists of WID rejected the trickle-down development theory stating that dividends of development processes are not equally reaped by men and women. They contended that the development process had accentuated the deterioration of the position of women. WID approach emphasized that women should not be merely reduced to passive recipients of welfare programmes, rather they should be integrated into development process by providing equal employment opportunities.[12] WID gave primacy to women's productive roles and integration into the economy as a means of improving their status. One of the main protagonists of this approach, Boserup, challenged the assumptions of welfare approach or trickle-down development theory and citing examples of sub-Saharan countries posited a positive correlation between the role played by women in agricultural production and their status vis-à-vis men.[13] Insights provided by Boserup's research led to the rejection of the narrow view of women's roles as mothers and wives. It provided intellectual underpinnings to WID advocates for characterizing women as productive members of society by mainstreaming them into the actual development process.[14] Unfortunately, advocates of WID distanced themselves from welfare issues and overemphasized the productive roles of women. This advocacy of women's productive roles was at loggerheads with the propagation of integration between production and reproduction roles by feminists of the time. In a nutshell WID suffered from lacuna of identifying women's subordination only to lack of access to resources while neglecting the importance of power, conflict and gender relations in understanding women's subordination.[15]

4.2(a) Gender and Development

Writings in the late 1970s drew distinction between sex and gender.[16] In 1977 feminists came together to form the Subordination of Women Workshop and published a volume in 1981, "Of Marriage and the Market", which marked a watershed in the evolution of thinking on feminism and development. The introduction to the volume clearly states, "We wanted to develop a theory of gender which was integrated into and informed by the general analysis of the world economy, but one that problematized the link between gender and economy in a less deterministic way".[17] Gender became a central theme for feminists to integrate with development. Thus the focus shifted to gender so that the problems of women should not only be viewed in terms of sex i.e., their biological differences with men, but in terms of their gender, i.e., in terms of the social relationship between men and women, a relationship in which women have been systematically subordinated.[18] Consequently, to operationalize gender two dominant approaches, namely, 'Gender Roles' and 'Social Relations Analysis' were put forth.

The *gender roles* framework:- Was developed by researchers at the Harvard Institute of International Development in collaboration with the Women in Development Office of United States Agency for International Development (USAID). This framework is based on '*sex role theory*'.[19] As per this framework, household is seen as a system of resource allocation. Gender equity connotes individual access and control over resources and women's productive contributions are regarded as basis for resource allocation. Gender equity and economic efficiency are thus, synergistic. Very synergy aims to highlight the key differences between the incentives and constraints under which men and women work; the insights gained from this analysis are incorporated in planning process for intervention of credit, education, training, etc. in such a way as to improve overall productivity.[20] Thus, gender roles framework primarily focuses on the distribution of roles and resources within the household and attempts to overcome the ideologies and stereotypes that try to veil women's work, especially reproductive roles.

Social Relations Analysis refers to those dimensions of social relations that create differences in the positioning of men and women in social processes. It exposes the social dimensions of hierarchical power relations embedded in social institutions and also its influence on 'the relative position of men and women in society'.[21] The discrimination occurs because men are given greater capacity than women to mobilize a variety of cultural roles and material resources in pursuit of their own interests. This approach integrates women in the social structures, processes and relations rather than in development process. Thus, this framework professes that in order to end women's subordination, social relations should be changed before allocating economic resources. Development agencies are urged to adopt a gender aware approach to development to improve development policy and practice.[22]

These two approaches converge on the issues of gender-disaggregated analysis of roles and access over resources. They diverge on account of degree to which gender analysis is extended beyond production to include the range of relations through which needs are met such as the rights and obligations, norms and values that sustain social life. The two frameworks also differ in assigning analytical weightages to social relations such as class, caste, etc. differently.[23]

4.3 Women Empowerment in India

Empowerment is a process of positive change that improves women's fallback position and bargaining power within a patriarchal structure, and identify different causal pathways of change; material, cognitive, perceptual and relational. More simply, empowerment is a process of awareness and capacity building leading to greater participation, decision-making power, control and transformative action. In addition, empowerment is both an individual and a collective process. Sometimes it involves people as groups that begin to develop their awareness and the ability to organize to take action and bring change.[24]

In the Indian context gender disparity exists in economic and social terms. Various initiatives have been undertaken by the government to lift people out of the poverty trap; majority of these had special provisions for women as poverty is multi-dimensional and gendered, equated with deprivation and lack of social power and connected mostly with social and spatial inequalities.[25] The language of women's empowerment in India entered the political discourse largely as a result of Indian women's movement challenging patriarchal gender relations and replacing official terminologies such as 'women's welfare', 'women's development', and 'women's upliftment'.[26] Gradually, empowerment of women turned from a politicised jargon into panoply of pro-poor development-intervention policy agendas. Government of India holds that empowerment through large-scale mobilisation of marginalised and poor women are the key to the problem of poverty. It has been seen that gender-based labour market segregation, wage gaps and mobility disparities tend to persist over time despite income growth. In rural India, labour markets in agriculture and off-farm work remain highly segregated, wage gaps continue to be substantial (with women's wages often still reaching just half of men's in 2011), and women's mobility and access to rural and urban employment severely constrained. Such inequalities are closely connected with disparities in power at home as well as with gendered norms and expectations.

4.4 Women Empowerment and MGNREGA

MGNREGA's central objective is to reduce poverty and empower women through increased self-reliance and job security.[27] The Act prescribe numerous provisions that have special bearing for rural women such as one-third of the workers be women, equal wages for men and women, childcare facilities at the work-sites, provision of work within five kilometres from the house, social audit forum must be conveniently scheduled for MGNREGA workers so that women and marginalised sections can participate without constraints. The Act also provides for women's representation in local committees.[28] All these provisions of MGNREGA have pro-women ramifications.

MGNREGA's advocacy of GAD professes that gender biased power structures and relations lead to gender-lopsided development outcomes which may ultimately cause women's deprivation. The empowerment aspects of MGNREGA have potential to equalize gender relations in the long run.[29] As per GAD, women's needs can be divided into strategic and practical.[30] Strategic needs are long term goals which help in changing women's position of subordination and discrimination. These are in the form of abolition of the sexual division of labour, alleviation of the burden of domestic labour and childcare, removal of institutionalized forms of discrimination, attainment of political equality, establishment of freedom of choice over childbearing and adoption of adequate measures against male violence and control over women. Practical needs are related to immediate goals and unlike strategic needs do not entail long run goals such as women's emancipation or gender equality. These are related to food, clothing, housing, etc.[31]

MGNREGA tends to meet practical needs in the short run while strategic needs are met long term. Wages earned by women workers helps raise their purchasing power to buy clothes, food, medicines, etc. In the long run, their economic power reduces dependency on male members for their basic needs thus, addressing issues of subordination and subjugation.[32]

It is in this context that the benefits of MGNREGA for women workers have been studied. It was hypothesised that "MGNREGA has been instrumental in improving the socio-economic conditions of women workers".

Primary survey data was collected through structured questionnaires from 180 women respondents. Amongst these, 135 women were beneficiaries and 45 women were job-card holders who had not done any work under MGNREGA. Focus group discussions were also held with the women in the selected villages to understand the socio-economic impacts of MGNREGA in their lives.

4.5 Women Empowerment through Employment Generation Under MGNREGA

MGNREGA attained universal coverage throughout India in three phases on 1st April, 2008. The secondary data reveals that women workforce participation has been above 45 percent since its inception against the statutory requirement of 33 percent. In 2008-09, the women work force participation was 47.87 percent. It increased to 49.90 percent in 2009-10 and then decreased to 48 percent in 2010-11. The women participation rate showed a steady rise from around 50 percent in 2011-12 to 53.13 percent in 2012-13 and 54.40 percent in 2013-14. In 2014-15, the participation rate for women was 55.52 percent till 31st December, 2014.[33]

To evaluate the impact of MGNREGA on gender the states were classified into three categories, namely, states with high percentage of women person-days (More than 66 percent of women person-days generated); states with medium percentage of women person-days (Between 33 percent to than 66 percent of women person-days generated) and states with low percentage of women person-days (Less than 33 percent of women person-days generated) (Table 4.1).

Table 4.1: Classification of States on Account of Percentage of Women Person-days (Percentage in Brackets)

Classification	2008-09	2009-10	2010-11	2011-12	2012-13	2013-14	2014-15
States with high percentage of women person days (More than 66 percent of women person-days generated)	Kerala (85.00) Tamil Nadu (79.66) Rajasthan (67.10)	Kerala (86.24) Tamil Nadu (78.89) Rajasthan (68.43)	Kerala (90.00) Tamil Nadu (83.00) Rajasthan (68.00) Goa (68.00)	Kerala (93.01) Goa (75.60) Tamil Nadu (75.57) Rajasthan (68.96)	Kerala (92.62) Goa (81.47) Tamil Nadu (74.68) Rajasthan (68.96)	Kerala (93.45) Tamil Nadu (84.00) Goa (73.88) Rajasthan (67.27)	Kerala (92.53) Tamil Nadu (85.71) Goa (74.82) Rajasthan (67.80)
States with medium percentage of women person-days (Between 33 to 66 percent of women person-days generated)	Andhra Pradesh (58.15) Tripura (51.01) Karnataka (50.42) Chhattisgar h (47.43) Maharashtr a (46.22) Manipur (45.92) Madhya Pradesh (43.00) Gujarat (42.82) Meghalaya (41.35) Himachal Pradesh (39.01) Sikkim (37.66) Odisha (37.58) Uttarakhan d (36.86) Nagaland (36.70) Mizoram (36.58)	Andhra Pradesh (58.25) Tripura (53.52) Goa (50.50) Chhattisgarh (49.17) Meghalaya (46.60) Manipur (46.41) Karnataka (45.22) Himachal Pradesh (44.71) Madhya Pradesh (43.03) Nagaland (41.50) Maharashtra (41.25) Gujarat (41.10) Sikkim (40.71) Uttarakhand (38.84) Mizoram (36.89) Odisha (36.50) Haryana (34.95) Jharkhand (34.73)	Andhra Pradesh (57.00) Arunachal Pradesh (33.00) Chhattisgarh (49.00) Gujarat (44.00) Haryana (36.00) Himachal Pradesh (48.00) Jharkhand (33.00) Karnataka (46.00) Madhya Pradesh (44.00) Maharashtra (46.00) Manipur (35.00) Meghalaya (44.00) Mizoram (34.00) Nagaland (35.00) Odisha (39.00) Punjab (34.00) Sikkim (47.00) Tripura (39.00) Uttarakhand (40.00) West Bengal (34.00)	Himachal Pradesh (59.19) Andhra Pradesh (57.54) Sikkim (46.61) Maharashtra (46.51) Gujarat (46.00) Karnataka (45.65) Chhattisgarh (45.50) Punjab (43.63) Madhya Pradesh (42.47) Uttarakhand (42.28) Meghalaya (42.09) Odisha (38.52) Tripura (38.20) Haryana (36.20) Manipur (33.51)	Himachal Pradesh (61.30) Chhattisgarh (47.20) Punjab (46.87) Sikkim (46.77) Karnataka (46.53) Maharashtra (44.78) Uttarakhand (44.17) Gujarat (42.79) Madhya Pradesh (42.56) Tripura (41.44) Meghalaya (41.05) Haryana (40.17) Odisha (37.65) Manipur (35.96)	Himachal Pradesh (62.59) Andhra Pradesh (58.43) Punjab (52.98) Chhattisgar h (48.26) Tripura (47.50) Karnataka (46.65) Sikkim (46.01) Gujarat (45.02) Maharashtr a (43.29) Meghalaya (43.08) Haryana (41.92) Uttarakhan d (41.61) Madhya Pradesh (41.36) Manipur (34.68) Bihar (34.14) West Bengal (33.53)	Telangana (60.80) Himachal Pradesh (60.80) Andhra Pradesh (58.45) Punjab (57.55) Chhattisgarh (49.93) Sikkim (49.23) Tripura (48.74) Karnataka (46.82) Uttarakhand (45.62) Maharashtra (43.44) Madhya Pradesh (43.31) Gujarat (42.86) Meghalaya (41.46) Haryana (41.32) Mizoram (40.21) West Bengal (39.82) Manipur (37.51) Bihar (37.29) Odisha (33.16)

States with low percentage of women person-days (Less than 33 percent of women person-days generated)	Haryana (30.64) Bihar (30.02) Jharkhand (28.50) Assam (27.16) West Bengal (26.52) Arunachal Pradesh (26.12) Punjab (24.61) Uttar Pradesh (18.10) Jammu And Kashmir (5.76)	West Bengal (30.47) Assam (27.70) Punjab (26.53) Arunachal Pradesh (24.84) Uttar Pradesh (20.27) Jammu And Kashmir (5.22)	Assam (27.00) Bihar (28.00) Jammu and Kashmir (7.00) Uttar Pradesh (21.00)	West Bengal (31.95) Jharkhand (31.00) Bihar (27.75) Arunachal Pradesh (25.45) Assam (25.19) Mizoram (23.85) Uttar Pradesh (17.25) Jammu And Kashmir (15.08)	West Bengal (32.87) Jharkhand (32.40) Arunachal Pradesh (32.00) Bihar (30.38) Nagaland (24.82) Assam (24.80) Mizoram (22.71) Jammu And Kashmir (19.89) Uttar Pradesh (18.76) Andhra Pradesh (10.00)	Odisha (32.97) Arunachal Pradesh (31.43) Jharkhand (31.31) Mizoram (27.01) Nagaland (26.29) Assam (24.53) Jammu And Kashmir (22.36) Uttar Pradesh (22.15)	Jharkhand (31.99) Nagaland (31.73) Arunachal Pradesh (30.39) Assam (27.38) Jammu and Kashmir (25.64) Uttar Pradesh (24.41)

Source: Compiled from Government of India (2015), MGNREGA – Report to the people: 2014-15, Ministry Rural Development, Department of Rural Development, New Delhi, p. 38; MGNREGA website (www.nrega.nic.in).

Three states namely, Kerala, Tamil Nadu and Rajasthan have continued to be the states with high percentage of women work days since 2008-09 to 2014-15. Goa is another state which had shown a high proportion of work days for women workers since 2010-11 from a moderate proportion in 2009-10. The number of states with high percentage of work days for women has remained between 3 to 4.

The number of moderately performing states have oscillated between 14 to 19 from 2008-09 to 2014-15. Eleven states have remained consistently in this category since the inception of the programme, namely, Tripura, Karnataka, Chhattisgarh, Maharashtra, Manipur, Madhya Pradesh, Himachal Pradesh, Gujarat, Sikkim, Uttarakhand and Meghalaya. The states of Andhra Pradesh and Odisha have also been the consecutive members of this category with the exception in 2012-13 and 2013-14 respectively. Haryana and Punjab were low performing states in 2008-09 and 2009-10 respectively but ultimately showed a rise in the percentage of women work days and entered the category of moderately performing states since 2011-12. Two states, i.e. Bihar and West Bengal, were continuously low performing states but finally jumped to the medium category in 2013-14 and 2014-15.

The number of low performing states has hovered between 6 to 10. The states namely Jammu and Kashmir, Uttar Pradesh, Arunachal Pradesh and Assam have been permanently in this category. Jharkhand too has been in this category with the exception of 2009-10. Mizoram and Nagaland entered in the low category in 2011-12 and 2012-13 from the medium category classification. This fluctuation from 6 to 10 in number of states in low percentage category is a matter of concern as the statutory provision of 33 percent of women's participation is not fulfilled.

The inter-state variation in terms of women participation in MGNREGA works can be explained by comparing the labour force participation of women as per NSSO data[34];[35] and MGNREGA women participation rate. The women participation varied due to the fact that states such as Kerala, Tamil Nadu and Goa which had less than 40 percent women participation in total labour force had increased the women participation in MGNREGA more than 73 percent. This is meant that these states used MGNREGA to bridge gender gap in labour force through MGNREGA. On the other hand, Rajasthan performed well on account of generating more persondays for women workers under MGNREGA because it has more women participation in its labour force as per NSSO survey. States such as Odisha, Jharkhand, Assam, Jammu and Kashmir and Uttar Pradesh had low women participation in total labour force as well under MGNREGA. It can be derived that policy perspective of these states had impact on women participation. States such as Sikkim, Chhattisgarh, Meghalaya and Mizoram had high women participation rate as per NSSO survey but less in terms of MGNREGA.

In Punjab, the work participation rate for women was 24.61 percent in 2008-09 which increased to 26.53 percent in 2009-10. It again rose to 43.63 percent in 2011-12 and 46.87 percent in 2012-13. In 2013-14, the women work participation rate was 52.98 percent which rose to 57.55 percent in 2014-15 (Table 4.1).

During the field survey, it came to light that MGNREGA has been helpful/ effective in promoting women empowerment. As a rural wage employment programme, MGNREGA recognised the relevance of incorporating gender equity and empowerment in its design MGNREGA served as a new opportunity to the women workers. The women share on works under MGNREGA is greater than their share of work in the casual wage labour market across all states.[36] Women are participating in the scheme much more actively than they participated in all forms of recorded work.[37] This has been attributed to a number of factors such as equitable and easy access to work, decent working conditions, equal payment of wages and representation on decision-making bodies.[38] The field survey results for evaluating socio-economic impacts of MGNREGA on women has been done on the basis of few parameters namely, easy access to work, social acceptability of work, decent and favourable working conditions, direct account payments, wage parity, gender equality, income consumption effects and intra household effects. These have been discussed in the following sub-sections:-

(i) Easy Access to Work: The Act stipulates the provision of MGNREGA work within 5 kilometres of residence; as work is being provided locally, it attracted many women workers.[39] A study conducted across ten sample districts of Bihar, Chhattisgarh, Jharkhand, Madhya Pradesh, Rajasthan and Uttar Pradesh confirmed these findings; only 30 percent of the women in the sample recalled earning cash income from a source other than MGNREGA in the three months preceding the survey. Of the total women in the sample, 50 percent stated that in the absence of MGNREGA they would have worked at home or remained unemployed.[40]

The field survey revealed that all the women workers were provided employment in the vicinity of their village (radius of 5 kilometers). Thus, as they do not have to travel for sake of employment the family members allowed them to work. This participation caused the family wage earnings, which would not have been possible had the opportunity for work close to home not come their way.

(ii) Social Acceptability of Work: MGNREGA work is offered by the local government. This has led to an increase in social acceptability of the work on account of a number of factors. Firstly, there are stipulated working hours[41] which makes women and their family feel safe and free from uncertainty. Secondly, this employment is believed to be more professional than domestic labour which is at the whim of the employer.[42]

During the field survey, all the responses complied with this finding. In the rural areas, the primary responsibility of household work lies with the women. However, all the respondents were willing to accept work despite their domestic duties as due to fixed working hours they could handle the twin responsibilities of household work and earning easily. They found the work remunerative over the traditional employment opportunities. The payment in cash instead of kind is another important factor for women as it increases their expenditure choices. The respondents also felt that fixed working hours and remuneration are the special features which were not a part of traditional informal employment opportunities.

(iii) Decent and favourable working conditions: MGNREGA mandates the provision of worksite facilities in the form of crèche, rest hours, shaded area for rest, drinking water facilities, etc. which tend to act as an incentive for the women workers.

During the field survey, respondents concurred that the working conditions during MGNREGA works were decent and favourable. Although the provision of crèche was not found anywhere during the field survey, however, during the focus group discussions, majority of the respondents stated that conditions like shaded rest area, drinking water facilities, rest hours, etc. were favourable for work.

(iv) Direct Account Payments: MGNREGA mandate the payment of wages through individual or joint savings account of workers as far as possible.[43]

During the field survey, it was found that women used to work in farms through contractors or their husbands. The contractors would negotiate the wage rates with the landlords and kept their commission thus paying less to the women workers. Women would never know what amount of wages the contractors had negotiated with the landlords. Also their wages were received either by the contractor or their husbands; the latter used the money at will, often for alcohol. However, under MGNREGA, they receive wages through bank or post-office accounts. The accounts could be individual or joint savings accounts. Women reported that due to account payments under MGNREGA, they got control over their wages.

(V) Wage Parity: MGNREGA mandate equal wages for men and women. This was a great attraction for women to participate in MGNREGA works. The National Sample Survey Organisation (NSSO) 66th Round[44] indicates that MGNREGA has reduced the traditional wage discrimination in public works. As per the data, average wage for labour in MGNREGA was Rs. 90.9 per day for men and Rs. 87 per day for women. The difference was larger for labour in other public works; Rs. 98.3 per day for men and Rs. 86.1 per day for women.[45] Other studies also suggest an upward movement of unskilled wages for women post-MGNREGA. For instance, in Kerala, the wages for women in agriculture and forest work rose from Rs. 70-80 in 2007 to Rs. 110-125 in 2009.[46] In fact, real wages increased more rapidly for female workers than for male workers.[47]

Wage parity appears to be positively affecting participation of women in the scheme. States with high wage differential in casual labour market are likely to have a greater participation of women in MGNREGA which assures wage equity. An intra-household substitution effect appears to be at work. In other words, when casual labour market opportunities are better for men than they are for women, it is easier for women to avail work under the scheme.[48]

Primary data revealed that more women workers were found at the work-sites. Women in villages where no MGNREGA work was initiated were also keen to work under the programme. This may be attributed to the fact that due to the existing wage disparity in the local market and wage parity in MGNREGA, women prefer to work under MGNREGA. Secondary data also revealed that women participation has increased in MGNREGA over the years in Punjab (Table 4.1). This clearly showed that had MGNREGA not been implemented, women participation in total workforce would likely have become much lower.

(vi) Gender Equality: Pre-MGNREGA, women in the rural areas used to work on private farms. Though women worked the same hours but were paid less than men.[49] However, MGNREGA clearly mandate equal wages for men and women. Hence, the women were only able to earn equal wages under MGNREGA.

Further, MGNREGA not only led to increase in wages of women but also increase in the local market wage rate.[50] At many places, where market wages are higher than MGNREGA, men undertake jobs in the market and women seek employment under the scheme.[51] Research suggests that improvements in gender equations across various spheres (social, political and economic) coupled with positive changes in self-perception gradually has resulted in the empowerment of women and engendered lasting social change.[52]

During the field survey, all women respondents stated that their wages were equal to men. Around 51 percent of the respondents subscribed to this view while 13.6 percent of the respondents were of the view that work was not divided as per the physical strength. 35.2 percent of the women respondents could not comment on this aspect of work division. It was found that informally work was identified and allotted to workers on the basis of the nature of activity in terms of physical strength required. However, the local social and cultural norms also greatly influence the division of work. Generally, men undertake tasks like shovelling and hoeing while the women perform tasks like carrying silt or construction mixture on their heads. Thus, the worksites that had only female workers were problematic; the officials complained that the women refused to perform hoe related work stating that it is 'men's work'. Generally, in Punjab and Haryana, as per the cultural and social norm-women do not perform hoe or spade related tasks; which was not the case in other states. This revealed that work was gendered in the minds of women and this caused problems at the workplace.

(vii) Income-consumption Effects: The paid work under MGNREGA has empowered women economically.[53] MGNREGA has led to increase in the income of women workers with a better control over their earnings. Improved access to economic resources and paid work has a positive impact on the socio-economic status of the women. In a study conducted in five districts of Chhattisgarh, 600 women workers with a household income below Rs 8,000 decreased from 94 percent to 57 percent due to MGNREGA, indicating the importance of MGNREGA for the poorest of the poor.[54] This was also apparent in the findings of another study conducted in Rajsamand and Dungarpur districts of Rajasthan, where in a large number of cases, women indicated that they had a substantial say in the way this money was spent.[55] They were able to utilise the money for food, repaying small debts including education of children and medical expenses. Another study reported that 81 percent of the women in Cuddalore district of Tamil Nadu and 96 percent in Rajnandgaon district of Chhattisgarh stated that they had spent their earning from MGNREGA on food and consumer goods. Similar tends were reported in the field.

Women Views About MGNREGA

During the focus group discussions, many women reported that the monetary payment under MGNREGA has given them financial independence. Women stated that their choices for expenditure has increased with monetary payments and they could spend as per their need and choice on things like clothing, medical services, education of their children and so on.

Women can take charge of their lives in small ways which has brought respite from the anxieties associated with fulfilling their basic needs. The primary data reports that 97.6 percent of women workers are of the view that MGNREGA has helped in improving their social as well as economic conditions. Around 73 percent of the respondents felt improved financial condition because of more money in hand to spend as per their discretion. Thus substantive fallout of MGNREGA for women is independence in aspects of spending money as initially, they had to depend on money from a male family member, either from husband, father or brother for meeting their basic needs. Now, majority of the respondents agreed that their income is either spent by them only or in consultation with them. The respondents also reported that they feel satisfied because of improved credit worthiness as the fear of hunger prevails no longer and also they do not have to migrate in search of work. Altogether MGNREGA has proved beneficial for fulfilling practical needs of women.

During the field survey, one of the women respondents narrated that she was working at homes of landlords and earning Rs. 800 per month. However, when MGNREGA work was initiated in the village, she was able to convince her husband to let her daughter, who was a school drop-out, resume her studies as there is no fee for the underprivileged and expenditure is of books alone. Moreover her earnings from MGNREGA work were more than what she and her daughter used to earn jointly.

MGNREGA is also a relevant and steady source of employment for women-headed households. In a survey across six states, 82 percent of the widows in the sample regarded MGNREGA as a very important source of income. Further, 67 percent of the women stated that MGNREGA had helped them avoid hunger and 46 percent said it had helped them avoid illness.[56]

During the field survey, many cases were reported where the elderly parents have been left or discarded by their children and have no source of income. They were also unable to get employment as daily labourers because of their old age. However, as MGNREGA has no upper age limit to be employed, such elderly people were able to get work and earn food for themselves. Similarly, MGNREGA was also a huge respite to the women-headed households like widows.

(viii) Intra-Household Effects: Various studies have cited narratives where women feel a sense of pride and achievement contributing to the household income. The women's contribution has led to the change in gender relations at the household level.[57] Studies also indicate that women exercise independence in collection and spending of MGNREGA wages, indicating greater decision-making power within the households.[58]

The primary data reported 27.2 percent of the respondents being of the view that MGNREGA has helped in improving their social position as they feel change in respect from their family members especially husbands. They are actively engaged in household decision making process. Although strategic needs[59] seems to be fulfilled but it is too early to comment on this aspect as programme is of recent origin.

4.6 Accounts of Women Workers in Villages with Non-MGNREGA Work

The women workers in villages with no MGNREGA work reported that they had heard about MGNREGA from their relatives in other villages. Most of the respondents stated that they were willing to work under MGNREGA as they faced gender disparity in their current employment. They also reported that most of the times they work as farm labourers on contractual basis. They were paid less wages as compared to men. In many cases their wages were collected by the contractors. In other cases, the male members collected wages form the contractors who would deduct their share from the worker's wages and disbursed the remaining amount to the workers. In such a scenario, the women were left with very small amount of money for themselves. Thus, they were unable to meet their consumption needs on par with women in with-work villages.

4.7 Conclusion

Women empowerment was not an intended goal of MGNREGA. However, the secondary data bring forth a disturbing fact that despite the statutory requirement of 33 percent of person-days to be generated for women, many states such as West Bengal, Assam, Uttar Pradesh, Arunachal Pradesh, etc. are unable to comply with this provision. As shown in Table 4.1, the number of non-complying states had been oscillating from 6 to 10 in the period of study.

The factors like provision of employment within 5 kilometers of residence, decent and favourable working conditions, gender equality, wage parity, etc. served as an attraction to women to work under the programme. The programme has empowered women economically as well as socially to a great extent. On one hand, women narrated stories and incidents of how earnings from the programme has led to their increased economic position i.e. economic empowerment in the form of more income in hand, equal wages, more control over their earnings, increased choices for expenditure, direct account payments, etc. While on the other hand, cases were reported which showed a change in the social position of women i.e. their social empowerment such as more say in the house-hold decision making, pride and achievement and increased levels of confidence through contribution to the family income, etc. Therefore, through MGNREGA, the women tend to meet their practical needs while their strategic needs are met long term.

However, due to non-initiation of MGNREGA work in certain selected villages, women in these villages stated that they were being deprived of the economic and social benefits of the programme which their counterparts in other villages were availing because of the work opportunity available at their doorsteps.

Further, the discussions held with MGNREGA women workers revealed that although they were facing minor problems in the form of non-availability of crèche facility, however, the benefits reaped from the programme outnumbered the flaws in the implementation of the programme. On the same lines, the non-MGNREGA women workers also reported that they would like the programme to be initiated in their villages in order to reap the benefits of the programme.

Hence, the hypothesis namely, "MGNREGA has been instrumental in improving the socio-economic conditions of the women workers", stands all approved & affirmed.

Endnotes

1. Naoko Otobe (2011), "Global Economic Crisis, Gender and Employment: The Impact and Policy Response", Employment Working Paper No. 74, International Labour Organization, Geneva, p. 4; International Labour Organization (2013), Global Employment Trends 2013, ILO, Geneva, pp. 1-170.
2. International Labour Organization (2013), op. cit., p. 93.
3. World Development Report (2012), Gender Equality and Development, World Bank, Washington, pp. 1-44.

4. S. Razavi (2012), "World Development Report 2012: Gender Equality and Development: A Commentary", Development and Change, Volume 43, Number 1, pp. 423-437.
5. Naoko Otobe (2014), "Promoting women's economic empowerment through productive employment and social protection", Working Paper 2014/091, United Nations University-World Institute for Development Economics Research, Helsinki, Finland, pp. 1-32.
6. S. Razavi (1997), "Fitting Gender into Development Institutions", World Development, Volume 25, Number 7, pp. 1111-1125.
7. C. Luttrell, S. Quiroz, C. Scrutton and K. Bird (2009), "Understanding and Operationalizing Empowerment", Working Paper 308, Overseas Development Institute, [Online} Available from http://www.odi.org.uk/resources/download/4525.pdf, [Accessed on 15th June, 2015].
8. S. Batliwala (2007), "Taking the Power Out of Empowerment – An Experiential Account", Development in Practice, Volume 17, Number 4, pp. 557-565.
9. Ibid, p. 561.
10. Andre Beteille (1999), "Empowerment", Economic and Political Weekly, Volume 34, Number 10-11, pp. 589-597.
11. Judy El-Bushra (2000), "Rethinking Gender and Development Practice for the Twenty-first Century", Gender & Development, Volume 8, Number 1, pp. 55-62.
12. S. Razavi and C. Miller (1995), "From WID to GAD: Conceptual Shifts in the Women and Development Discourse", Occasional Paper 1, United Nations Research Institute for Social Development and United Nations Development Programme, pp. 5-40.
13. E. Boserup (1970), Women's Role in Economic Development, St. Martin's Press, New York, pp. 19-28.
14. Razavi and Miller, op. cit., p. 39.
15. Ibid, p. 41.
16. F. Edholm, O. Harris and K. Young (1997), "Conceptualizing women", Critique of Anthropology, Volume 3 Numbers 9 and10, pp. 101-130; G. Rubin, (1975), 'The Traffic in women: Notes on Political Economy of Sex", in R. Reiter (ed.), Towards an Anthropology of Women, Monthly Review Press, New York, pp. 157-210.
17. Ruth Pearson, A. Whitehead and K. Young (1981), "Introduction: The Continuing Subordination of Women in the Development Process" in Kate Young et. al. (eds.), Of Marriage and the Market, CSE Books, London, pp. 1-19.
18. Caroline O.N. Moser (1989), "Gender Planning in the Third World: Meeting Practical and Strategic Gender Needs", World Development, Volume 17, Number 11, pp. 1799-1825.
19. R.W. Connell (1987), Gender and Power: Society, the Person and Sexual Politics, Polity Press, Cambridge, p. 42.
20. Razavi and Miller, op. cit., p. 32.
21. *Ibid,* p. 11.

22. *Ibid*, p. 28.
23. *Ibid*, p. 33.
24. Md. Aminur Rahman (2013), "Women's Empowerment: Concept and Beyond", Global Journal of Human-Social Science, Volume 13, Number 6, pp. 6-13.
25. P. Golding (1986), Excluding the Poor, CPAG Publishers, London, p. 34; S. Granzow (2000), Our dream: A World Free of Poverty, Oxford University Press and The World Bank, p. 121; P. Shaffer (2008), "New Thinking on Poverty: Implications for Globalisation and Poverty Reduction Strategies", Real-World Economics Review, Volume 47, pp. 192-231.
26. R. Bhattacharyya (2009), Examining the Changing Status and Role of Middle Class Assamese Women: Lessons from the Lives of University Students, PhD thesis, Newcastle University, UK, p. 65.
27. Reetika Khera and Nandini Nayak (2009), "Women Workers and Perceptions of the National Rural Employment Guarantee Act", Economic & Political Weekly, Volume 44, Number 43, pp. 49-57.
28. Government of India (2013a), op.cit., pp. 5-125.
29. Pankaj and Tankha, op. cit., pp. 45-55.
30. Maxine Molyneux (1985), "Mobilization without Emancipation? Women's Interests, the State, and Revolution in Nicaragua", Feminist Studies, Volume 11, Number 2, pp. 227-254.
31. *Ibid*, p. 230.
32. Pankaj and Tankha, op. cit., p. 47.
33. Government of India (2015), Mahatma Gandhi National Rural Employment Guarantee Act, 2005 – Report to the People: 2014-15, Ministry of Rural Development, Department of Rural Development, New Delhi, p. 46.
34. National Sample Survey Organisation (2014), Employment and Unemployment Situation in India, (July 2011 - June 2012), Ministry of Statistics & Programme Implementation, Government of India, p. 56.
35. McKinsey Global Institute (2015), The Power of Parity: Advancing Women's Equality in India, McKinsey and Company, New York, p. 71.
36. Dutta, et. al., op. cit., p. 19.
37. J. Ghosh (2009), "Equity and Inclusion through Public Expenditure: The Potential of the NREGS", Paper for International Conference on NREGA, New Delhi, p. 43.
38. Government of India (2012b), MGNREGA Sameeksha: An Anthology of Research Studies on the Mahatma Gandhi National Rural Employment Guarantee Act, (2005) – 2006-2012, Ministry of Rural Development, Orient Blackswan, New Delhi, p. 18.
39. Khera and Nayak, op. cit., p. 52; Pankaj and Tankha, op. cit., p. 47; Kiran Bhatty (2006), "Employment Guarantee and Child Rights", Economic & Political Weekly, Volume 41, Number 20, pp. 1965-1967.
40. J. Dreze and R. Khera (2011), The Battle for Employment Guarantee, Oxford University Press, New Delhi, pp. 13-39.

41. Khera and Nayak, op. cit., p. 54; Pankaj and Tankha, op. cit., p. 54.
42. Barbara Harriss-White (2003), India Working: Essays on Society and Economy, Cambridge University Press, Cambridge, p.28. ; Khera and Nayak, ibid, p. 55.
43. Government of India (2013a), op. cit., p. 69.
44. National Sample Survey Organisation (2010), Employment and Unemployment, 66th Round National Survey, (July 2009-June 2010), Government of India, New Delhi, p. 34.
45. Ibid, p. 36.
46. R.M. Sudarshan (2009), Examining India's National Rural Employment Guarantee Act: Its Impact and Women's Participation, Institute of Social Studies Trust, New Delhi, pp. 6-17.
47. J. Ghosh, op. cit., p. 45.
48. Dutta, et.al., op. cit., p. 15.
49. Sudha Narayanan (2008), "Women's Work Childcare and Employment Guarantee", Economic & Political Weekly, Volume 43, Number 9, pp. 10-13.
50. Khera and Nayak, op. cit., p. 48; Pankaj and Tankha, op. cit., p. 54; Ratna Sudarshan (2008), "Impact of NREGA on Rural Labour Market in Kerala: Preliminary Findings on Women's Work", International conference on "NREGS in India: Impacts and Implementation Experiences", New Delhi, 16-17 September.
51. R.M. Sudarshan (2011), India's National Rural Employment Guarantee Act: Women's Participation and Impacts in Himachal Pradesh, Kerala and Rajasthan, Institute of Development Studies, Centre for Social Protection, New Delhi, p. 10.
52. C. Dheeraja and H. Rao (2010), Changing Gender Relations: A Study of MGNREGS across Different States, National Institute of Rural Development (NIRD), Hyderabad, p 11.
53. Khera and Nayak, op. cit., p. 51; Pankaj and Tankha, op. cit., p. 48.
54. Dheeraja and Rao, op. cit., p. 61.
55. T. Shah, S. Verma, R. Indu and P. Hemant, (2010), Asset Creation through Employment Guarantee?: Synthesis of Student Case Studies in 9 States of India, International Water Management Institute (IWMI), Sri Lanka, p. 15.
56. Khera and Nayak, op. cit., p. 53; National Federation for Indian Women (2008), Social-Economic Empowerment of Women under NREGA, Report Submitted to the Ministry of Rural Development/UNDP, NFIW, p. 13.
57. Khera and Nayak, ibid, p. 52; Pankaj and Tankha, op. cit., p. 52; Bhatty, op. cit., p. 1966.
58. Dheeraja and Rao, op. cit., p. 43.
59. Molyneux, op. cit., p. 248.

5

Political and Administrative Capacity Building in MGNREGA

5.1 Introduction

In the late 1980s decentralization gained momentum globally and democracies experimented with policies promoting decentralization. Decentralization posits enhanced accountability mechanisms by developing principal (central government) and agent (local government) relationship. With increased autonomy, decentralization results in improved allocative efficiency as the 'agent', being aware of local needs, tries to reflect local preferences in the planning process.[1] Recent literature on participation has emphasized the role of active and engaged civil society which can articulate the demands and needs of the citizens and responsive and effective state to deliver public services so as to deepen democratic governance.[2] India professed its commitment to decentralization with the enactment of the 73rd and 74th Amendment Acts constitutionally empowering rural and urban local bodies. The success of decentralization largely depends on devolution of 3Fs, namely, Functions, Finances and Functionaries to the local bodies.[3] Along with these it also demanded a commensurate increase in capacities of local units for effective implementation of development programmes. The talk of 'capacity building' has been loud in development programmes.[4]

The literature reviewed revealed that the implementation of the policies has been relatively poor even when finances have not been a constraint. Programme implementation has suffered due to weak administration, understaffing, lack of capacity of the existing staff, and sometimes on account of lack of will among the political and administrative apparatus. It is therefore to be recognised that the availability of funds, though necessary, is not sufficient for the successful implementation of a programme. The capability of the staff, both political and administrative, to optimally utilize funds and produce results is equally important.[5]

The present chapter attempts to study the role and capacity of local political leadership and administrative apparatus in the planning and implementation of MGNREGA and to identify the factors affecting the delivery of services. Further, a study of human resource availability (both elected and administrative) at the village and block level for the planning and implementation of works under MGNREGA, their existing capacity needs and the capacity building measures needed for better implementation of MGNREGA are explored. Thus, it was hypothesized that, "The local bodies have the capacity to plan and implement MGNREGA works at the village level".

(i) Adequate human resource is available with the local bodies to undertake MGNREGA works.

(ii) The elected and appointed officials have the capacity to plan and implement MGNREGA works.

(iii) Regular training programmes are conducted for the officials to build their capacities for the implementation of MGNREGA.

5.2 Capacity Building

Capacity building is considered a serious and pressing need for the government organisations.[6] Over a period of time, it became apparent to the government that capacity building is a prerequisite for not only enhancing the managerial quality and skills of its workforce but also improving service delivery. Thus, capacity building can be progressively built as an approach to development. According to United Nations Development Programme (UNDP), there is need to first assess the existing capacity needs; secondly, possible future needs are to be planned; and finally, the gaps between these two needs are to be identified.[7] The identification of the gaps can help in devising strategies and development plans that could enhance capacity both at the organizational and the individual level.

Capacity building is variously described either as an approach or process to achieve goals like poverty reduction or as an objective in itself for the development of individual and organizational effectiveness.

UNDP defines capacity as "the ability of individuals, organizations and societies to perform functions, solve problems, and set and achieve goals. Capacity development entails sustainable creation, utilization and retention of that capacity to reduce poverty, enhance self-reliance and improve people's lives. It requires acquisition of individual skills, institutional capacities and social capital as well as the development of opportunities to put these skills and networks to productive use in the transformation of society".[8]

World Bank Africa Region defines capacity as the "proven ability of key actors in a society to achieve socio-economic goals on their own. This is demonstrated through the functional presence of a combination of most of the following factors: viable institutions and respective organizations; commitment and vision of leadership; financial and material resources; skilled human resources. In short, Capacity = Institutions + Leadership + Resources + Skills + Practices – Constraints".[9]

Thus it can be said that capacity building is the process to enhance capabilities and skills of individuals, institutions and societies to solve problems, make informed choices, define their priorities and plan their futures.

5.3 Evolution of Capacity-Building

The emergence of capacity building as a concept can be traced back in the history of international development assistance. Capacity building has generally evolved through six phases, namely, Institution Building, Institutional Strengthening, Development Management, Institutional Development, Capacity Development and Systems Perspective.[10] **Phase I** – In 1950s and 60s the main focus was on institution building. It normally involved importing models from developed countries. The stress was on the design and functioning of individual organizations with little emphasis on contextual issues. **Phase II** – In late 1960s and 70s the focus shifted towards the strengthening of existing institutions and adoption of western administrative techniques. e.g., redesigning of administrative systems or training to upgrade capacities of individuals. **Phase III** – In 1970s development management reflected emphasis on the implementation of development programmes. During this phase the primary focus was on the delivery systems of public programmes and ability of governments to reach target groups. This stage was also characterized by greater support for decentralization, involvement of local groups and institutions as well as integration of public programmes with rural development programmes.[11] **Phase IV** – During the 1980s the concept of institutional development was applied to the private sector, NGOs as well as the government. Institutional development sought to address the sustainability issue of not only 'what works' but 'what lasts'. **Phase V** – During late 80s and early 90s the emergence of capacity development was closely tied to the growing emphasis on sustainability and the need for developing countries to be self-sustained. Local capacities became the central focus of attention during this time. **Phase VI** – From 1990s to 2000s, capacity development continued to evolve with increased importance of systems perspectives. This led to greater emphasis on more comprehensive approaches like poverty reduction strategies and support for development networks. The capacity building literature noted the importance of issues such as motivations, incentives and building on local traditions and practices to capacity building and effective capacity utilization.[12] Further, the Institutional and Development framework developed by Elinor Ostrom went far beyond the public and private institutional designs. She demonstrated how the top-down government management systems tended to underperform with lower rates of return than systems where incentives to government officials were aligned to those of locals with their active participation.[13]

Despite broad consensus on some of the fundamentals of capacity building, the concept is still evolving. Some consider capacity building as a development objective while others considers it as an approach to development.

5.4 Capacity-Building in India

In India, after the implementation of the 73rd and 74th Amendment Acts, local bodies were entrusted with the responsibility of delivering a large number of services in the local areas. The Constitution also provided for the devolution of powers and responsibilities to the rural local bodies including the 29 matters listed in the Eleventh Schedule. Further, the local bodies are also at the centre-stage of various development schemes. Hence, with the increase in responsibilities of local bodies and the role and reach poised for future enlargement, the local bodies must have the capability to face the challenges in undertaking and implementing major national programmes apart from being able to fulfil their statutory functions. Therefore, the greatest challenge was to ensure the capability of local bodies to effectively perform the responsibilities entrusted to them.

However, the crucial issue of capacity building of the local bodies remained a largely neglected area for a long time. It took a long time to realise that along with devolution of powers, the local institutions need special capacity building and enhancement efforts in order to deliver efficiently and effectively. For example, implementation of the provisions of Part IX of the Constitution requires capability building of the Panchayats to the fullest sense. This includes training, provision of adequate functionaries, technical assistance and other support to Panchayats. Further, the local bodies also lack specialised and technical skills required for delivering services pertaining to engineering design, project management, maintenance of high-tech equipment, accounting etc.[14] Hence, in the post-decentralised period, the need was felt to build upon the capacities of the local bodies in order to perform their functions effectively.

Several efforts were made by the Government of India in working out the capacity building of the local bodies including training plans, funding and implementing the capacity building measures under various programmes. However, the implementation of capacity building efforts has been uneven across states.[15] Subsequently, in order to build capacities of the local bodies,

National Capability-Building Framework (NCBF) was brought out in August 2006 by the Ministry of Panchayati Raj (MoPR) following extensive discussions and consultations with the various state governments. The NCBF aims at comprehensively building, effective and sustainable capacity of all stakeholders of local governments to enable them to achieve the goal of developing local governments into independent institutions of local governance.[16]

The foremost purpose of the NCBF:- Was to lay down the minimum standards in terms of content and strategies for rolling out a training programme for elected and appointed officials. One of the non-negotiable standards adopted in the NCBF was that there ought to be universal coverage of all elected representatives and officials to training programmes of high quality and that too within a brief time-frame.[17]

NCBF has following four objectives –

(i) ***Upgradation of knowledge and skills of elected representatives***: It attempts to enable elected panchayat representatives to upgrade their knowledge and skills to perform their responsibilities better by exposing them to the modalities of implementing several programmes equitably and equip them with the operational skills required for day-to-day performance of their executive duties.

(ii) ***Panchayat officials to function as technical advisors***: It aims to equip the key officials associated with panchayats to function as technical advisors and trainers and orient them to respect, be more receptive and learn from the ground-level experience of elected panchayat representatives.

(iii) ***Improving grass-root democracy***: It attempts to improve vigour of practice of grass root level democracy through promotion of effective functioning of the gram sabha by providing space for the community, particularly the poor, to assert their demands through participative planning, monitoring and implementation of plans and holding their panchayats accountable through Right to Information Act and social audit.

(iv) ***Sensitization of stakeholders***: It aims to sensitize media, political parties, representatives in the legislatures, civil society organisations and citizens for effective local government.[18]

5.4(a) Principles of NCBF

The Framework describe the preparatory activities, building up of training infrastructure, developing a pool of resource persons, the range of handholding activities required to sustain a capacity development effort, planning the logistic of implementation, and monitoring and evaluation of capacity building efforts. The NCBF is based on some basic principles which are as follows :

(i) Capability building is a multifaceted exercise aimed at promoting effective functioning of panchayats, of which training is one of the facets, which must be repeated periodically as a continuous process of development with the active participation of all the stakeholders.

(ii) Training is not only information dis-semination but a process of exploration, discovery and growth in which both trainers and participants are enriched through mutual learning.

(iii) Training is not about providing ready-made answers to the problems but providing space and time for trainees to analyse the situation and seek solutions to their problems.

(iv) Mutual learning uses several modes to sustain interest. Trainers must encourage togetherness among learners, accept differences and recognise people's right to make mistakes.

(v) The participants in the Panchayati Raj system have well-honed knowledge, experience and native wisdom about grass-root reality, which must be respected and should constitute the base for their further learning. No member can be scorned or maligned on account of his/her social and economic background.

(vi) The training programme should ensure participation of all members through activities that involve creativity and provide scope for thinking and right degree of challenge.

(vii) Trainers should be objective and non-judgmental with whom the trainees can communicate freely. Trainers should evoke and stimulate thinking and accept criticism from the trainees.

(viii) Training must enable panchayat members, particularly women and representatives of disadvantaged groups, to understand within their own context how to increase their overall exposure, learning and comprehension through regular participation in the training programmes.

(ix) The framework must constantly develop and evolve on the basis of regular impact assessment. Training must become a two-way process so that feedback is ploughed into reforming of content and process of training.[19]

5.4(b) Components of NCBF

The NCBF envisaged that training programmes for elected representatives would be fast tracked. With respect to quality, certain basic minimum standards were set down, such as the number of elected representatives per classroom session (20 per batch); the various styles and pedagogies to be used (interactive satellite training, film screening, and local face-to-face training, etc.); the qualifications for resource persons (persons with right attitude and aptitude) and the standards and detailed methodology for orientation and training of resource persons. While the Ministry and the State departments of Panchayati Raj would contribute towards the content creation and rolling out of generic programmes focused on panchayat governance, sector-specific programmes would be funded by the respective ministries and departments. The buckling together of general and sector-specific training programmes would be undertaken by the respective State Institutes of Rural Development (SIRD) which would prepare a training calendar that would logically progress from general to specific matters. Thus, the delivery of content to the participants was carefully thought out and envisaged to be sensitively sequenced to ensure that the learning experience was effective.[20]

The Framework aims at segregating the training content and phasing the training programme into three parts (Table 1). (For detailed description of courses comprising Part I, II and III, see Annexure VIII).

Table 5.1: Phases and Contents of Training Programmes

	Theme	Description of the manner of interaction	Area covered in Brief	Category covered	Duration	Timeline for Completion
Part I	Building the right mindset for implementation of Panchayati Raj and learning basic functions	Course 1(a): Foundation Course	Overview of Panchayati Raj	Elected Panchayat representatives (about 22 lakh); Panchayati Raj Officials (about 8 lakh)	4 days	Within 20 weeks of election
		Course 1 (b): Basic Functional Course	Internal Housekeeping, including understanding accounts, Social Audit, Right to Information, Panchayat Revenues	Elected leaders of Panchayats at all levels and Chairpersons of Standing Committees (5 per Panchayat, About 10 lakh); Panchayati Raj Officials (about 5 lakh)	4 days	Within 20 weeks of election (Including foundational course, each office bearer would undergo8 days of training)
		Course 1(c): Functional Literacy Course	Give those who need to an exposure to functional literacy	Illiterate or semiliterate elected representatives (about 8 lakh people)	One month, or as required, preferably at the village level itself.	6 months

Part II	Basic skill building for planning and implementation	Course II(a): Sectorally focused training programme	Coverage of core functions of Panchayats aimed at improving capacities to deliver services and development programmes	Elected Panchayat representatives (about 22 lakh); Officials associated with Panchayati Raj (about 8 lakh)	At least 6 days (2 phases of 3 days each)	Within 40 weeks of election
		Course II(b): Computer Training	Training in basic computer skills and selected software for Panchayat level Training	At least 2 persons per Panchayat (about 5 lakh)	At least 6 days, with local handholding from the resource centre	Within 52 Weeks
Part III	Consolidation through interaction and networking	III(a): Gram Sabha level campaigns	Awareness Creation	Gram Sabhas, NGOs, SHGs and CBOs	At least 3 days a week	Coverage of all Gram Panchayats at least once a year
		III(b): Panchayati Raj TV channel and radio programmes		People at large	At least 3 days a week	All-India coverage
		III(c): Panchayati Raj Newsletter		Panchayati Raj members and individual subscribers	Once a month	All Panchayats
		III(d): Formation of networks of Panchayat elected representatives	Experience Sharing	Elected Panchayat representatives (about 22 lakh)		Within the first year after election
		III(e): Yearly refresher course		Elected Panchayat representatives (about 22 lakh)	At least 4 days	Once a year for remaining 4 years
		III(f): Visits to identified 'beacon' Panchayats	On the site Training	At least 10 lakh elected leaders of Panchayats	At least one full day each, excluding travel	At least two exposure visits every year
		III(g): Intermediate Panchayat level Resource Centres	Daily assistance to support Panchayat-level planning and implementation	Elected Panchayat representatives (about 22 lakh)	Every working Day	To commence by 20 weeks, when members have finished Part I training
		III(h): Helplines			16 hours a day, every working day	
		III(i): Certificate Courses	More intensive and academic study	Interested Stakeholders	6-month course	For about 100 persons per state

Source: Government of India (2010), National Capability Building Framework for Panchayati Raj Elected Representatives and Functionaries, Ministry of Panchayati Raj, New Delhi, pp. 7-8.

5.4(c) NCBF: An Assessment

Various efforts were made by the MoPR for training and capability building of elected representatives of panchayat through the NCBF. For this, NCBF was implemented through various existing and new schemes like Rashtriya Gram Swaraj Yojana (RGSY), Panchayat Mahila Evam Yuvak Sashaktikaran Abhiyaan (PMEYSA), Backward Regions Grant Fund (BRGF), etc.[21]

BRGF programme, implemented from 2008 onwards in 250 backward districts of the country, provided a launching pad for the implementation of the NCBF though in a limited sense. An allocation of Rs.1 crore was provided for capacity building of panchayat representatives and officials in the backward districts of each state. Further, the United Nations Development Programme-Capacity Development Local Government (UNDP-CDLG) project assisted seven states in the implementation of NCBF. The project also initiated an annual cycle of Panchayati Raj Institutions Capacity Building and Training workshops.[22]

Another programme, Rajiv Gandhi Panchayat Sashaktikaran Abhiyan (RGPSA), launched in 2013, aimed to strengthen Panchayati Raj Institutions by undertaking activities, ranging from administrative and technical support for panchayats, enhancing panchayat infrastructure, improvement in the quality of panchayat processes such as accounting procedures and strengthening e-governance at the panchayat level, undertaking capacity building and training (CB&T) of elected representatives and functionaries and up-gradation of CB&T institutional systems. On the demand side the programme focused on supporting gram sabhas to actively strengthen accountability processes like social audit.[23]

However, the performance in implementing capacity building efforts has been uneven across states. Efforts were generally intermittent and discontinuous with one-off training programmes consisting of routine lectures by inadequately equipped resource persons. Though some states prepared plans in accordance with NCBF but were not able to implement them as per the schedule. In many states, the continuing aspects of training and handholding, such as setting up of helplines, newsletters and functioning of intermediate panchayat-level resource centres did not take off.[24] Specifically, following deficiencies were observed –

(i) Less backward states which had comparatively better facilities in place like infrastructure and training personnel were able to absorb the enhanced allocations for training and conducted programmes of a good quality while on the other hand, the states that had greater need for implementation of the NCBF were unable to conduct programmes in accordance with the NCBF due to lack of infrastructure facilities and training personnel to undertake the implementation of the programme.

(ii) The overall allocation of funds in six years of the BRGF programme has only been 55 percent of the entitlement.

(iii) Monitoring formats for tracking the physical and financial progress of each state in juxtaposition with its agreed programme were not used. Consequently the states deviated from the programme once the perspective plans were approved and funds released to the states. This amounted to serious deficiencies in the implementation of the NCBF.

(iv) SIRDs are approached by various other government departments besides the MoRD to impart training on various aspects to elected members and officials. In the process, the realization of the importance of the NCBF as the foundation of capacity building of three-tier local governance system was missed out. Further, SIRDs receive requests and funds from the concerned line departments for the same training programme. For instance, training on MGNREGA is covered in NCBF and also separate funds are released to SIRD by MoRD to train elected representatives and implementing agencies on MGNREGA. This causes duplication of activity and funds.[25]

5.5 Capacity Building Under MGNREGA

Capacity building of state, district, block level and village level functionaries and agencies together form the most strategic aspect in effective implementation of MGNREGA. The amendments to MGNREGA, 2005 has necessitated enhancement of capacity building of all stakeholders to achieve expected outcomes. The stakeholders need to fully internalize new implementation architecture of the programme such as the importance of social mobilisation, procedural details as well as the relevant technical issues.

At all India level 300 MGNREGA officials were trained as State Resource Trainers. In case of Punjab eleven officials were trained, namely, State Nodal Officer MGNREGA, Assistant Manager Finance, Block development and Panchayat Officer, Technical Assistant, Assistant Project Officer, District Coordinator MGNREGA, Accountant, and faculty of State Institute of Rural Development in 2013-14.[26] Further, 41 MGNREGA officials were imparted training for trainers as District Resource Trainers. These include mainly Assistant Engineer, Technical Assistant, Assistant Programme Officer and IT Manager during the same year.[27]

In this study, the capacity of MGNREGA officials (elected and appointed) to implement MGNREGA works has been analysed on the basis of various indicators namely, adequacy of human resource available with the local bodies, administrative and technical staff available with the local bodies for planning and implementation; and training programmes conducted for the elected and appointed officials.

It was hypothesised that "The local bodies have the capacity to plan and implement MGNREGA works at the village level."

The sub-hypotheses investigated in this regard are –

(i) Adequate human resource is available with the local bodies to undertake MGNREGA works.

(ii) The elected and appointed officials have the capacity to plan and implement MGNREGA works.

(iii) Regular training programmes are conducted for the officials to build their capacities for the implementation of MGNREGA.

The data was collected through interviews conducted with three Additional Programme Officers, three Junior Engineers, three Computer Operators-cum-Accounts Clerks, twelve Sarpanches, thirty Panchayat members, eight Gram Rozgar Sahayaks, eight Panchayat Secretaries and four officials of the State Institute of Rural Development at Nabha and Mohali.

5.5(a) Adequacy of Human Resource Available at the Block and Village Level

The adequate number of human resource is important for the implementation of the programmes. The insufficiency of man power has adverse impact not only on implementation but also on the performance of functionaries who are assigned additional duties in the absence of sufficient man-power. Therefore, the key pre-requisite for proper implementation of any scheme is to ensure that adequate number of personnel is available.

The MGNREGA Operational Guidelines, 2013 mandate for the deployment of separate staff for the implementation of MGNREGA. In the initial years of the programme, it was prescribed that the existing staff can be given additional responsibility of implementation in order to get the things started. However, subsequently, separate staff was to be appointed for the implementation of the programme. For the effective implementation of the programme, appointed officials to be engaged include Additional Programme Officer (APO), Gram Rozgar Sahayak (GRS), Technical Assistant (TA), Computer Operators-cum-Accounts Clerk while elected officials include Sarpanch and other Panchayat members.

The sub-hypothesis investigated is "Adequate human resource is available with the local bodies to undertake MGNREGA works".

Appointed Officials

(i) Availability of Additional Programme Officers

The Additional Programme Officer (APO) is the implementing authority at the block level. As per the Act, a full-time Programme Officer has to be appointed at the block level under MGNREGA. However, normally block level executive authorities like Tehsildars or Block Development and Panchayat Officers (BDPOs) are designated as Programme Officers. They are required to discharge responsibilities of Programme Officer in addition to their normal duties. Therefore, in order to reduce the excessive workload, the APOs were hired to assist the Programme Officers in discharging their MGNREGA responsibilities at the block level.[28]

During the field survey, it was found that one APO was available per block. The APOs were full-time officials appointed exclusively for MGNREGA. In Punjab, APOs were hired on contractual basis with remuneration of Rs. 8000 initially which was increased to Rs. 16000 in 2012-13. As the APOs were the non-permanent employees, therefore the BDPOs in the capacity of Programme Officers were the signatory authorities for MGNREGA works in the block.

(ii) Availability of Gram Rozgar Sahayaks

The Gram Rozgar Sahayak (GRS) has to be appointed at the village level to assist gram panchayats in executing MGNREGA works. As per the Operational Guidelines, GRS should be engaged exclusively for MGNREGA works and not assigned any other work. The guidelines further prescribe for the deployment of GRS in every gram panchayat. More than one GRS can be deployed in GPs having high labour potential and GPs with scattered habitations and tribal areas.[29] The Comptroller and Auditor General of India (CAGI) Report of 2013, revealed that Punjab tops the list of states with shortage of GRS (Table 5.2).

Table 5.2: Shortage of Gram Rozgar Sahayaks

S.No.	State / UT	Required	Actual	Shortage	Percentage of Shortage
1.	Punjab	12,776	772	12,004	93
2.	Jammu and Kashmir	4,131	889	3,242	78
3.	Haryana	202	54	148	73
4.	Madhya Pradesh	23,336	6,438	16,898	72
5.	Himachal Pradesh	3,243	1,055	2,188	67
6.	Uttarakhand	1,811	648	1,163	64
7.	Gujarat	13,715	5,371	8,344	61
8.	Assam	243	136	107	44
9.	Uttar Pradesh	15,145	12,050	3,095	20

Source: Government of India (2013c), "Performance Audit of Implementation of Mahatma Gandhi National Rural Employment Guarantee Act (MGNREGA)," Comptroller and Auditor General of India Report No. 6 of 2013, New Delhi, p. 26.

During the field survey, it was found that GRS had not been appointed in every GP. In fact, the number of GRS in all the three blocks visited was far below their required number. In block Nabha, only nine GRSs had been appointed to cover 171 GPs while in Samana, only seven GRSs had been appointed for 96 GPs. In block Sanour, the number of GRS was six while the number of GPs in that block is 107.

The GRS' revealed that when work starts in five to six villages under their charge it becomes very difficult for them to manage all the works at the same time. They attributed the reason for ignoring other permissible works to this over-burdening.

(iii) Availability of Technical Assistants

Technical Assistant (TA) has to be appointed to assist GPs in identifying and conducting measurement of works. TA should be appointed for a cluster of villages depending upon the potential labour demand in the villages.[30] In Punjab, against the requirement of 2,555, only 74 technical assistants were deployed (one for five GPs) leaving a shortage of 2,481 technical assistants (97 percent).[31]

During the field survey, it was found that TAs had not been appointed for MGNREGA works in Patiala district. The Junior Engineers (JEs) for Panchayati Raj working with the block office had been given additional charge for MGNREGA. The JEs revealed that they were overburdened due to MGNREGA works as simultaneously they were also discharging duties in their parent department. The APOs stated that due to delay in measurement of works by JEs, the payment to MGNREGA workers got delayed. In some cases, the GPs were unable to prepare shelf of works[32] and send work proposals in time as estimation of works could not be completed due to unavailability of JEs.

Further, it came to light that the shortage of staff, especially engineers, has resulted in the implementation of works that were comparatively simple to implement and did not require much technical expertise such as renovation of ponds or plantation of trees. At many instances poor designing of the assets was observed, e.g. in village Boladi, the retaining wall around the de-silted pond was not erected which resulted in caving-in of the muddy boundary wall of the de-silted pond due to rain. In another instance the tree plantation was done without land-levelling which resulted in drying down of the trees due to unavailability of water.

A study documented that shortage of staff has hampered quality of works, people-centric planning and implementation, timely measurements of completed works and timely disbursal of payments to workers.[33] Further, the non-appointment of full time Secretary to the gram panchayats has also hampered the effective implementation of MGNREGA.

It came to light during the field survey that in district Patiala, the JEs had submitted a memorandum to the Additional Deputy Commissioner, Patiala stating that JEs were overburdened with their normal departmental duties due to which they were unable to discharge the additional duties assigned to them under MGNREGA.

(iv) Availability of Computer Operators-cum-Accounts Clerk

The guidelines prescribe for the appointment of Computer Operators-cum-Accounts Clerk at the block or GP level depending on the location of the computer centre. He has to assist the GP or PO exclusively in data entry work and maintenance of MGNREGA accounts. The guidelines further prescribe for the deployment of at least three Computer Operators at the block level.[34]

During the field survey, it was found that only one Computer Operators-cum-Accounts Clerk was appointed in each block. The Computer Operators revealed that although they were overburdened with work yet they did not complain because of the fear of the termination of their service as they were on contractual basis.

Elected Officials

The elected officials for the implementation of MGNREGA include the gram panchayat members. Their adequacy was not prescribed and therefore, not tested as per the Act. During the field survey, a Sarpanch and the other Panchayat members were available in every village visited.

Thus, the above discussion highlights the inadequate human resource availability for the implementation of MGNREGA. While the APOs were available in adequate numbers to assist the Programme Officers at the block level, an acute shortage of staff was found in the form of Gram Rozgar Sahayaks, Technical Assistants and Computer Operators-cum-Accounts Clerks. The main reasons were either the non-appointment of the GRSs, TAs and Computer Operators-cum-Accounts Clerks or the overburdening of the existing staff with additional responsibilities for implementation of MGNREGA. It is important that support staff in the form of Technical Assistants or Junior Engineers is adequately available to assist the gram panchayats. The Gram-Panchayats are dependent on the administrative staff for the preparation of estimates, supervision and execution of work, technical advice, measurement of works, quantification of the value of works, etc. Therefore, positioning the 'right' personnel in adequate numbers is important for the successful delivery of the programme.

5.5(b) Capacity of the Officials to Plan and Implement MGNREGA Works

Capacity on the part of officials is important to perform duties effectively using the knowledge and skills. MGNREGA works require capacity among officials for effective planning and implementation of the works. Most of the MGNREGA works require knowledge and expertise of technical nature on the part of officials. The gram panchayat, being an elected body, does not have the ability to understand the technicalities and other intricacies of planning, execution and measurement standards of higher degree required in these works. Further, the appointed officials also need to acquire expertise and sincere efforts in order to work as per their capacities.

Sub-hypothesis investigated in this regard is that, "The elected and appointed officials have the capacity to plan and implement MGNREGA works."

(i) Capacity of Gram Panchayat Members

Gram Panchayat is the core body entrusted with the planning and implementation of MGNREGA at the village level. It is an elected body comprised of members called Panches or Panchayat members and their leader called Sarpanch. Gram Panchayat is responsible for registering households and issuing job cards, identifying, planning and executing works, allotting employment to the job card holders, maintaining records, convening the gram sabha meetings for planning and conducting social audit, awareness generation and social mobilization, monitoring and implementation at the village level, etc.[35]

During the field survey, it was observed that the almost all the gram panchayats were initiating or focussing more on the works which were simpler to plan or implement in comparison to other permissible works e.g., tree plantation, renovation or de-silting of ponds while works which require expertise of some type were largely ignored e.g., agriculture related works like vermi-composting, liquid bio-manure, solid and liquid waste management, etc. The reason that came to light was that the gram panchayats were not adequately skilled to identify or implement MGNREGA works on their own. They were not capable enough to plan and implement works of technical or expert nature. Gram Panchayats admitted that in place of renovation or de-silting of ponds other works could have been initiated which were important for the development of the village like water harvesting or flood control works. However, due to lack of capacity and their dependency on the appointed officials such works of technical nature could not be initiated.

Further, the CAGI Report, 2013 reported that in the renovation of ponds in Punjab, due to non-maintenance, jungle weed grows up again and again. Therefore, the expenditure incurred on renovation of ponds was rendered infructuous.[36] Similar observations were made during the field survey also.

(ii) Capacity of Gram Rozgar Sahayaks

Gram Rozgar Sahayak (GRS) assists gram panchayats in executing the MGNREGA works at the village level. The GRS is responsible for overseeing the process of registration, distribution of job-cards, allocation of work to the applicant, facilitating gram sabha meetings and social audit, recording attendance of labour at the worksites, ensuring worksite facilities, providing group mark-outs to every group of labourers required to earn daily wage rate, maintaining MGNREGA related registers at the GP level.[37]

During the field survey, it came to light that the GRS were only able to perform the routine tasks or tasks of non-technical nature like registration of households, distribution of job cards, allocation of work to the applicants, etc. However, the tasks which required little technical knowledge on their part or non-routine activities were ignored such as providing mark-outs to the group of labourers or individual labourer for earning minimum wage, facilitating gram sabha meetings for planning of works or conducting social audit and so on.

(iii) Capacity of Additional Programme Officers

The Additional Programme Officer (APO) is responsible for preparing a consolidated plan at the block level from the project proposals received from the gram panchayats in the block and submit it to the district level. He is also responsible for maintaining and updating all the documents related to MGNREGA works in the block such as job-card register, muster rolls, gram sabha resolutions, work estimates, measurement books, Action Taken Reports on previous social audits, grievance redressal, etc. Further, he is also responsible for providing technical support to gram panchayats, act as a liaison between gram panchayats and block and between block and district.[38]

During the field survey, it came to light that APOs were able to discharge their duties efficiently. However, only few permissible works other than routine works were initiated in the locale of study. Even if the gram panchayat sent proposal of any new work involving technical or engineering expertise i.e. the works other than normal works being initiated in the area, their proposals were changed at the block level. The APOs stated that due to the lack of capacity on their part to undertake works of technical nature, such proposals were not encouraged by the higher authorities. The shortage of technical staff has further accentuated the situation.

Thus, the above discussion draws attention to the lack of capacity of the officials, both elected as well as appointed, to plan and implement MGNREGA works efficiently. Due to this, only few works were initiated in the villages like renovation or de-silting of ponds, tree plantation, etc. Other works requiring expertise and important for the development of the villages were not taken up. For example, water harvesting, flood control works, solid and liquid waste management works etc. were not initiated due to lack of technical expertise required to prepare such proposals or the incapacity of the officials like APOs, GRSs, Gram Panchayats to implement such works.

5.5(c) Training of the Officials Involved in Planning and Implementation of MGNREGA Works

Training is an important element to build the capacities of the functionaries entrusted with the responsibility of implementing the programme. The effective implementation of the programme depends upon the capacities of the functionaries to deliver successfully. Training is required to update the skills and knowledge of the implementing authorities along with their educational background and experience. It provides the functionaries a number of opportunities to keep themselves updated with new and recent happenings in their work. Hence, regularity of training programmes is also important to enhance the ability and performance of elected as well as appointed officials.

MGNREGA has mandated compulsory training for its new and existing staff so as to achieve the intended objectives of the programme. The on-going discussion seeks to evaluate the efficacy of training of officials such as APOs, GRS, Sarpanches and Panchayat members as well as Panchayat Secretaries under MGNREGA. The training module suggested in MGNREGA Operational Guidelines, 2013 for the various stakeholders has been described in Table 5.3.

Table 5.3: Suggested Training Module for Various Stakeholders

Stakeholder	Trainer	Suggested Training Modules
DPCs and other district level officers	Resource agencies empanelled by the State for each district/ cluster of districts	Course I
District Trainer Team	Resource agencies empanelled by the State for each district/cluster of districts	Course I and II For new recruits, there must be field posting for a period of 6 months to a year after undergoing a Basic Training Course to give them a hands-on grasp after which they should be certified as trainers
Programme Officer, Assistant Programme Officer	District Master Trainers	Course I Regular field based support from the District Unit is necessary to ensure that training is not a one off affair. Additional refresher courses may be designed as per need by the State/District
Junior Engineers, Cluster Facilitation Teams, Technical Assistants, PIA Teams	District Master Trainers	Course III
GRSs/EGAs and Mates	Cluster Facilitation Team/PIA Team	Course III
Gram Panchayat Leaders	Cluster Facilitation Team/PIA Team	Exposure Visits
MGNREGA Workers	EGAs and Mates	As per IEC

Source: Government of India (2013a), Mahatma Gandhi National Rural Employment Guarantee Act, 2005, Operational Guidelines, 2013, 4th Edition, Ministry of Rural Development, Department of Rural Development, New Delhi, p. 41.

The sub-hypothesis investigated in this regard is that "Regular training programmes are conducted for the officials to build their capacities for the implementation of MGNREGA."

(i) Training of Additional Programme Officers

MGNREGA guidelines mandate that the training programmes be conducted for the APOs upon induction. The suggested training module prescribes Course I training for the APOs (Annexure IX). It include imparting knowledge about workers' rights under the Act, registration for work and job-cards, planning and execution of works, maintenance of records at the gram panchayat and block level, technical resource support, measurement of work, wage payment through banks and post offices, provisions of transparency and accountability with emphasis on social audit and right to information, methods of generating awareness among the people regarding the scheme, etc. The training module also includes their sensitization towards rights-based development, gender justice, social justice and eco-restoration and good governance.[39]

During the field survey, the APOs reported that they had been trained at the State Institute of Rural Development at Nabha or Mohali. Their training focused on various aspects of MGNREGS such as planning and execution of works, maintenance of records, registration for work, preparation of job-cards, etc. All the respondents stated that the training lasted for one to three days and it has benefitted them in the execution of MGNREGA works. It has also informed them regarding the diverse nature of works under the scheme, various provisions of the Act and other mechanisms for the speedy transaction of works. All the respondents opined that they were able to use the learnings from the training in the field. The APOs expressed satisfaction with the training provided to them and would be happy to undertake follow-up training as ambit of works has widened under MGNREGA in wake of convergence of works.

(ii) Training of Gram Rozgar Sahayaks

The Operational Guidelines prescribe for conducting Course III (Annexure IX) training for the GRS. The training module for GRS include instruction about the workers' rights under the Act; planning, execution and measurement of works; work-site facilities; conduct of gram sabha meeting; awareness generation methods; potential of MGNREGA with specific reference to poverty reduction; natural resource management and local economic development. He should be trained in work-site management and measurement of works undertaken by MGNREGA.[40]

During the field survey, out of eight GRS interviewed, three reported that they had received on-the-job training at the State Institute of Rural Development, Nabha for 2 to 3 days while the other five had not received any orientation or on-the-job training. Out of these five GRS, two said that they were likely to attend training in the near future. One stated that he received on-the-job training while working with a Panchayat Secretary. Two of the GRS stated that they were unlikely to receive any in-service training in the near future.

The three GRS who attended training were sent for the same after ten to twelve months of their appointments, however, by that time they had figured out on the job, most of what was covered by the training module(s), i.e. their duties and functions. They reported that some components like preparation of job-cards, providing work-site facilities, etc. were found to be useful.

(iii) Training of Gram Panchayat officials

The training module for the Sarpanches includes 'exposure visits' while the provision of training and guidance to the panchayat members is the responsibility of the Cluster Facilitation Teams (CFTs). Exposure visits enable

Sarpanches from different regions to interact with and learn from each other, allowing them to get first-hand information and view practical examples of best practices. CFTs are entrusted with serving the cluster of gram panchayats.[41]

During the field survey, out of twelve Sarpanches, six reported that they had not been imparted any form of training for MGNREGA. The remaining six Sarpanches stated that they had received formal training at the block office. The six Sarpanches who received training stated that they were apprised of various works which could be undertaken by gram panchayats under MGNREGA. The duration of training for Sarpanches was one to three days. Few Sarpanches reported that the works undertaken in the village were the result of the training. All Sarpanches who received training expressed satisfaction with the training. The Panchayat members interviewed had been trained at training camps organised by the State Institute of Rural Development in the village. As discussed earlier, no CFTs had been constituted in the state (for details, see discussion on page 95-97). All the Panchayat members stated that the training camps were useful in increasing their knowledge about the scheme and the works to be undertaken in the village. They recommended that such training camps must be organised more frequently by the authorities.

(iv) Training of Panchayat Secretaries

The Panchayat Secretaries were entrusted with the implementation of MGNREGA works before the Gram Rozgar Sahayaks were recruited in Punjab. MGNREGA works were initiated in 2008 in district Patiala while the GRS were recruited in 2009-10 in different phases. Until that time the Panchayat Secretaries were given the additional charge of MGNREGA. During the field survey, out of the eight Panchayat Secretaries interviewed, four reported that they had never received any formal training about MGNREGA while other four reported that they had received training. These four reported that they were told about the kind of works that could be started under MGNREGA and the formalities to be completed before initiating the works. These included preparing list for the job-cards, preparing job-cards, opening of bank accounts of the job-card holders, etc.

The satisfaction level of the Panchayat Secretaries was low as they revealed various problems faced by them while discharging their duties even after receiving training. These were problems of utilising wage and material within 60:40 ratio, meaning that out of the total grant sanctioned 60 percent must be utilised for paying the wages of unskilled workers and 40 percent must be used for procuring material cost, problems of record keeping of MGNREGA, absence of office space to store the record books, etc.

The above discussion discloses the lack of regular training programmes among both appointed and elected officials. While officials like APOs and gram panchayat members expressed satisfaction with the training provided, most of the other officials like Gram Rozgar Sahayaks, Panchayat Secretaries and Sarpanches, had not been provided any type of training. In fact Sarpanches were not covered by the training for the gram panchayat members either. Almost all the officials emphasized the need to organize training programmes more frequently and regularly.

5.6 Lacunae in Capacity Building Programmes

The field survey results revealed that although there was dearth of capacity among the officials involved in the planning and implementation of the programme, however, efforts have been made to enhance the capacity of officials. The in-depth analysis of the primary data collected through interviews and complemented through observation brought forth wide discrepancies between the official records and existing ground reality. The survey revealed that although the training programmes were conducted to build and enhance the capacity of the implementing authorities, the authorities at the village and block level suffered from certain shortcomings which hampered their performance. These have been identified as shortage of able resource persons with SIRD, lack of motivation and interest among trainees, apathy of district officials towards training programmes, irregular and unsystematic training programmes, training as a mere formality, delayed training, learnings of the training are not fully implemented and are discussed below.

(i) Shortage of Able Resource Persons with SIRD

The officials at the State Institute of Rural Development, Nabha admitted that the substantial share of responsibilities under MGNREGA devolves on the rural local bodies; therefore to impart training to these officials they need qualified and experienced resource persons. However, the SIRD officials reported shortage of qualified resource persons to impart training to the local government officials. Due to this, most of the times such resource persons were hired who lacked in-depth knowledge or experience in local governance. Therefore majority of the trainers were unaware of the ground realities and the problems of the trainees. Hence, the gap existed among the inexperienced trainers and the trainees who had first-hand experience of the rural local governance. This has seriously affected the quality of the training programmes.

(ii) Lack of Motivation and Interest among Trainees

The SIRD officials reported the lack of motivation and interest among the trainees. One of the officials revealed that the trainees show a great deal of lack of interest during the capacity building programmes. He stated that, "it is not the food we get energy from but the digestion of the food. Therefore the officials would not gain only by sitting in the training programmes but by paying attention in the training programmes." Therefore, the poor motivation and commitment of the officials towards the training programmes would not benefit them.

(iii) Apathy of District Officials towards Training Programmes

During the field survey, it was observed that the higher officials have an apathetic attitude towards the training programmes of the lower level officials. One of the APOs revealed that she along with the other APOs had requested the ADC to arrange for their training as they were facing many problems after the introduction of the new guidelines in 2013 but no training programme was conducted for them even after repeated requests.

(iv) Irregular and Unsystematic Training Programmes

Capacity building of the officials is not a regular and continuous process. During the field survey, the APOs reported that they were provided training only once in the last five to seven years of their appointment. The APOs admitted that irregular and unsystematic training programmes are the major reason for compromised staff capacity and this impeded the performance of the support staff. In fact the relevance of training has further increased in the wake of convergence, as more works have been added in the ambit of MGNREGA. Another study has also documented that training programmes for MGNREGA officials are irregular, slow to implement and have poor coverage.[42] Training is considered a one off affair.

(v) Training as a mere Formality/Training as a Casual Process

The officials reported that the training programmes were only a formality. The Sarpanches reported that they could get away with just marking their attendance at the block office during the training and not attending the programme. Two of them revealed that they were told about the various rural development schemes but no details were provided regarding their duties or functions with regard to MGNREGA. Moreover the APOs reported that higher officials casually pass on information regarding any training programme, and they simply demand that any one or two officials can come and join it. The Panchayat officials have stated that they had attended trainings for only one day. Is an unhealthy trend as per the report of Expert Committee on Leveraging Panchayats for Efficient Delivery of Public Goods and Services, Government of India, 2013.[43] The report has taken cognizance of such practices and discouraged the trend of conducting one day training programmes.

(vi) Delayed Training

The Act mandates that the APOs must be provided training upon induction while it was found that those who had been trained were not provided any training upon induction but instead after one year or more of their appointment. Similarly, the GRS's were also imparted training after one to two years of their appointment. It was also found that the newly appointed GRS have not received training even after six to eighteen months of their appointments. The time spent in learning the ropes compromises the working of the programme. Further, being thrown in at the deep end without support may end up placing them at the mercy of local established networks.

(vi) Learnings of the Training are not Fully Implemented

Almost all the officials reported that they were able to implement the learnings of the training while discharging their duties. However, it was observed that they only implemented those learnings which were part of their daily routine such as preparing list of gram sabha members, preparing job-cards, maintaining registers, marking attendance at the worksites, etc. The non-routine and qualitative aspects such as awareness generation amongst people regarding MGNREGA, social audit, convening gram sabha meetings, etc were not given due importance. Such tasks were simply completed on paper while in practice they never took place. These tasks demanded mass participation of all the stakeholders; the officials did not render them properly and the stakeholders almost never demanded these services or held anyone accountable for lack of their provision.

5.7 Conclusion

It is clear from the above discussion that capacity building has been narrowly understood and implemented badly. There is a lot of rhetoric that surrounds capacity building, but when it comes to implementing an agreed set of standards, both the Centre and the States have been found wanting. The National Capability Building Framework of the Ministry of Panchayati Raj has failed to comprehensively build capacity of all the stakeholders of local governments in the country. The states failed to promote effective functioning of the panchayats and conduct training programmes in accordance with the guidelines of the NCBF in order to enhance capacity of the elected as well appointed officials.

The primary data findings revealed that there was shortage of support staff at the block as well as village level for the implementation of MGNREGA, e.g., adequate number of Technical Assistants, Gram Rozgar Sahayaks and Computer Operators-cum-Accounts Clerks were not appointed which has hampered not the initiation but also the quality of MGNREGA works. The non-appointment of two Diploma Engineers per 6000 households had not been done in Punjab. Also, the additional responsibilities assigned to the existing staff like Junior Engineers had further affected the implementation of the programme. The Junior Engineers stated that due to additional charge they were overburdened and their regular work suffered. The Comptroller and Auditor General of India's Report, 2008 has also highlighted that there was no appointment of full time dedicated staff for MGNREGA, which is a deviation from the national MGNREGA guidelines. Failure to appoint full time dedicated staff for MGNREGA has resulted in routing of the MGNREGA works through normal departmental channels which were already overburdened with their existing responsibilities. As a consequence of the overburdening, smooth and effective implementation of the programme has been hampered.[44]

The findings revealed that the elected and appointed officials did not possess the required capacity to plan and implement MGNREGA works. This has resulted in the implementation of only two or three types of permissible works which were simpler to plan and implement like tree plantation and renovation of ponds while other agriculture and environment related works which require expertise were largely ignored.

Impact of Irregular Training Programme for Officials

The capacity of the elected as well appointed officials has suffered due to the irregular training programmes for the officials. There is lack of quality in the delivery of training programmes. Further, as the quality of training is not being monitored, one cannot conclude that the training standards prescribed have been met or not. In other words, the capacity building of officials is irregular, delayed and a casual process which hampers the efficiency and effectiveness of the officials. As capacity of officials has not been enhanced from time to time it was observed that the gram panchayats continue to undertake only one or two types of works such as renovation of traditional water bodies and tree plantation. Officials lack capacity to undertake other types of works which may require technical skills at their end. After convergence the ambit of works has increased but it is seen that simple works such as cleaning the road berms off wild growth are undertaken while other works which are important from the ecological and economic perspectives are ignored.

Hence, the hypothesis namely, "The local bodies have the capacity to plan and implement MGNREGA works at the village level", stands invalidated.

Endnotes

1. J. T. Bossert and C.J. Beauvais (2002), "Decentralization of Health Systems in Ghana, Zambia, Uganda and the Philippines: A Comparative Analysis of Decision Space", Health Policy and Planning, Volume 17, Number 1, pp. 14-31; A. Mitchell and J.T. Bossert (2010), "Decentralization, governance and health-system performance: Where You Stand Depends on Where You Sit", Development Policy Review, Volume 28, Number 6, pp. 669-691.
2. Samuel Hickey and Giles Mohan (2004), "Towards Participation as transformation: critical themes and challenges", in Samuel Hickey and Giles Mohan (eds.), Participation: from tyranny to transformation? Exploring new approaches to participation in development, Zed Books Limited, New York, pp. 3-20.
3. Government of India (2013b), Towards Holistic Panchayat Raj, Twentieth Anniversary Report of the Expert Committee on Leveraging Panchayats For Efficient Delivery of Public Goods and Services, Policy Issues, Volume 1, New Delhi, p. 9.
4. J. Ahmad , S. Devarajan, S. Khemani, and S. Shah (2005), "Decentralization and service delivery", Policy Research Working Paper 3603, The World Bank, Washington, DC, p. 16.
5. Nupur Tiwari (2011), "Reinforcing the implementation and monitoring of the schemes under NREGA through Panchayatti Raj", [Online] available from: http:indiagovernance.gov.in/files/Involvement-of-PRIs-in-the-implementation-and-monitoring-of-the-schemes-under-NREGA.pdf, [Accessed on 13th Feb, 2012].
6. Patricia W. Ingraham, G. Joyce Phillip and Amy Kneedler Donahue (2003), Government Performance: Why Management Matters, Johns Hopkins University Press, Baltimore, Maryland, pp.140-143.
7. United Nations Development Programme (2008), Capacity Assessment Practice Note, UNDP, New York, pp. 1-31.
8. World Bank (2006), Capacity Development Resource Center-Perspectives and Definitions, World Bank Africa Region, pp. 45-47.
9. *Ibid,* p. 34.
10. CHF (2007), The CHF Capacity Building Approach, Cynthia Farrell, Ottawa, Canada, p. 5.
11. *Ibid,* pp. 5-6.
12. *Ibid,* p. 6.
13. Vikram Dayal, Rucha Ghate, Nilanjan Ghosh, Kanchan Chopra and Nagendra, Harini (2012), "Remembering Elinor Ostrom", Economic and Political Weekly, Volume 47, Number 34, pp. 23-25.
14. Government of India (2010), National Capability Building Framework for Panchayati Raj Elected Representatives and Functionaries, Ministry of Panchayati Raj, New Delhi, p. 1.
15. Government of India (2013b), op. cit., p. 180.
16. *Ibid,* p. 183.
17. Ibid, pp.186-189.

18. Government of India (2010), op. cit., p. 2.
19. *Ibid,* pp. 3-4.
20. Ibid, p. 7.
21. Government of India (2013b), op. cit., pp. 195-207.
22. *Ibid,* p. 198.
23. *Ibid,* p. 201.
24. Ibid, p. 205.
25. Ibid, p. 206.
26. Government of India (2014), Report on Capacity Building of Functionaries on Operational Guidelines under MGNREGA, MGNREGA Division, Department of Rural Development, Ministry of Rural Development, New Delhi, pp. 9-12.
27. Ibid, pp. 19-23.
28. Government of India (2013a), op. cit., p. 7.
29. Ibid, p. 27.
30. Ibid, p. 29.
31. Government of India (2013c), Performance Audit of Implementation of Mahatma Gandhi National Rural Employment Guarantee Act (MGNREGA), Comptroller and Auditor General of India Report No. 6 of 2013, CAG, New Delhi, p. 173.
32. The shelf of works are the works which the gram panchayats are interested in initiating their villages in the next financial year.
33. Ambasta, op. cit., p. 19.
34. Government of India (2013a), op. cit., pp. 29-30.
35. Ibid, p. 6.
36. Government of India (2013c), op. cit., p. 222.
37. Government of India (2013a), op. cit., p. 27.
38. Ibid, p. 7.
39. Ibid, p. 42.
40. Ibid, pp. 44-45.
41. Ibid, p. 41.
42. T.R. Raghunandan (2012), 'Introduction', in T.R. Raghunandan, (ed.), Decentralisation and Local Governments: The Indian Experience, Essays from Economic and Political Weekly, Orient Blackswan Private Limited, New Delhi, pp. 134-157.
43. Government of India (2013b), op. cit., p. 205.
44. Government of India (2013c), op. cit., p. 27.

6

Transparency and Accountability in MGNREGA

6.1 An Introduction

Transparency and accountability are intrinsic part of governance. There has been a growing emphasis for enhancing transparency and accountability in public services over the last few years. As per the World Development Report, lack of transparency and accountability is one of the major reasons for poor public service delivery in developing countries. According to the report, there were not enough mechanisms to ensure that the poor could directly interact with the public service providers and provide continuous feedback on the quality of services being provided.[1] Therefore, streamlining service delivery systems and ensuring transparency and accountability is very important.[2]

In India, designing appropriate systems for ensuring transparency and accountability and institutionalizing them has always been a challenge. Historically, none of the public service delivery programmes have had an explicit public monitoring component. The government also not pro-actively disseminated information in a demystified and simplified manner which the common public or beneficiary can understand.[3] However, in recent years, the government has acknowledged public monitoring in various policy measures in the form of Right to Information Act, social audit, public opinion surveys, citizen's report cards, community score cards, participatory poverty assessments, monitoring public service provision, networking with non-governmental actors and use of Information and Communication Technology (ICT) for ensuring transparency and accountability in its working. Government while implementing MGNREGA imbibed mechanisms such as annual reports, vigilance and monitoring committees, grievance redressal mechanisms, pro-active disclosures by the gram sabha, regular updation of the website, etc. for ensuring transparency and accountability.

6.2 Concept of Transparency

In the last two decades, the transparency movement has gained momentum. International organizations and Non-Government Organisations (NGOs) advocate transparency as an important instrument for enhancing service quality, greater accountability and limiting scope for corruption.[4] The concept of transparency has been the subject matter of a number of studies in different fields such as negotiation theory[5] to make the operations of the international organisations more transparent by presuming that international negotiations should be open to the same level of outside scrutiny as it prevails in bargaining in domestic contexts, international security,[6] regime effectiveness,[7] etc. However, a consensual definition of transparency is missing.[8]

Christopher Hood traces the history of the concept and identifies the "broadest doctrine of openness" as "...the doctrine that the general conduct of executive government should be predictable and operate according to published (and as far as possible non-discretionary) rules rather than arbitrarily". Hood's analysis illustrates the tendency for transparency to bleed conceptually into other equally compelling normative standards such as rule of law, accountability, public participation and deliberative democracy.[9]

Precedent Conditions of Transparency

The World Trade Organization states that ensuring "transparency" in international commercial treaties involves three core requirements –

(i) to make information on relevant laws, regulations and other policies publicly available.

(ii) to notify interested parties of relevant laws and regulations.

(iii) to ensure that laws and regulations are administered in a uniform, impartial and reasonable manner.[10]

This definition includes not only making information available and accessible to stakeholders, but also laws and regulations administered and implemented in an impartial and predictable manner.[11]

Transparency is also narrowly defined as "the release of information which is relevant for evaluating institutions".[12] Using a terminology derived from the principal-agent framework, a distinction is made between agent controlled and non-agent controlled transparency. The release of government information by governments is a typical example of agent controlled transparency while the use of that information by external actors such as the media, NGOs or citizens is non-agent controlled.[13]

According to Vishwanath and Kaufmann, transparency is the "increased flow of timely and reliable economic, social and political information, which is accessible to all relevant stakeholders".[14] This perspective emphasizes not only the availability of information, but also its reliability and accessibility to a range of potential agents.

In all the above definitions, the concept of transparency revolves around information sharing. Therefore, information access and provision is the central thrust of transparency.

6.2(a) Transparency and Information

Provision of information is an important step towards transparent governance and service delivery. With the provision of information the citizens can be sensitized about what to expect of their government, and thus to benchmark service delivery and expose misdoings, biases and inefficiencies. Transparency also brings decision-making processes closer to citizens. To this extent, the provision of information in the public domain is an effective mechanism to facilitate mobilization to bring greater transparency in the system.[15]

Management of Information

However, simply making information available is not sufficient to achieve transparency. Large amounts of raw information in the public domain may breed opacity rather than transparency. Information should be managed and published so that it is relevant and accessible; timely and accurate. For information to be relevant and accessible it should be presented in plain and readily comprehensible language and formats appropriate for different stakeholders. It should retain the details and disaggregation necessary for analysis, evaluation and participation. Information should be made available in ways appropriate to different audiences. In terms of timely and accurate information, it should be made available in sufficient time to permit analysis, evaluation and engagement by relevant stakeholders. This means that information needs to be provided while planning as well as during and after the implementation of policies and programmes. Information should be properly managed so that it is up-to-date, accurate and complete.[16]

In general, transparency imbibes provision of information to the public along with establishing mechanism for people's participation and mobilization in the governance process.

Transparency is a multifaceted concept that is often conflated with good governance, accountability, impartiality and rule of law.[17] Transparency is a powerful force that can help fight corruption, improve governance and promote accountability when consistently applied.[18] However, it is not only transparency that is the most important thing. Transparency has a purpose and that is ensuring accountability. Accountability is the reason why transparency is introduced into governance systems.[19]

6.3 Concept of Accountability

Accountability is "a relationship between power-holders and those affected by their actions and consists of two key elements: 'answerability' (making power-holders explain their actions) and 'enforceability' (punishing poor performance)".[20] Accountability mechanisms are classified into "vertical" and "horizontal" mechanisms. Horizontal accountability is ensured internally through rules and regulations of the government while vertical accountability is ensured through the citizen who is able to demand accountability from the government and its officials directly.[21] Both types of accountability mechanisms ensure transparency in governance. Hence, accountability in public service delivery is comprised of two things – a system of institutions designed to make transparency and accountability structurally possible; and an informed and mobilized citizens that can demand accountability from the system[22] (Figure 6.1).

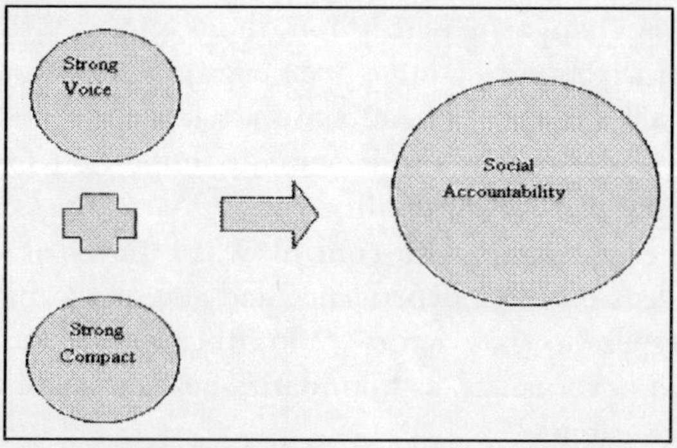

Figure 6.1: Concept of Accountability

Source: Yamini Aiyar, Bala Posani, Abhijit Patnaik and Mandakini Devasher (2009), "Institutionalizing Social Accountability: Considerations for Policy", Accountability Initiative Policy Paper 2, Centre for Policy Research, New Delhi, p. 13.

The degree of citizen engagement is classified as *consultation*, *presence* and *influence*, based on the extent of policy impact they could create.[23] In the words of Anne Marie Goetz, "consultation can occur in a range of spaces with dialogue, information sharing or awareness rising",[24] e.g., public opinion surveys, citizen's report cards, community score cards, participatory poverty assessments, etc. The second category of engagement, i.e. presence can ensure that organization has "a greater presence and access to decision-making processes to represent the concerns of excluded groups",[25] e.g., participatory budgeting exercises in South Africa, Brazil, Sri Lanka, Uganda and Mexico.[26] The most effective form of engagement is influence, i.e. degree of pressure on policy making and service delivery through mechanisms premised on people's right to seek accountability from power holders.[27]

Amongst these, consultation is expected to create the least impact while influence is expected to create the maximum impact.[28]

6.3(a) Accountability and Citizen Participation

Accountability in public service delivery can be improved if the traditional 'hierarchical controls' are replaced by the citizen's willingness and ability to participate.[29] In other words, service providers will be accountable if there is an emphasis on citizens' input and feedback resulting in appropriate, responsive and accountable service delivery. The literature reviewed revealed that the participation of citizens in planning and implementation of projects has not only increased the effectiveness of public service delivery and made it more appropriate, but also increased accountability and reduced corruption.[30] People's participation in development activities of the state is no longer considered as a hindrance. Instead, citizens are encouraged to participate in order to ensure responsiveness and accountability.[31]

Thus, there is change in perception about society's role from "well-behaved" local participation to a more open engagement with the government; however, there is still a distant relation between state and the society. Autonomy from the state was deemed as fundamentally, important for legitimacy of civil society in its pro-accountability role.[32] According to Cunill, "co-management is irreconcilable with control. The efficacy of societal control is directly dependent on the independence and autonomy that societal actors maintain with respect to state actors".[33] In other words, accountability can be ensured in "co-governance" as boundaries between state and society are blurred to a large extent.[34]

Numerous examples are available around the world where citizen groups have been engaging themselves directly with the state apparatus, its core functions, monitoring and influencing the policy from inside. For example, Participatory Budgeting in Porte Allegre, Brazil where ordinary citizens were directly involved within the governmental apparatus in the planning and supervision of public spending activities which were normally under the exclusive purview of public officials.[35]

In India, a grass-root organization, Mazdoor Kisan Shakti Sangthan (MKSS), mobilized citizens to directly engage with institutions of horizontal accountability. Through social audits, MKSS empowered ordinary citizens and turned them into auditors to have an access to the state documents such as muster rolls in order to expose corrupt practices. This form of "hybrid" accountability broke the state's monopoly over official oversight and legitimized citizen's inclusion into the state affairs,[36] thereby moving towards "co-governance".

Thus, societal role in accountability emphasizes empowerment of citizens to have a direct say in formulation and monitoring of services and holding service providers accountable. Reforms like decentralization and institutionalization brought the state and its decision-making processes closer to the citizens by creating new spaces where citizens could engage directly with service providers.[37] The emphasis is to strengthen and integrate citizen voice into the working of the state and create avenues for direct monitoring of service providers by citizens. On the one hand features like formal computerized complaint systems and citizen charters enable citizens to interact with the service providers directly while on the other hand, decentralization of services and creation of Community based Organizations provide the communities a more direct role in planning, delivering and monitoring of the services. There has also been access to information legislations in many countries that has further facilitated the process by opening up state operations to free scrutiny by the citizens.[38]

Hence, over the last few years there has been a transformation in the manner in which accountability is sought from the state. From a division of labour approach that segregated horizontal and vertical accountability efforts, there is now a distinct trend towards 'hybrid' accountability where citizens are increasingly involved directly in the monitoring and decision-making processes of the state.[39]

6.4 Transparency and Accountability

Transparency and Accountability are two elements of good governance, transparency facilitates accountability. The links between the two are neither implicit nor automatic. In order to ensure better accountability, there is a need to understand what to do with the information received through transparent mechanisms and to convert transparency gains into accountability gains. Much work has been done to understand the procedural need for transparency but relatively less attention has been paid whether this has led to any sustained improvements in accountability. For example, in India, the Right to Information Act (RTI) has made significant inroads into making the state processes transparent. However, attention needs to be paid on how best to strengthen the state machinery in order to translate transparency gains into accountable service delivery and governance.[40]

Another issue in strengthening the links between transparency and accountability is to identify what kind of information is most effective in ensuring accountability.[41] Any information about services has to be regular, reliable and relevant (3Rs) in order to be effective in improving the quality of services.[42]

Therefore, transparency and accountability are inter-linked in which transparency is a tool to ensure effective accountability.

6.5 Transparency and Accountability in India

In India the governance structure has under-performed in terms of accountability. The reasons for these institutional failures are numerous and complex. The institutional mechanism is plagued with structural weaknesses such as the multiplicity of institutions, overlapping responsibilities or jurisdictions, lack of enforcement powers, poor performance standards, etc. This has led to an adverse incentive structure ultimately reducing efficiency and accountability.[43]

Due to multiple institutional failures, civil society in India has emerged as an important arena for mobilization of people to demand action for accountability from the state. A wide variety of accountability instruments and mechanisms are employed by citizen groups within this space. As a consequence, the state has initiated efforts to create new structures for closer citizen engagement and to strengthen accountability. For example, RTI Act, 2005 has facilitated citizen mobilization as well as created opportunities and provided tools to citizens to engage with and scrutinize the state.[44]

As a result, accountability in India today is diverse and vibrant addressing various issues in governance and service delivery. Instruments such as RTI and social audit have the potential to significantly empower citizens and initiate critical steps towards establishing accountability.[45]

6.6 Transparency and Accountability in MGNREGA

Commitment to transparency and accountability is an integral part of MGNREGA. The poor for whom the scheme is being implemented must be aware of their rights and entitlements and participate in the programme design and decision-making processes. Further, they must be empowered to monitor and evaluate the scheme regularly. For this, the Central Employment Guarantee Council (CEGC) constituted a working group on transparency and accountability in 2010 for strengthening the process of transparency and accountability within MGNREGA. The objective was to facilitate workers and citizen's access to the rights granted under the Act. The working group in its first meeting constituted five sub-groups on the various issues to be addressed. The issues were –

(i) Transparency and proactive disclosure.

(ii) Grievance redressal and Ombudsman.

(iii) Social Audit.

(iv) Management Information System (MIS).

(v) People's entitlement and transparency.[46]

These sub-groups recommended several measures to strengthen the implementation of the scheme in different arenas, most of which were later incorporated in MGNREGA Operational Guidelines in 2013.

The following discussion attempts to evaluate efficacy of various provisions made in MGNREGA to promote transparency and accountability like proactive and mandatory disclosure mechanisms, social audit, vigilance and monitoring committees and grievance redressal mechanism. It was hypothesized that "The mechanisms to ensure transparency and accountability under MGNREGA are functional". The sub-hypothesis investigated were –

(i) The mechanisms of information disclosure under MGNREGA are working to ensure transparency.

(ii) Regular social audit of the works is conducted under MGNREGA.

(iii) Vigilance and Monitoring committees are actively involved in the monitoring of MGNREGA works.

(iv) Grievance redressal mechanisms are functional under MGNREGA.

The subsequent sections i.e., section 6.7, 6.8, 6.9 and 6.10 discusses the information disclosure mechanisms, social audit, vigilance and monitoring committees and grievance redressal mechanisms under MGNREGA.

The data was collected through interviews conducted with twelve Sarpanches and thirty Panchayat members in twelve villages, three Additional Programme Officers (APO's); eight Gram Rozgar Sahayaks (GRS); eight Panchayat Secretaries; five volunteers of the Nehru Yuva Kendra, Patiala, who were involved in conducting the social audit in the selected blocks and eight members of the Vigilance and Monitoring Committees (one ex-serviceman, one local school teacher, one anganwadi worker, two former panchayat members and three MGNREGA workers) in order to investigate the detailed aspects of implementation. Focus group discussions were held with the beneficiaries, job-card holders and gram sabha members in the villages. Informal interviews were also held with the staff of Joint Development Commissioner's Office at Mohali and MGNREGA Cell at the district level. Observation was used to supplement the data.

6.7 Information Disclosure Mechanisms

To ensure transparency, the MGNREGA Operational Guidelines, 2013; prescribe for proactive dissemination of information of different aspects of MGNREGA regarding realization of workers' rights such as number of person-days generated, details of the workers and wages paid, expenditures on items and assets created and so on. MGNREGA provides for information disclosure through wall paintings, gram sabha meetings, website updation, annual reports, information boards at the work-sites and so on. The findings of the field survey regarding the working of information disclosure mechanisms have been discussed below.

6.7(i) Information Disclosure through 'Wall Paintings'

The operational guidelines mandate that the information available in the Management Information System (MIS) has to be painted on the walls. This includes number of days of work provided and payments made to every job-card holder in a year, list of works sanctioned, expenditure on labour and material component, quantity of various material items and rates at which these were procured. The guidelines also prescribe that report cards on local works, employment and funds must be pasted by the gram panchayat at other prominent places in the village like schools and community centres; office of intermediate panchayat, Programme Officer, District Programme Coordinator and district panchayat.[47]

During the field survey, no such information was found displayed on the walls in any of the villages visited. However, some information was found so displayed at one of the block offices and the district office. This was about the basic features of MGNREGA; it was not a report card regarding the local works initiated or completed in the area or the employment generated or funds allocated or utilized in the area.

Apart from pro-active disclosure, the operational guidelines mandate that the information must be displayed in the vernacular at public places like the gram panchayat office or at the worksites. The guidelines call for the involvement of Bharat Nirman Volunteers, youth clubs, women's groups and local civil society organizations in the dissemination of information related to MGNREGA.[48]

During the field survey, no display of information was found at the public places like gram panchayat office regarding the workers' rights, expenditures on items and assets created. Further, there was no involvement of the civil society organizations or women groups during the field survey. Only worker unions or MGNREGA union members were found to be involved in generating awareness among people in a few selected villages.

6.7(ii) Information Disclosure through Gram Sabha Meetings

In order to ensure compliance with the statutory requirements of transparency, accountability and proactive disclosure of key documents, the guidelines prescribe that the information should invariably and proactively be placed in the domain of the gram sabha. The gram sabha has to be convened regularly for the effective and efficient implementation of the scheme regarding the updated data on employment demanded or received, number of job-cards issued, list of people who have demanded and given or not given employment, funds received and spent, payments made, works sanctioned and works started, cost of works and details of expenditure, duration of work, person-days generated, reports of local committees, copies of muster rolls has to be placed by the gram panchayat before the gram sabha once in every quarter.[49]

During the field survey, it came to light that virtually no Gram Sabha meetings are convened for the above mentioned tasks. The meetings are shown to be organized only to furnish the paper work while in actual practice, few gram sabha members from the village are called upon to get their thumb impressions or signatures by the authorities in order to show compliance with the guidelines. Further, some gram sabha members revealed that they had no idea regarding the material component used in the work or the procuring agency. However, the authorities stated that as most of the people were daily wage labourers, either they were not available for the gram sabha meetings during the day or were unable to read the official documents because of illiteracy. So in order to finish the work in time they had to resort to such methods. They stated that their records were open to anyone who wanted information about the scheme.

6.7(iii) Information Disclosure through Regular Website Updation

The guidelines mandate that all the MGNREGA records must be regularly uploaded on the MGNREGA website (www.nrega.nic.in).

The MGNREGA website was regularly updated and the various records related to employment generation, person-days generated, job-card holders, works initiated, funds allocated and utilized, etc. could be accessed through it.

6.7(iv) Information disclosure through Annual Reports

The guidelines mandate that the Central Employment Guarantee Council is responsible for preparing an annual report regarding implementation of the scheme. The report must be laid before Parliament by the Central Government. Correspondingly, every State Employment Guarantee Council has to prepare an annual report to be placed before the State Legislatures by 31st December of the succeeding year. Further, the District Programme Coordinator, Programme Officer and gram panchayat must prepare an annual report containing the facts, figures and achievements relating to the implementation of the scheme within its jurisdiction.[50]

As MGNREGA annual reports were available on the website, it clearly showed compliance with the guidelines related to annual reports.

6.7(v) Information Disclosure at the Work-sites

Work-sites are the prime location concerned with conduct of MGNREGA works, labour amenities, entitlements, etc. It is essential to disclose the information at work-site so as to ensure transparency and also prevent elite capture of entitlements. As per the operational guidelines, pro-active disclosure at the work-site shall be through the following –

(i) Display of information through citizen information boards

(ii) Reading out of muster rolls information regarding attendance, work done and wages paid in the presence of workers at the end of the day by the person authorized,

(iii) Reading of the measurements in the Measurement Book to the workers during the measurement of works.[51]

During the field survey, apart from one village, there was no display of information through citizen information boards at any of the work-sites visited. The picture below shows that although display boards existed at the work-sites for completed and ongoing works but columns in the board were not filled. Thus panchayats had displayed boards to complete the formality but information on the boards was missing which is against the essence of the MGNREGA guidelines.

Completed Work	**Ongoing Work**
	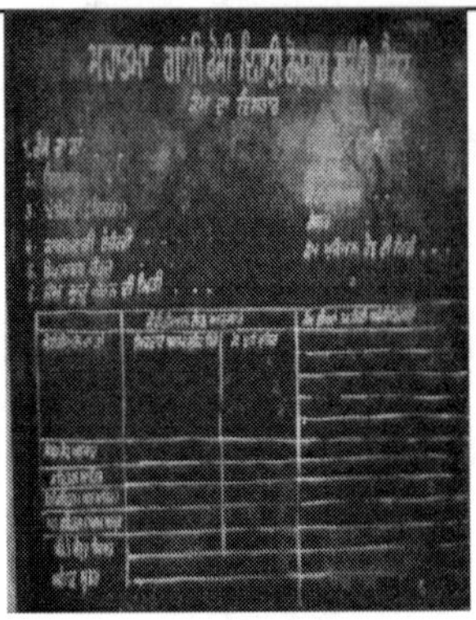

Image 6.1:Citizen Information Boards at the work-sites

Similarly, the muster rolls were not available at the worksites, although, they were produced by the gram panchayat members when demanded. The workers reported that there was no reading out of muster roll information at the work-sites. Few workers reported that the measurements were done in their presence by the authorities. However, majority of the workers were found to be unaware about the measurement records at the work-sites.

The guidelines also prescribe that work-site file shall be maintained for each work and be accessible to all residents of the gram panchayat, members of Vigilance and Monitoring Committee, elected representatives etc. The file must contain the following information about–

(i) details of the work

(ii) details of administrative and technical sanction

(iii) period of work and generation of person days expected

(iv) details of workers and wages paid

(v) initiation meetings

(vi) labour amenities provided

(vii) materials used item-wise indicating source, unit cost, total cost, etc

(viii) grievances raised by workers

(ix) entries by Inspecting Officers, Report of the Vigilance and Monitoring committee.[52]

It was found during the field survey that some of the above mentioned information was available in the files maintained by the gram panchayats for the MGNREGA works.

It is prescribed that the photographs of worksite (at least three stages – before, during and after completion of work) be uploaded on the website (www.nrega.nic.in).[53] During the field survey, it was found that the photographs of the works were available with the Gram Rozgar Sahayaks and also uploaded on the website.

The above discussion highlights that some of the mechanisms of information disclosure available under MGNREGA were not in place like wall paintings, report cards, awareness through involvement of civil society organisations, information boards at the worksites, gram sabha meetings. These mechanisms were either not resorted to or not put to good use. However, the annual reports and updation of information on the website was regularly done to ensure information disclosure.

Social Audit

Social audit is a process for ensuring transparency and accountability in public works by involving various stakeholders such as service seekers, service providers, civil society organizations and so on. It is a process through which government expenditure details at the local level (usually at the village level) are obtained and discussed in a public hearing attended by both the service providers and the people who have benefited from that particular government programme. This provides an opportunity to the citizens, especially the poor, to directly engage with the service providers and provide continuous feedback on the implementation of large government programmes. It also exposes corruption in the implementation of the government programmes.

Charles Medawar pioneered the concept of Social Audit in 1972 with its application in medicine policy, drug safety issues and on matters of corporate, governmental and professional accountability. According to Medawar, the concept of social audit is based on the principle that "in a democracy the decision makers should account for the use of their powers with the consent and understanding of all concerned".[54]

The basic component of social audit is people's participation for ensuring transparency. In recent times, the research around the world acknowledged that participation of stakeholders in state's activities could play an important role in strengthening transparency and accountability leading to increased responsiveness in service delivery. Various studies have documented how participation of citizens in planning and implementation of government programmes has not only increased the effectiveness of public service delivery but also reduced corruption.[55]

The concept of social audit is based on the philosophy that citizens have the right to know how they are governed and to participate actively in auditing elected representatives, the services delivered and programmes implemented.[56] It provides an opportunity to the citizens, especially the poor, to directly engage with the service providers and provide continuous feedback on the implementation of the programme. Simultaneously, it also provides an opportunity to the government to take corrective action and improve the level of service delivery.[57]

Therefore, social audit performs three intrinsic democratic functions. First, it produces informed citizens. Second, it encourages citizens to participate in local affairs through the provision of information and third, it helps create a sense of civic responsibility by bringing people together to address issues of collective concern.[58]

Social Audit in India

In India, there were few organized spaces for citizens to directly participate in regular monitoring and evaluation of the government programmes. However, civil society experimented with evidence-based advocacy using social audits to create more space for citizen engagement. As stated earlier, a Rajasthan based grass-root organization, Mazdoor Kisan Shakti Sangathan (MKSS) involved ordinary citizens in verifying government records and supposed expenditures on entitlements against testimonies of the beneficiaries.[59] The theme of MKSS's struggle was that people have the right to know what the government is doing and how funds are being spent. MKSS demanded access to information related to local development works. It analyzed the official records; cross checked the information with residents of relevant villages and shared it with the assembled villagers at the public hearing meetings. Local residents who were victims of fraudulent practices were invited to give testimonies. The government officials and local politicians were also given an opportunity to defend their actions publicly during the meetings.[60]

Considering the significant impact of public hearing in ensuring accountability, the Government of India attempted to include social audit in almost all the flagship social sector programmes like MGNREGA, National Rural Health Mission, Mid-Day Meal Programme, Sarv Shiksha Abhiyan and so on.

Social Audit in MGNREGA

In MGNREGA, social audit provided the primary stakeholders (daily wage labourers) an opportunity to participate in the audit of the programme. Section 17 of the MGNREGA mandate regular conduct of social audits on all aspects of the scheme. The MGNREGA operational guidelines provide step by step guidance for conducting social audit of the MGNREGA works.[61] The association of all stakeholders in the conduct of social audit helps in ensuring transparency in the implementation of the Act.

At the All-India level, a total of 2,91,434 social audits had been conducted in 2011-12 while 3,27,510 social audits were conducted in 2012-13. In 2013-14 the number of social audits conducted was 1,87,117 across the country. In 2011-12, 1,32,160 issues were raised and actions taken during social audit across the country while in 2012-13, the figure was 1,52,753. In 2013-14, 1,17,573 issues were raised and actions taken at the pan India level (Table 6.1).

Table 6.1: Social Audit at All-India Level

Year	Number of Social Audits	Number of Issues Raised and Actions Taken
2011-12	2,91,434	1,32,160
2012-13	3,27,510	1,52,753
2013-14	1,87,117	1,17,573

Source: MGNREGA website: http://nrega.nic.in/netnrega/home.aspx

In Punjab, 22,286 social audits were conducted in 2011-12. In 2012-13, the number of social audits conducted was 23,376 in the state while in 2013-14, it was 22,276. The number of issues raised and actions taken was 6,845 in 2011-12 while in 2012-13, it was 8,678 in Punjab. In 2013-14, 15,912 issues were raised and actions taken in the state (Table 6.2).

Table 6.2: Social Audit in Punjab

Year	Number of social audits	Number of issues raised and actions taken
2011-12	22,286	6,845
2012-13	23,376	8,678
2013-14	22,276	15,912

Source: MGNREGA website: http://nrega.nic.in/netnrega/home.aspx

In district Patiala, the number of social audits conducted in 2011-12 was 1,958 while two issues were raised and actions taken in the same year. In 2012-13, 1,938 social audits were conducted while no issues were raised and actions taken during the same year in the district. Further, in 2013-14, a total of 994 social audits were exercised while 804 issues were raised and actions taken in the district (Table 6.3).

Table 6.3: Social Audit in District Patiala

Year	Number of social audits	Number of issues raised and actions taken
2011-12	1,958	2
2012-13	1,938	0
2013-14	994	804

Source: MGNREGA website: http://nrega.nic.in/netnrega/home.aspx

This section discusses the findings from the field survey with respect to the social audits conducted, attendance and participation in the social audit meetings, findings of the meetings and increased awareness regarding MGNREGA entitlements in the locale of study.

The sub-hypothesis investigated in this regard was that "Regular social audit of the works is conducted under MGNREGA".

(i) Social Audit Unit

The operational guidelines prescribe that a Social Audit Unit (SAU) has to be established by the state government to facilitate the conduct of social audit of MGNREGA works. SAU can be a society or a directorate but independent of the implementing agencies.[1]

During the field survey, it was found that no SAU has been established in the state. During interactions with the officials of Joint Development Office, Mohali, it was reported that SAU was in the process of being established. However, in its place the State Institute of Rural Development (SIRD) has been given the responsibility to facilitate the process of social audit. The SIRD officials when contacted confirmed facilitation of social audit process in the state. However, they complained of shortage of capable resource persons to conduct programmes.

The guidelines also prescribe that an annual calendar is to be framed to conduct at least one social audit in each gram panchayat every six months and a copy of the calendar has to be sent to all the District Programme Coordinators (DPCs) for making necessary arrangements. The SAU must be provided with the required information and records of all the implementing agencies by the Programme Officer at least 15 days before the date of Gram Sabha meeting to conduct social audit properly.[2]

During the field survey, it was found that an annual calendar was framed to conduct the exercise of social audit twice a year. The volunteers of the Nehru Yuva Kendra, Patiala were engaged in conducting social audit in the villages. During inter-actions with them it was reported that the necessary records required to conduct the audit were made available to them by the officials.

(ii) Conducting social audit

Social audit provides a good, accurate platform to the citizens for making direct claim on the state. It is an effective means for the local people to interact with the MGNREGA officials.[3]

During the field survey it was found that social audit has been undertaken for the various works completed in the villages. All the officials reported that they have exercised social audit in their villages with the help of Nehru Yuva Kendra, Patiala. The village officials also reported that they were informed about the social audit to be conducted in the village, well in advance by the block level officials. Interviews with the volunteers of Nehru Yuva Kendra, Patiala also revealed that they informed the Sarpanch of the village an hour in advance before visiting the village for conducting social audit.

(iii) Attendance in the Social Audit Meetings

The MGNREGA guidelines mandate that the labourers and the village community shall be informed about the gram sabha conducting social audit by the resource persons as well as the Programme officer to ensure full participation.[4]

During the field survey, the volunteers of the Nehru Yuva Kendra, Patiala expressed that the attendance of the people in the social audit meetings was satisfactory. Even if the attendance was low, the village officials would call few beneficiaries or job-card holders from the village to attend the meetings. The online social audit reports revealed that the attendance of the gram sabha members was between 15 to 20 members during the audit in majority of the villages. However, during the focus group discussions it came to light that most of the gram sabha members had no prior knowledge of the social audit meetings to be conducted in the village. The village authorities claimed that as most of the people were daily wage workers, they were not available during the social audit exercise even when informed in advance. Therefore, they conducted the audit in the presence of workers who were available in the village during the social audit meetings.

(iv) Participation in the social audit meeting

It is believed that social audit provides an opportunity to the primary stakeholders to participate, express views and air their grievances freely. The focus group discussions held with the beneficiaries during the field survey revealed that majority of those who attended the social audit meetings actually participated and expressed their grievances. Majority of them complained about the delay in wage payments. A few of them also complained about the late measurement of works due to which their payments got delayed.

(v) Findings of the Social Audit Meetings

The Act mandate that gram sabha shall be convened to discuss the findings of the verification exercise, review the compliance on transparency and accountability, fulfilment of rights and entitlements of labourers and proper utilisation of the funds.

The interviews conducted with the volunteers of the Nehru Yuva Kendra, Patiala revealed that the social audit team did not find any irregularities in the conduct of the scheme. There were no complaints regarding irregularities in the meetings. Therefore, the social audit reports did not mention complaints from the beneficiaries. However, it was reported that in most of the villages, the gram sabhas were defunct; therefore, no discussions took place on the findings of the report

(v) Increased Awareness Regarding Entitlements in the Scheme

Various studies report that social audit has helped in increasing the awareness among the respondents regarding their entitlements in the scheme e.g. provision of safe drinking water, shaded area for rest, appointment of a crèche minder for the children at the work-site, mandatory unemployment allowance in case work was not provided within a fortnight of submitting a demand for work, 10 percent of additional wages if employment was provided beyond five kilometres from their residence, etc.[5]

The field survey, however, revealed mixed results. While the awareness with regard to job-cards, rest hours, safe drinking water and shade facility existed; majority of them were ignorant about unemployment allowance, travelling allowance, crèche minder, medical aid and insurance, conduct of gram sabha meetings, social audit meetings, etc.

Lacunae in Social Audit Process

The mobilization of the community by the social auditors can provide impetus to the social audit process.[6] A study conducted in Andhra Pradesh reported that overall enforcement of social audit in the state was slow and has created a perception amongst workers and officials that the audit has limited impact.[7] The lacunae in the social audit process revealed by this study are discussed below. These were mainly low awareness among the respondents, absence of formal feedback mechanism, lack of technical skills among the auditors, social audit missing social aspect, social audit – a mere formality, indifferent attitude of officials, discrepancies and social audit and non-involvement of NGOs.

(i) Low Awareness among the Respondents

As per the mandate, the Social Audit Unit (SAU) is responsible for building capacities of gram sabha for conducting social audit. It is also responsible for creating awareness amongst the labourers about their rights and entitlements under the Act and facilitating verification of records with primary stakeholders and work-sites. For this, SAU needs to identify, train and deploy appropriate number of State Resource Persons, District Resource Persons, Block Resource Persons and Village Resource Persons to facilitate the gram sabha in conducting social audit. The resource persons can be drawn people from amongst the primary stakeholders, civil society organisations or Bharat Nirman Volunteers who have the knowledge and experience of working for the rights of the people. The trained resource persons, in turn, will train the village community in carrying out the verification process.

Disclosure by Field Survey

During the field survey, it came to light that State Institute of Rural Development, Nabha has provided training to the volunteers of the Nehru Yuva Kendra for conducting social audit in the various districts of the state. In Patiala district, the volunteers worked as village resource persons and conducted social audit by verifying official records and filling proformas. One volunteer per village was involved in conducting social audit. The volunteers interviewed revealed that they were not trained with respect to building capacities of gram sabha for conducting social audit. Further, on inquiring it came to light that majority of the respondents were unaware of the concept of social audit, its mechanism and processes. Only the key persons or agencies in the village such as Sarpanch or panchayat members, GRS, whose participation is mandatory in the audit, knew about it. The gram sabha members were also not aware of the social audit exercise conducted in their village. However, few of the participants during the focus group discussions admitted that someone asked them regarding the work completed under MGNREGA and payment received by them but the reason of the whole exercise was largely unknown to them. Thus, the exercise of practically involving the gram sabha members was not complied with. The Gram Sabha members were the mute spectators of most part of the proceedings.

Further, little evidence was found of initiatives by the authorities in spreading awareness about social audit. A study revealed a link between participation in social audit assemblies and awareness of entitlements among the work-site beneficiaries. It reported that the elites were aware of the social audit while the non-elites and women had not even heard of it.[8] This was found to be the case here as well.

(ii) Absence of Formal Feedback Mechanism

An ideal social audit brings on board the perceptions of the people, examines outcomes and involves community in the task of verification and its findings are supposed to be enforced by the government.[9] However, studies reveal that due to the lack of feedback mechanism in the social audit process, the complainants are unlikely to have information about the outcome of their grievances.[10] Another study reported that due to the absence of written record of follow-up remedial action, it is unlikely that the guilty will be punished.[11]

During the field survey it came to light that due to the absence of the effective feedback mechanism, people had no idea regarding the status of their complaints. Majority of the respondents reported that neither their grievances were addressed, nor they were aware of any action taken to redress those grievances. The respondents showed their job-cards and pass-books to validate their claims of not having received the payments of the works completed two years ago while their fellow workers who worked with them on the same projects had received payments a long time ago. Further, the people had little idea whom to approach for the redressal of their complaints.

(iii) Lack of Technical Skills among Auditors

A study reported that the modest impact of the social audit reflects a problem of lack of capacity on the part of social audit team. Careful documentation of audit findings required improvements in the training of auditors and greater emphasis on the importance of more complete documentation in the training modules.[12] Further the efficacy of the social auditor is constrained by the fuzzy outcomes, multiplicity of goals and unclear weighing of these goals that characterize government implementing agencies.[13] Another study reported that social auditors lack technical skills to undertake the audit due to which the officials refused to recognise their findings as valid.[14]

During interviews with the volunteers of the Nehru Yuva Kendra, it came to light that they were unaware about the basic philosophy of social audit. Being technically incompetent to undertake the social audit exercise, the auditors relied only on the official version while ignoring the perceptions of beneficiaries. In other words, it has led to reduced citizens' space in the audit process. The auditors also revealed that they were given one-day training regarding filling-up the requisite proformas.

(iv) Social Audit Missing Social Aspect

Social Audit tends to accommodate the voices of people. However, the auditors focused on the books and accounts of the village functionaries while ignoring the 'social' aspect i.e., the social audit process focused more on the auditing of records rather than the social mobilization aspect.[15]

During the field survey, it was revealed that the local officials would call a few people from the village in case of low strength in the social audit meeting solely for the purpose of getting their thumb imprints on the required documents. Therefore, the local officials would connive and report compliance with the requirement by the above strategy.

(v) Social Audit – A mere Formality Ignoring Guidelines

A study reported that even though some states have recently responded to the Act by conducting 'regular' social audits, the exercise has largely been superficial with claims of no irregularities in programme implementation.[16]

During the field survey, similar tendency was reported on the part of the auditors. The volunteers of Nehru Yuva Kendra revealed that it took only half an hour for them to complete the process of social audit in a village. Their only focus was to finish audit in as many villages as they could in a day. One of the volunteers revealed that he was asked by the district officials to conduct social audit in one block for Rs.12000 and he was permitted to take help from any of his friends or family members to finish the audit. The auditors accepted that their main focus during the audit was to fill the proformas. Further, majority of them reported that they did not find any discrepancy during the audit conducted by them.

As per the guidelines social audit shall be convened at a neutral public space by the gram sabha. However it was reported that majority of the social audits took place at the house of the Sarpanch. Further, the Act mandates that the meeting shall be chaired by an elderly villager who is not a part of the gram panchayat or implementing agency. During the field survey it was reported that in majority of the cases, the Sarpanch presided over the meeting or if any block official was present, then he was the chairman. Thus neither was the social audit conducted on neutral ground nor was an elderly villager made to chair the audit.

(vi) Indifferent Attitude of Officials

The enhanced citizen engagement has not resulted in significant shifts in state behaviour. The audit process itself is bureaucratised. It has been pushed through a top-down, state-heavy bureaucratic hierarchy rather than as a social movement like the launch of the initiative in Rajasthan which was later diluted on account of vested interests of the officials. A study reported that due to multiple changes and innovations in MGNREGA in the recent years, the understaffed and indifferent lower bureaucracy is only racing to meet the new guidelines and implementation requirements.[17]

During the field survey, the APOs complained that they were not consulted by the higher authorities in finalising the dates for social audit in their blocks. Being an implementing authority at the block level, the Act mandates them to be present during the social audit proceedings in the village. However, it was reported that barring one APO, other APOs were not present during the social audit proceedings in the village. The online social audit reports also confirm the findings. The reports mentioned that APOs were present only in two villages during the audit. Among the block and district officials, only Gram Rozgar Sahayaks were present during the audit meetings. Further, the auditors revealed that one of the APOs told them to carry back social audit reports with them as he has no place to keep the reports in his office. The reports were found to be lying in the office of Nehru Yuva Kendra, Patiala. Another APO said that their work was over once the reports were uploaded online; the submission of the hard copies of the reports in the district office was the responsibility of the auditors. However the auditors were found to be unaware regarding the submission of the reports and kept them in their office with no one even concerned about their submission to the concerned authority.

(vii) Discrepancies and Social Audit

Social audit helps in bringing out various discrepancies or malpractices in the implementation of the scheme. It also helps in adherence of laid down norms and standards by the implementing authorities. It has been said that the absence of complaints in a social audit report is a result of poor attendance in the gram sabha and low level of awareness among the beneficiaries.[18]

During the field survey, a volunteers of the Nehru Yuva Kendra reported that during his training a field visit was organised in village Gurdaspura in Nabha block, where during the audit, many malpractices were found on the part of Sarpanch; the work was done with the help of machines but the workers were showed to be paid wages in the documents. When questioned, the Sarpanch claimed that the work was done during the tenure of the previous Sarpanch. When the ex-Sarpanch was called in the meeting, there was a heated exchange between the two Sarpanches and social audit meeting had to be called off. The volunteer reported that although he later tried to follow-up through the training officials of the State Institute, he could not find whether anything had been resolved in that case. His submission was that when as trainee he failed to get information, he could well-imagine the plight of a poor labourer who has no idea whom to approach for seeking justice.

(viii) Non-involvement of NGOs

NGOs role in the success of social audit in other states like Rajasthan and Andhra Pradesh was believed to be an important factor in mobilization of the beneficiaries. However, during the field survey, absolute absence of involvement of NGOs was observed in the locale of study. The absence of the NGOs has not only affected the active involvement and participation of the people but it has also deprived them of the benefits they could derive from their participation in the social audit process.

Vigilance and Monitoring Mechanism

The vigilance and monitoring of a scheme is important for its effective implementation. It provides a continuous feedback to the agencies regarding the performance and opportunities to take remedial action in case of any deviation from the guidelines. The vigilance and monitoring mechanisms under MGNREGA has been established as a watch-dog and provides mechanism for inspection at the local level. The operational guidelines prescribe that all states shall make an arrangement for a three-tier vigilance mechanism to proactively detect irregularities in the implementation of MGNREGA and to follow up detected irregularities and malfeasance, including those identified during social audit and to ensure that the guilty are punished and recoveries of mis-spent funds duly made.[19] The sub-hypothesis tested in this regard was: "Vigilance and Monitoring Committees are actively involved in the monitoring of MGNREGA works."

State Level

The operational guidelines mandate that a Vigilance Cell has to be constituted at the state level consisting of a Chief Vigilance Officer (CVO). The CVO can be a senior government officer or a retired officer supported by at least two senior officials (serving or retired), one Civil Engineer and an Auditor.

The State Vigilance Cell is responsible for receiving complaints about the implementation of MGNREGS in writing or orally or through mobile, telephone or internet and get it verified either directly or through the District level Vigilance Cell depending on the seriousness of the complaint. It is also entrusted with conducting regular field visits to detect irregularities and taking suo-moto action on reports appearing in the media. It is also expected to review the inspection system, transparency arrangements and functioning of the field and district level vigilance system. It is also responsible for recommending initiation of disciplinary action against the officials found guilty and framing charges if the reply to the initial memo is unsatisfactory. It is also responsible for developing a plan of action for the functioning of the vigilance mechanisms in respect of MGNREGAs and sending an annual report to State Employment Guarantee Council with suggestions on controlling irregularities and malfeasance.[20]

During the field survey, the officials at the Joint Development Commissioner's (JDC) office, Mohali reported that the vigilance and monitoring system was functional in the state. The officials stated that although there was no vigilance cell formulated at the state level, however, the employees of the Engineering wing and the JDC office were appointed to monitor and invigilate the works and records of the gram panchayats from time to time. The general tendency of the officials was to check and verify the works and records of those gram panchayats who had spent the maximum amount of funds in the state. These officials also submit report to State Employment Guarantee Council with suggestions and recommendations.

District level

The guidelines prescribe for the establishment of a Vigilance Cell at the district level. It is to be headed by a district level officer and supported by an Engineer and an Auditor of appropriate seniority. Engineer and Auditor can be appointed on contractual basis. The District Vigilance Cell is responsible for performing the following functions –

(i) Carrying out directions of the State Vigilance Cell.

(ii) Performing inspections on its own and taking follow up actions for recovery, disciplinary action and filing of criminal cases in respect of non-officials and officials whose disciplinary authority is at the district level.

(iii) Overseeing the inspection schedule of officials, the observance of transparency provisions at the district level and below and the functioning of Vigilance and Monitoring Committees at the local level.

(iv) Sending annual reports to the State Vigilance Cell.[21]

During the field survey, it was reported that District Vigilance Cells has been established in Punjab. In Patiala district, the Vigilance Cell invigilates all the development schemes in the district. For its vigilance functions, it maintained coordination with VMCs formed at the village levels.

Local level

The guidelines prescribe for the establishment of Vigilance and Monitoring Committee (VMC) in the gram panchayat area. The VMCs must be comprised of about ten members half of whom shall be women with representation for Scheduled Castes and Scheduled Tribes in proportion to their population. The members of the VMCs can be identified from among local school teachers, anganwadi workers, self-help group members, social audit volunteers, members of various Community-based Organisations and youth clubs. The VMC team is to be appointed/nominated/elected by the gram sabha for a period of 6 months but not exceeding one year.[22]

The guidelines further provide that the report of VMC must be placed at the gram sabha meeting. The VMC is responsible for visiting work sites and interacting with workers, verifying records and onsite facilities, assessing quality of materials and cost, providing end-of-work report on its satisfactory completion including a qualitative assessment of the nature of the work and its usefulness.[23]

During the field survey, it was reported that VMCs were formulated at the village level from amongst the gram sabha members, anganwadi workers, local school teachers, local ex-servicemen, educated youths, etc. However it came to light that in some of the villages, even the members of the VMCs were not aware of their membership. The Sarpanches admitted that the authorities had to nominate the members of the VMC and could not find many literate persons in the village, so they nominated whosoever was available in the village. The Sarpanches also admitted that in some cases they failed to inform few members. Further, in the villages where members were not aware of their membership, not many were aware of their role in VMC also. One of the ex-servicemen who was a member of VMC revealed that when he was informed about his being a member of the VMC, he initially refused to be the member because of personal problems but the Sarpanch of the village insisted him to be a member on the pretext that his role won't be more than signing a few documents to complete the formalities. The authorities also admitted that they failed to make VMC members aware of their role as they were themselves not much aware of it. Some of the Sarpanches reported that they were asked by the Panchayat Secretary to suggest a few names of literate people from the village in order to constitute a committee which is a sheer formality, hence they complied.

One of the Sarpanches reported that he had informed the VMC members about their role. However, the local school teacher and the anganwadi worker complained that they were forcefully made the VMC members as they had already informed the Sarpanch about their busy schedule. The officials complained that they had difficulties in convincing people to become members of the VMCs.

Out of the six work-sites visited during the field survey, the workers at only one of the work-sites reported that the VMC members had visited the work-site and interacted with them. At the other five work-sites, it came to light that most of the VMC members did not visit the work-sites, verified records or work-site facilities and assessed the quality of materials used as the onus for these lies with the same authorities who are also nominating VMC members. So, all in all, without visiting the work-sites, it was assumed that all is well at the work-sites and satisfactory completion reports of the works were approved.

In one of the villages, one of the VMC members reported that he urged other members of the committee to visit the work-site on and off, however, none of the members paid heed to him. He reported that VMC was only a formality the authorities are completing as practically in most of the villages VMCs were defunct committees.

The above discussion reveals that VMCs are not actively involved in the monitoring of MGNREGA works. The Vigilance Cell had not been established at the state level as per the guidelines. At its place, the officials at JDC office, Mohali were appointed to monitor and invigilate the works and records from time to time in the state. However, at the district level, District Vigilance Cell had been established. At the local level, the VMCs were formulated only in paper. Most of the times, the members were either not aware of their membership or of their duties. All in all these committees were dysfunctional at the village level.

Grievance Redressal Mechanism

The redressal of grievances is important for the effective implementation of a programme. The satisfactory redressal is equally important as timely redressal of grievances. Under MGNREGA, various mechanisms have been adopted to deliver timely and satisfactory redressal of the grievances such as appointing Programme Officers and District Programme Coordinator as grievance redressal officers at the block and district levels respectively, establishment of helplines, complaint boxes and Ombudsman at the district level. In order to investigate the effective working of these mechanisms, the sub-hypothesis tested in this regard was, "Grievance redressal mechanisms are functional under MGNREGA." The findings of the field survey have been discussed in the following paragraphs.

Block and District Level

Under MGNREGA, the state governments are responsible for determining the appropriate Grievance Redressal mechanisms at the block and district level for dealing with any complaint in respect of implementation of the scheme. It is entrusted with laying down the procedure for disposal of such complaints. The Programme Officer (PO) is the Grievance Redressal Officer at the block level and the District Programme Coordinator (DPC) at the district level. The action taken on the complaints received by the PO and the DPC has to be placed before the meetings of the intermediate and district panchayats respectively. A complaint register has to be maintained with the name and address of the petitioner, nature and date of the petition and uploaded on the website on a weekly basis. The complainant must be given a receipt with number and date to follow up the status of the grievance from a counter in the office of the PO. The failure to dispose of the complaint in seven days is a contravention of the Act by the PO punishable under Section 25 of the Act. [24]

During the field survey, it was reported that generally the workers approach the gram panchayat or the Sarpanch if they had a complaint. The Sarpanch or the panchayat members informed the block office which then try to address it. It was also reported that in case the block office is unable to address the grievance, it send the complaint or the complainant directly to the district level.

The nature of complaints reported during the field survey was usually regarding the delay or non-payment of wages to the workers, delay in sanctioning or receiving of grants by the gram panchayats, non-measurement of works, non-estimation of work proposals etc.

It came to light that the workers did not have much information regarding the grievance redressal mechanisms under MGNREGA. One of the gram panchayat members' reported that even though they had filed complain to the highest level, their complaints had not been addressed even after two years. He further stated that if the panchayat members had not been heard, it was impossible that a poor worker could be entertained by the authorities.

There were numerous cases reported during the field survey, where payments were not made to the workers of the works completed two years ago. The block and village level authorities blamed the online system of payments for the delay in wage payments to the workers. The APOs stated that due to the newly introduced online system of wage payments, they were unable to comment where exactly the problem was; the online system showed that the wages had been paid to the workers while the workers came to them with their pass-books with no entries for wages. Although

MGNREGA guidelines, prescribe that MIS report shall clearly point where the delay had occurred[25] but the APOs had no clue. They also reported that the online system had proved to be problematic in case of payments to the suppliers. The payment was done to the suppliers through online system but it was unclear which gram panchayat's payment had been done and which gram panchayat's payments were pending and thus gram panchayats were not in a position to draw materials from the supplier.

Helplines

The guidelines prescribe for the setting up of helpline for grievance redressal. Complaint boxes must be installed in the offices of PO and DPC to facilitate submission of complaints. A state level officer must be designated to monitor the disposal of complaints. Further, monthly reports on complaints received and disposed must be sent from the gram panchayat to PO, from PO to DPC, DPC to State Government and from State Government to Government of India and should be placed on the website also.[26]

During the field survey, it was reported that helpline had been established to facilitate the process of grievance redressal. The officials at the JDC office, Mohali reported that in case of any grievance it was immediately marked to the concerned district office which further marked it to the concerned block office. The JDC office had also received complaints through the central office, New Delhi which they had transferred to the concerned district. Therefore the helpline was functional to address the grievance of the stakeholders.

However, no complaint boxes were installed at the block or district level.

Ombudsman

The operational guidelines prescribe for the appointment of Ombudsman at the district level by the State Government for the speedy and effective redressal of grievances regarding MGNREGA. The Ombudsman is supposed to receive complaints from MGNREGA workers and other stakeholders on specified matters and facilitate their disposal in accordance with law. He is also mandated to engage experts for inquiring into the technical aspects relating to the complaint.

The Ombudsman is responsible for addressing the issues alleging irregularities regarding registration of households and issue of job-cards, custody of job-cards, demand for work, issue of dated acknowledgement receipt against submission of application for work, payment of wages and payment of unemployment allowance. He is also responsible for redressal of procedural and substantive issues of Gram-Sabha, discrimination on the basis of gender/caste/religion, work-site facilities, measurement of work, quality of work, use of labour displacing machines, engagement of contractors, operation of accounts in bank or post offices, registration and disposal of complaints, verification of muster rolls and other documents and use and release of funds.[27]

During the field survey, the officials at the JDC, Mohali revealed that one ombudsman was appointed for a cluster of four to five districts in Punjab. At the time of field survey, there were only four Ombudsmen in the state while the other seats were lying vacant. As per the information revealed by the MGNREGA Cell of Patiala district, the Ombudsman of the Patiala district was also the incharge of Fatehgarh Sahib district. However, the seat of the Ombudsman was lying vacant since 2012 in Patiala.

Conclusion

The chapter has discussed various transparency and accountability mechanisms in MGNREGA available in the locale of study. While some of the information disclosure tools were found to be in place like annual reports and regular website updation, majority of them were not in place like irregular or no gram sabha meetings, absence of information display boards at the worksites, absence of detailed information of the works and the workers on the information display boards, lack of information provision through wall paintings or report cards at the gram panchayat, block and district office.

The process of social audits was also found more to be a formality to be completed rather than a social mobilization exercise. The officials were only interested in completing the paper work to comply with the guidelines. The auditors were also found to be unaware regarding the basic philosophy of social audit. They were only trained to fill-up the proformas without being imparted any information on the importance of people's participation. In addition to this, no civil society organisation was found to be engaged in social mobilization in the locale of study. The absence of civil society organisations and lack of people's participation has resulted in official capture of the works under MGNREGA.

Similarly, the Vigilance and Monitoring Committees were formulated in order to comply with the operational guidelines of the Act. Most of the members of these committees were unaware of their membership while those who were aware had no idea regarding their duties as VMC members. The elected and appointed officials were merely completing the formalities in case of VMCs as well. At the state level, no Vigilance Cell was in place.

For grievance redressal, although helplines were functional, the block and district level officials were unable to address large number of complaints on their own. Most of the complaints were related to delay or non-payment of wages to the workers, non-measurement of works or non-preparation of work proposals. Further, the office of Ombudsman at the district level was vacant since 2012. Thus, considering the number and nature of the grievances, the grievance redressal mechanism was also found to be wanting.

Hence, the limitations of the transparency and accountability mechanisms under MGNREGA need to be done away with. Pro-active information disclosure mechanisms, regular social audits, gram sabha meetings will help in reflecting people's felt needs and minimising official capture of the works under MGNREGA. Further, the vigilance and monitoring as well as the grievance redressal mechanisms needs to be established and strengthened up. It is only through redressing of such issues of strong participatory mechanisms that transparency and accountability can be enhanced.

Hence, the hypothesis namely, "The mechanisms to ensure transparency and accountability under MGNREGA are functional", stands partially validated.

Endnotes

1. Government of India (2013a), op. cit., p. 116.
2. *Ibid.*
3. Y. Aiyar and S.K. Mehta (2015), "Spectators or Participants: Effects of Social Audits in Andhra Pradesh", Economic and Political Weekly, Volume 50, Number 7, pp. 66-71.
4. Government of India (2013a), op. cit., p. 114.
5. S. Shankar (2010), "Can Social Audits Count?", Australia South Asia Research Centre Working Paper 2010/09, Centre for Policy Research, New Delhi, pp. 1-26.; F. Afridi and V. Iversen (2014), "Social Audits and MGNREGA Delivery: Lessons from Andhra Pradesh", IZA Discussion Paper Number 8095, Institute for the Study of Labour, Germany, pp. 2-48; Aiyar, Mehta and Samji, op. cit., pp. 4-5.
6. Goetz and Jenkins (2001), op. cit., p. 370.
7. Aiyar and Mehta, op. cit., pp. 2-3.
8. Shankar, op. cit., p. 13.
9. *Ibid,* pp. 13-14.
10. Aiyar and Mehta, op. cit., pp. 3-5.
11. Shankar, op. cit., p. 14.
12. Afridi and Iversen, op. cit., p. 34.
13. J. Tirole (1994), "The Internal Organization of Government", Oxford Economic Papers New Series, Volume 46, Number 1, pp. 1-29.
14. Aiyar and Mehta, op. cit., pp. 36-37.

15. Shankar, op. cit., p. 23.
16. Afridi and Iversen, op. cit., pp. 45-46.
17. Aiyar and Mehta, op. cit., pp. 3-6.
18. *Ibid,* p. 6.
19. Government of India (2013a), op. cit., p. 117.
20. Ibid, pp. 117-118.
21. Ibid, p. 118.
22. Ibid.
23. Ibid, pp. 118-119.
24. *Ibid,* pp. 121-122.
25. Ibid, pp. 121-122.
26. Ibid, p. 122.
27. Ibid, pp. 123-124.

7

Conclusions and Suggestions

7.1 Introduction

The study of Mahatma Gandhi National Rural Employment Guarantee Act, 2005 in district Patiala in Punjab focused on the implementation aspect of the programme. It aimed at studying the administrative machinery of MGNREGA, awareness generation of the job-card holders through the outreach of the programme, impact of the programme on the socio-economic conditions of women workers, capacity of the implementing agencies and working of transparency and accountability mechanisms under MGNREGA. A comprehensive research methodology was adopted to test the pre-determined hypotheses and to deduce logical conclusions with respect to various implementation aspects of MGNREGA.

The study used both primary and secondary data. The secondary data was taken from MGNREGA website, annual administrative reports, journals, newspapers, books and the internet. Primary data was collected through questionnaires, formal interviews, face-to-face and telephonic interactions, discussion meetings and focus group discussions. Observation was an important source of information gathering. The researcher conducted survey and collected data from 360 job-card holders from the villages. Interviews were held with twelve Sarpanches (Panchayat Heads) and thirty Panchayat members of the selected villages; and three Assistant Programme Officers (APO's) at the block level. Face-to-face and telephonic interactions were held with other officials concerned with the implementation of MGNREGA, namely, eight Panchayat Secretaries, three Junior Engineers, three Computer Operators-cum-Accounts Clerks, eight Gram Rozgar Sahayaks (GRS) and three mates (work-site supervisors) in order to investigate the detailed aspects of implementation. Discussion meetings were also held with five volunteers of the Nehru Yuva Kendra, Patiala who conducted social audit in the selected villages to investigate the details of the social audit process. Apart from these, face-to-face interactions were also held with eight members of the Vigilance and Monitoring Committees, namely, one ex-serviceman, one local school teacher, one anganwadi worker, two former panchayat members and three MGNREGA workers to analyze the functioning of VMCs at the local level. Discussion meetings, face-to-face and telephonic interactions were also held with four officials at the State Institute of Rural Development, Nabha and Mohali; two officials at MGNREGA Cell of Zila Parishad Office, Patiala; and seven officials at MGNREGA Cell of Joint Development Commissioner's Office, Mohali for seeking detailed information regarding capacity building measures and training programmes organized; grievance redressal mechanisms and vigilance and monitoring mechanisms at the state and district levels. Further, observation was used to supplement the data.

7.2 Main Findings

Main findings of the study have been organized hypotheses-wise. An introduction to the context of each hypothesis is followed by sub-hypothesis wise discussion.

Hypothesis I

The administrative machinery for the implementation of MGNREGA does not fulfil the provisions of the Act.

The administrative machinery responsible for implementing MGNREGA has been studied at the central, state, district, block and village level. In addition to that, the roles and duties of the various authorities were also analyzed. Following are some of the main findings regarding the administrative machinery evaluated in the field.

Non-establishment of Administrative Agencies

Some of the important administrative agencies for MGNREGA prescribed under the Act had not been constituted at the central, state, district, block and village levels. At the central level, Central Employment Guarantee Council had not been constituted since 2012 while no information existed in the Annual Reports and MGNREGA website regarding the National Management Team (NMT) or any of its five prescribed divisions. The officials at the state level were also not aware about NMT. At the state level, the State Employment Guarantee Council had also not been constituted since 2013. The non-constitution of the apex bodies for the last 3-4 years at the Central and state level has reflected the non-seriousness of the government regarding the programme. Further, there were limited number of experts appointed by the State Employment Guarantee Mission in the State Management Team while some of the important fields were ignored such as Human Resource Development, Knowledge management and learning including research, social inclusion, rights and entitlements, etc.

Inadequate MGNREGA Staff and Practice of Additional Charge to the Permanent Staff

An acute shortage of MGNREGA staff was found at the block and village levels in the form of Computer Operators-cum-Accounts Clerk, Gram Rozgar Sahayaks, mates (worksite supervisors), Junior Engineers and Technical Assistants. The shortage of MGNREGA staff and additional duty (charge) of MGNREGA to the permanent staff at the district, block and village levels had hampered the implementation of the programme.

The permanent employees were assigned additional duties for MGNREGA e.g., the District Programme Coordinator at the district level and the Programme Officers at the block level were assigned additional charge for MGNREGA. Due to work overload, they had delegated their authorities to the Additional District Programme Coordinator and Additional Programme Officer at the district and block levels respectively.

Lack of Technical Expertise

The number of officials providing technical expertise for MGNREGA was very less. Due to the additional charge of MGNREGA assigned to the Junior Engineers (Panchayti Raj) and non-appointment of the Technical Assistants in the district, the measurement of works, wage payments to the workers and work proposals has suffered e.g., in one of the villages, Sarpanch reported that a traditional water body was renovated at the cost of Rs. 2 lakhs. The wages were supposed to be sanctioned after measuring the silt removed in consonance with the person-days. However, the visit of the technical expert for measurement took place after 3 months of work completion. In the meantime, the substantial amount of silt got eroded due to natural degrading agents like wind and rain. Thus, the amount of money spent mismatched with the excavated silt found on site after three months. This resulted in further delay in releasing the pending wages to the workers. The Sarpanches also reported that due to unavailability of technical experts, the work proposals to be sent to the block level by the village authorities also got delayed.

Delay in Payment of Salaries to MGNREGA Staff and Wages to Workers

MGNREGA staff hired on contractual basis was paid less as compared to permanent staff of similar ranks. The officials complained that the salaries had been delayed for over six months. On the other hand, in case of the workers who were leading a hand to mouth existence, the payment had been delayed for over six months. Keeping in mind the gravity of situation it could be inferred that the practice of payment of salaries and wages was contrary to the basic philosophy of the Act that mandates payment of wages to workers within 15 days. Due to prevalence of such practices, financial security and stability of the workers could not be ensured.

Problem of Wage-Material Ratio

The officials stated that in case of construction works under MGNREGA, they faced difficulties in abiding to the 60:40 ratio. As per the guidelines, the cost of construction material like cement and bricks, wages of the skilled workers like mason had to be paid from 40 percent of the grants while 60 percent of the grants had to be utilized for paying the wages to the unskilled workers only. However, the construction material and wages of the skilled workers costs more in the construction works. Further, less number of unskilled workers were required in the construction works, hence they were employed in less numbers. Thus, according to them, the requirement of 60 percent of the amount to be spent on the wages of unskilled workers was too much.

Inadequate Infrastructure

The officials also complained of inadequate infrastructural facilities like separate building or space for record keeping. One of the female APOs reported that APOs had not been given any vehicle for field visits and the BDPO (PO) was reluctant to give his official vehicle for official field visits to the APO. In such a situation, she was dependent on her husband for field visits to the villages. But as her husband also had his own job to do, it was not possible for her to visit the field with his help every single time.

Lack of Inter-Agency Coordination

Post-convergence, the ambit of MGNREGA works has expanded. To carry out these works, the involvement of various departments such as agriculture, land development, animal husbandry, irrigation, Mandi Board, etc. was required. The officials complained that there was lack of inter-department coordination due to the disinterest of the officials of various departments to undertake works falling within their jurisdiction.

No Revised Schedule of Rates

The officials reported that the Schedule of Rates (SoRs) under MGNREGA was of the British times. The Operational guidelines prescribe that new SoRs can be developed under MGNREGA. However, SoRs had not been revised under MGNREGA and the measurements were done as per old SoRs. The officials reported that it was nearly impossible for the workers to meet those old standards, especially women and elderly people.

Absence of Bottom-up Approach

The officials at the block level complained of lack of bottom-up approach. They reported that the senior level officials did not pay heed to their requests or complaints. The grievances of the lower level officials were not taken seriously by the higher officials e.g., one of the APOs requested the ADPC for arranging training programmes for the APOs to equip them for the expanded ambit of works after the new operational guidelines in 2013. However, no training programmes were conducted for them even after repeated requests. Similarly, due to the apathetic attitude of the higher officials, the repeated requests of the lower level officials to avoid the delay in payment of wages to the workers were not heeded.

However, in some instances, it was also observed that the senior officials had apprehensions regarding the lower level officials; that they were trying to evade the responsibilities of carrying out works in villages by giving such excuses. Therefore, the pressure exerted by the senior officials could be justified for carrying out the works. In some villages, the researcher observed that the existence of political groups had hampered the progress of MGNREGA works. In these cases, the senior officials need to exercise their authority at village level for undertaking the works rather than pressurizing the lower level officials.

Cumbersome Process of Muster-roll Approval

The village level officials reported that muster-roll has to be approved prior to the initiation of works. Although there is electronic approval of muster-roll but it takes time for approval. In the meantime, the workers whose names were sent for approval get involved in other employments such as farm labour, Mandis, etc. In certain cases, the delayed approval of muster-rolls rendered the approved muster-rolls as futile because the workers got disinterested to work under MGNREGA or were able to find alternative employment elsewhere.

Hence, primary and secondary data support the hypothesis that the existing administrative machinery for the implementation of MGNREGA does not fulfil the provisions of the Act.

Hypothesis II

The outreach of MGNREGA has generated awareness of its key provisions among the job-card holders in the rural areas.

Information dissemination is the key to the success of any development programme. Awareness amongst the targeted population regarding various provisions of the programme can help in accessing the guarantees or claiming the entitlements. Similarly in case of MGNREGA, for improving the access and outreach of the programme, information has to be disseminated through institutions of gram sabha, gram panchayats, self-help groups, Bharat Nirman Volunteers and Nehru Yuva Kendra in the form of wall writings, awareness generation campaigns, information display boards, and so on. The mechanisms and institutions were supposed to be involved in disseminating information regarding MGNREGA; however, the study found that respondents lacked information regarding certain key provisions of the programme due to which they were unable to make claims. Thus, inspite of the rights and entitlements being legally stipulated, people were unable to access them due to lack of information and awareness. These have been discussed below:–

Low Awareness Regarding Possession of Job-cards

Although majority of the respondents in with-work villages stated that they possessed job-cards but around 23 percent respondents reported that their job-cards were not in their possession; rather they were with the Sarpanch. This practice of keeping workers job-cards by some person or official is against the basic philosophy of MGNREGA as this can lead to misuse of job-cards by the officials for their personal gains such as

Low Awareness Regarding Unemployment Allowance

MGNREGA mandates work on demand but if work is not provided on demand then unemployment allowance has to be paid. It was found that majority (88.3%) of the respondents were unaware about the provision of unemployment allowance under the Act. It was also found that the officials deliberately concealed this information from the workers as they were unable to pay the allowance. Due to this skewed information and apathetic attitude of the officials to disburse unemployment allowance, none of the respondents was paid the allowance.

Low Awareness Regarding Payment of Wages within 14 days

Majority of the respondents (77.5%) were not aware regarding the provision that wages are to be paid within 14 days. Due to this, they were unable to exert pressure on the authorities to pay wages on time in case of delay in wage payments. A significant number of cases were reported where wages were delayed for over six months.

Low Awareness Regarding Compensation for Delay in Payment

The Act prescribes that compensation has to be paid in case of delay in wage payment to the workers beyond 15 days of work completion. It was found that 97.5% of the respondents were unaware of it and none of the respondents had ever been paid compensation.

Low Awareness Regarding Travelling Allowance and Insurance

Majority of the respondents (93.9%) were found to be unaware about the travelling allowance and thus, they never made a request for the allowance. The respondents were also unaware (96.1%) about the insurance provision under MGNREGA.

Lack of Participation in Gram Sabhas

Gram Sabha is the primary forum for selection of MGNREGA works. However, 82.5% of the respondents were not aware of this. Further, 73.1% of the respondents had never participated in the gram sabha meetings. It was found that gram sabha meetings were not held regularly; also the agenda of these meetings was usually hijacked by the local groups with different political affiliations. Due to this, the gram sabha meetings became fractious and ended without any resolution being approved. Therefore, the gram sabha meetings were only a formality to be completed in paper.

Low Awareness Regarding Worksite Facilities

Under MGNREGA, the worksites are to be provided with various facilities such as muster-roll, marking daily attendance, availability of shaded rest area, provision of drinking water, etc. in order to provide decent working conditions to the workers as well as to maintain transparency. The respondents were found to be aware of worksite facilities such as muster-rolls (65.3%), record of daily attendance (54.2%), shaded rest area (54.2%) and availability of drinking water (65%). However, the workers were unaware regarding the provision of crèche facility (80.6%), appointment of a woman as crèche incharge (90%) and the prescribed wage-material ratio (90.8%).

Hence, the primary and secondary data revealed that the outreach of MGNREGA has only partially generated awareness among the respondents in the rural areas.

Hypothesis III

MGNREGA has been instrumental in improving the socio-economic conditions of women workers.

MGNREGA has been helpful in improving social and economic conditions of the women workers, thus, empowering them to some extent. The economic position of the women improved with more income in hand, more control over their earnings facilitated by direct account payments, increased choices for expenditure and so on. Cases were also reported of improved social position of women in the form of more say in the household decision-making processes, pride and achievement and increased levels of confidence through contribution to the family income. On the other hand, the women in the villages where no MGNREGA works were initiated reported that they were deprived of economic and social benefits of MGNREGA which their counterparts in other villages were availing on account of the work opportunities available through MGNREGA. The non-MGNREGA women workers also reported that they would like the programme to be started in their villages so they can reap its benefits.

Although MGNREGA can be viewed as a tool to women empowerment but the researcher noted a number of issues in its working that were detrimental to the interest of women like preference for male workers over female workers in the household, lack of crèche facilities at the worksites, activities unsuitable to women's strength, lack of participation in the decision-making bodies and so on. These have been discussed earlier and are briefly outlined here.

Preference for Male Over Female Workers in the Household

The work under MGNREGA is provided to a household rather than an individual. Thus whenever a demand is made by both male and female members of a household. Normally the preference for work is given to male members. Primary data findings had confirmed this discrimination. This intra-household gender discrimination may also be one of the causes for skewed women participation.

Lack of Crèche Facilities at the Work-Sites

The Act provides that when there are more than five children under the age of six years present at a work-site, a female worker has to be appointed to take care of them. However, no child care facilities were provided anywhere in the locale of study. During discussions, it came to light that lactating mothers were either not preferred for MGNREGA work or they were to leave their children at home. The non-availability of work-site facilities like crèche was a huge disincentive for women and this was in complete contravention of the letter and spirit of the Act.

Activities Unsuitable to Women's Physical Strength

Certain types of MGNREGA works also limit the participation of women e.g., tasks related to hoeing and shovelling. In such a situation, the provision of equal pay was resented by men when they undertook strenuous work which women were not in position to undertake on account of lower physical strength. However, the philosophy of minimum wage was related to equal hours of allotted work undertaken and nature of work

Lack of Participation of Women in Decision-Making Bodies

Participatory decision making structures such as gram sabha meetings, social audit, vigilance and monitoring committees and grievance redressal committees prescribed under the Act were defunct in the most of the villages selected for study. It was found that wherever such bodies were functional, women participation was very low. 78.4 percent of women respondents stated that they did not attend gram sabha meetings or social audit meetings as they did not see the importance of their participation. It was also found that women, in particular, were not aware of their right to participate in a gram sabha. Further, no women were found to be appointed as mate i.e. in a supervisory capacity at any worksite or as MGNREGA staff.

While a number of issues need to be addressed, in the balance it was seen that socio-economic conditions of MGNREGA women workers had improved.

Hence, the primary and secondary data supported the hypothesis that MGNREGA has been instrumental in improving the socio-economic conditions of women workers.

Hypothesis IV

The local bodies have the capacity to plan and implement MGNREGA works at the village level.

Under MGNREGA, the local bodies have been entrusted with the responsibility of planning and implementing MGNREGA works. The gram panchayat is responsible for selection of works through gram sabhas, prioritizing those works, preparing shelf of works and submitting the proposals to the BDO. In order to perform these functions the gram panchayats must have adequate number and capacity of officials to plan and implement these works. Further, regular and timely training programmes are required to enhance capacities of the officials. These three aspects were analysed in the field survey and it was found that the local bodies were not able to plan and implement the works efficiently due to varied reasons. These have been discussed sub-hypotheses wise.

Sub-hypothesis (i)

Adequate human resource is available with the local bodies to undertake MGNREGA works.

The field survey highlighted that although the elected officials involved in the implementation of MGNREGA, i.e., the Sarpanch and other Panchayat members were available in every selected village, there was inadequate human resource availability amongst the appointed officials. While one Additional Programme Officer was available per block to assist the Programme Officers at the block level, there was acute shortage of Gram Rozgar Sahayaks, Technical Assistants and Computer Operators-cum-Accounts Clerks.

The inadequacy of support staff such as GRSs, TAs and Computer Operators-cum-Accounts Clerks had led to the over-burdening of the existing permanent and contractual staff of MGNREGA with additional responsibilities for implementation of the programme. The overburdening of the officials with additional responsibilities of MGNREGA had serious impact on the overall implementation of the programme. On account of non-availability of technical experts, the authorities were found to be more interested in initiating the works which required less technical expertise. The gram panchayats were also unable to prepare complete work proposals in the absence of preparation of estimates of works and costs by Junior Engineers; this forced officials at the block level to discourage initiation of new works. This also resulted in delay in payments to the MGNREGA workers as the measurement of works could not be completed on time.

Sub-hypothesis (ii)

The elected and appointed officials have the capacity to plan and implement MGNREGA works.

The field survey drew attention towards lack of capacity of the officials, both elected as well as appointed, to plan and implement MGNREGA works efficiently. It was found that only few works were initiated in the villages like renovation or de-silting of ponds and tree plantation while other works important for the development of the villages were not taken up such as water harvesting, flood control works, solid and liquid waste management works. These works were not taken up due to lack of capacity of the elected and appointed officials.

The gram panchayat members admitted that they were dependent on the appointed officials for the planning of works of technical nature like water harvesting, flood control works, solid and liquid waste management, liquid bio-manure etc. Therefore, due to their own lack of capacity and their dependency on the appointed officials, such works of expert and technical nature could not be initiated.

The appointed officials like Gram Rozgar Sahayaks were also found to be incapable of performing tasks that required some technical knowledge on their part for providing mark-outs to the labourers for earning minimum wage. The APOs corroborated the problem saying that they had to change the proposals of new works requiring technical expertise sent by gram panchayats at the block level. The APOs stated that due to their own lack of capacity to undertake works of technical nature and shortage of technical staff, such proposals were not encouraged by the higher authorities.

Sub-hypothesis (iii)

Regular training programmes are conducted for the officials to build their capacities for the implementation of MGNREGA.

The field survey disclosed lack of regular training programmes for both appointed and elected officials. While officials like APOs and panchayat members expressed satisfaction with the training provided, majority of the other officials amongst Gram Rozgar Sahayaks, Panchayat Secretaries and Sarpanches, had not been provided any type of training. In fact, Sarpanches were not covered by the training for the Gram Panchayat members either. Out of 12 Sarpanches interviewed, 6 reported that they had not been imparted any form of training under MGNREGA. Other 6 reported that during the training, they went to the block office to complete the formality of marking their attendance. No details were provided regarding their duties and functions relating to MGNREGA. However, almost all the officials emphasized the need for more frequent and regular training programmes.

The APOs stated that the training programmes had benefitted them in the execution of their duties under MGNREGA; they were ready to undertake follow-up training due to widened ambit of works under the programme. However, majority of the GRSs revealed that they had not attended any formal training programme. Out of eight GRS, three reported that they had received on-the-job training at the State Institute of Rural Development, Nabha for 2 to 3 days while the other five had not received any orientation or on-the-job training. Out of these five GRS, two said that they were likely to attend training in the near future. One stated that he received on-the-job training while working with a Panchayat Secretary. Two of the GRS said that they were unlikely to receive any in-service training in the near future.

The three GRS' who attended training were sent for the same after ten to twelve months of their appointments, by which time they had figured out, on the job, most of what was covered by the training module(s), i.e. their duties and functions. They reported that some components like preparation of job-cards, providing worksite facilities, etc. were found to be useful.

Hence, the primary and secondary data did not support the hypothesis that the local bodies have the capacity to plan and implement MGNREGA works.

Hypothesis V

The mechanisms to ensure transparency and accountability under MGNREGA are functional.

Under MGNREGA, various mechanisms have been established to ensure transparency and accountability such as information display boards, regular updation of the MGNREGA website, social audit, vigilance and monitoring committees and grievance redressal mechanisms. An attempt was made to analyze these mechanisms available in the locale of study.

Sub-hypothesis (i): The mechanisms of information disclosure under MGNREGA are working to ensure transparency.

During the field survey it was found that while some of the information disclosure tools were in place like annual reports, regular website updation, work-site file and photographs of the work-sites, majority of them were not in place. There was no pro-active information available through wall paintings in the villages as prescribed under the Act. Although some basic information in the form of availability of work under MGNREGA was displayed at one of the block offices out of three and the district office but the details of the ongoing or completed works in the block or the district was not displayed. Further, no information was found displayed at the public places through notice boards or report cards in the gram panchayat's office.

It was also found that the gram sabha meetings were not held. Therefore, the information related to MGNREGA works was not imparted. At most of the work-sites, no information display boards were found and wherever the Information Boards existed, no detailed information regarding works and workers, number of work-days generated and expenditure incurred was mentioned. Similarly, no muster-rolls or measurement records were available at the work-sites but these records were with the Sarpanch and were shown to the researcher when demanded.

Sub-hypothesis (ii): Regular social audit of the works is conducted under MGNREGA.

Social audit is a mandatory process under MGNREGA with the philosophy of a social mobilization exercise for accountability in the use of public funds in welfare schemes. During the field survey, it was found that social audit was conducted in the locale of study with the help of volunteers of the Nehru Yuva Kendra, Patiala every six months. However, it was found that the exercise was considered merely a formality to be completed by the concerned authorities; the officials were only completing the paper-work to comply with the guidelines. The auditors were also found to be unaware regarding the basic philosophy of social audit. They reported that they were trained only to complete the formalities of filling-up the proformas; the importance of people's participation in development and the need for transparency and accountability served by social audit has been discussed with them. In addition to this, no Social Audit Unit had been established in Patiala district though prescribed in the guidelines; the State Institute for Rural Development (SIRD) had been assigned the responsibility of facilitating social audit in the state. The officials at SIRD complained of shortage of able resource persons to conduct training programmes.

Further, it was found that no Civil Society Organisation (CSO) was engaged in social mobilization in the locale of study. Due to the interest of the authorities to only complete the formalities and non-engagement of CSOs, the participation of people was low. The absence of civil society organisations and lack of people's participation has resulted in official capture of the works under MGNREGA.

Sub-hypothesis (iii) :Vigilance and Monitoring committees are actively involved in the monitoring of MGNREGA works.

The Vigilance and Monitoring Committees (VMCs) are important to detect irregularities in the implementation of MGNREGA. At the state level, the Vigilance Cell was not in place. In its place, the Engineering wing's officials of the Joint Development Commissioner's office were appointed to monitor the works in the villages. These officials only visited those worksites or verified the records of those villages which had utilised maximum amount of funds in the state.

At the local level, the Vigilance and Monitoring Committees were only formulated on paper to comply with the operational guidelines of the Act. The VMCs were found to be dysfunctional in the locale of study. It was reported that in many cases, the members of these committees were unaware of their membership while those who were aware had no idea regarding their duties as VMC members. The elected and appointed officials complained that they faced difficulties in convincing literate people to become the VMC members.

Sub-hypothesis (iv): Grievance redressal mechanisms are functional under MGNREGA.

The satisfactory and timely redressal of grievances is important for the implementation of MGNREGA. During the field survey, it was found that helplines were functional for grievance redressal. The officials at the Joint Development Office, Mohali reported that they had received complaints through helplines on a number of occasions. At the block and district level, the Programme Officer and District Programme Coordinator officials were appointed to deal with complaints at the block and district levels respectively. A large number of complaints reported were mainly related to delay or non-payment of wages to the workers, non-measurement of works or non-preparation of work proposals. It was found that most of these complaints were not addressed. Further, the complaint boxes were supposed to be installed at the block and district levels to facilitate the process of grievance redressal but no such complaint boxes were installed at these offices. The office of Ombudsman at the district level was vacant since 2012.

Hence, the primary and secondary data partially support the hypothesis that the mechanisms to ensure transparency and accountability under MGNREGA are functional.

Discussion

This field based study revealed that MGNREGA, through its information dissemination mechanisms, has helped in generating awareness amongst the beneficiaries regarding the provision of job-cards, wage provisions, maintenance of muster-rolls, daily attendance at the work-site, rest hours, requirement of availability of shaded area for rest and provision of drinking water facility at the work-site. This awareness equipped the beneficiaries to claim their rights and entitlements under MGNREGA.

The gender component of the programme has helped in improving socio-economic conditions of the women workers as they have wages on par with men without any gender discrimination. With an increased rate of participation and equal wages for women, there has been a positive impact on the economic well-being of women and children. The access to economic resources has a favourable impact on the social status of women. Women beneficiaries have control over their income due to direct transfer of wages in their bank accounts. With this control over finances they were more involved and also wielded influence in intra-household decision-making processes. Thus the change in socio-economic conditions of the women has positive impacts on children's education, food security and nutrition. Women have choice over spending of their wages on medicine, food, clothing, education of their children, which was missing earlier.

Further, 95 percent of the wage and material payments in the programme are made through electronic fund management system.[1] This increases transparency and reduces chances of misappropriation. Wage payment through post-office or bank accounts has substantial implications for financial inclusion of workers especially women. The percentage of women workers with bank accounts has risen more than five times from 9 percent in 2004-05 to 49 percent in 2011-12. In 2015-16, 56 percent women workers have bank accounts (till 31st December, 2015).[2]

Most Important Tool for GPs

Very programmes has given gram sabhas the mandate to plan and execute their own works. The availability of grievance redressal mechanisms has helped in addressing issues of the beneficiaries as they could use helplines to lodge their grievances. The capacity building programmes have helped the officials to undertake and discharge their roles and responsibilities effectively. MGNREGA has found endorsement across political affiliations; even when a political party with different ideology came to power, the budgetary allocation to the scheme increased to Rs. 34000 crore in 2014-15 – the maximum to the programme so far.

However, the study of MGNREGA in District Patiala of Punjab State showed that the implementation of the programme suffered from many lacunae at all levels. It was found that the important administrative agencies responsible for implementing, monitoring and evaluating MGNREGA and thus recommending measures to improve its implementation had not been constituted. The Central Employment Guarantee Council, the apex body at the central level entrusted with the implementation of the programme in the country had not been appointed since 2012. Similarly, the National Management Team responsible for maintaining and operating Management Information System on critical aspects and its five divisions entrusted with performing functions in specific areas such as human resource development and capacity building, programme management, IT, grievance redressal and so on had not been constituted.

A similar situation was found at the state level; the Punjab State Employment Guarantee Council responsible for implementing MGNREGA in the state had not been re-constituted since the expiration of its term in 2013. The State Employment Guarantee Mission responsible for recruiting experts to establish a professional State Management Team had failed to appoint the required number of experts in important areas such as rights and entitlements, human resource development, knowledge management and learning, social inclusion, participatory planning process for livelihoods and convergence. Similarly the Vigilance Cell responsible for receiving complaints or taking *suo-moto* action on media reports and conducting regular field visits to detect irregularities under MGNREGA has not been constituted at the state level. A make-shift arrangement was in place that authorized a few members of the Engineering wing in the Joint Development Commissioner's Office at Mohali to conduct inspections. At the village level, the Vigilance and Monitoring Committees had been constituted by the officials from amongst the gram sabha members; however, the members were not aware of their membership and role. These committees were found to be largely dysfunctional.

The field survey also revealed lack of adequate numbers of officials for implementing MGNREGA in the district. The Technical Assistants responsible for assisting gram panchayats for preparing work proposals and undertaking measurements of works had not been appointed in the district. Gram Panchayats are dependent upon technical experts for preparing estimates of projects and conducting measurements. Junior Engineers (Panchayati Raj) had been assigned additional duties for MGNREGA in the place of Technical Assistants. However, the JEs were not available in requisite numbers and believed themselves to be above the job. The shortage of TAs and JEs had an adverse impact not only on the shelf of works to be prepared by the gram panchayats but also on the measurement of works and wage payments of the workers. Due to the inadequacy of technical expertise, important works of technical nature such as water harvesting, solid and liquid waste management were not initiated by the higher authorities. Rather, works which were simpler to plan and required less technical know-how for implementation such as tree plantation or de-silting of traditional water bodies were taken up. However, despite the non-technical nature of work and ease of its measurement wage payments to workers were delayed. This was on account of inadequate technical staff to measure work performance. Further, the unavailability of technical experts has also led to poor designing of the assets at some places. Thus, the inadequacy of officials had not only affected the financial security and stability of the workers but also the people-centric planning and implementation and the nature and quality of the projects. The number of Gram Rozgar Sahayaks was also inadequate in the district. The GRS had not been appointed in all the gram panchayats. One GRS was appointed to cover more than 16 GPs on an average in a block. Similarly, one Computer Operator-cum-Accounts Clerk was appointed per block i.e. for more than 100 GPs.

The non-appointment of MGNREGA staff in adequate numbers has led to the over-burdening of the existing staff. The permanent staff of local government and bodies has been assigned additional duties for MGNREGA along with their routine work. Those at the higher levels, on the plea of work overload, have delegated their MGNREGA related duties, e.g., the District Programme Coordinator has delegated MGNREGA duties to the Additional District Programme Coordinator at the district level, while at the block level Additional Programme Officers have been specifically hired to look after MGNREGA duties of the Programme Officers. The researcher observed serious disaffection among the permanent staff at the lower levels. The Junior Engineers and Panchayat Secretaries were not ready to perform the additional duties for MGNREGA and JEs had submitted a memorandum against this to the Additional District Programme Coordinator.

It was also observed that the appointed as well as elected officials' inability to perform MGNREGA work effectively was in part due to inadequate capacity among them. The study revealed that the training programmes conducted for the officials were irregular and unsystematic. Out of the 12 Sarpanches, 6 had never been exposed to any form of training. Of the other 6 Sarpanches who had attended training programmes, half reported that these were only a formality; they could get away with just marking their attendance and not attending the training. On the other hand, the other half gave credit to the training programmes for the MGNREGA works initiated by them in their villages. Similarly, out of the 8 GRS, only 3 were provided on-the-job training for 2-3 days by SIRD and that too after 10-12 months of their appointment. Of the other 5, two were likely to attend training in the near future; one received in-service training while working with a Panchayat Secretary; and the remaining two believed they were unlikely to attend any training programme in the near future. The APOs said that the training programmes had benefitted them and they were ready to undertake follow-up training programmes in the wake of increased ambit of MGNREGA works. However, more training programmes were not arranged due to the indifference of the senior officials towards training.

Further, no training was provided to the mates while the volunteers of the Nehru Yuva Kendra in the district who conducted social audit were simply trained to fill-up the requisite proformas for social audit. This affected the implementation of the programmes in different ways. The incapacity of the volunteers (auditors) to go beyond furnishing the paper-work negatively affected the awareness levels of the people; they remained largely ignorant about the basic philosophy of social audit. The volunteers themselves also had no idea regarding this.

Majority of the job-card holders were found to be unaware regarding the key provisions of the programme. In some cases, it was found that the officials had deliberately concealed the information from the people on certain fronts like unemployment allowance, travelling allowance, insurance, etc. Due to lack of information, people were unable to claim their entitlements. Thus, the apathetic attitude of the officials deprived people of the information and their rights e.g., no gram sabha meetings were held for selection of MGNREGA works. Further the non-involvement of civil society organizations and NGOs has also largely compromised the social mobilization in the district.

The mechanisms of grievance redressal also failed to address a large number of complaints. No complaint boxes were installed at the block or district offices. The Ombudsman had also not been appointed in the district since 2012. Further, the workers were also not aware of the procedure to be followed for redressal of their complaints. Thus, the grievance redressal machinery can be said to be ineffective.

The above discussion revealed that the problem of implementation of MGNREGA is more of administration rather than planning. The uneven implementation across states points to the need to strengthen service delivery and improve governance structures. In light of the above shortcomings, the study has offered some recommendations to work towards realising the potential of MGNREGA as a game changer.

7.4 Suggestions

Effective implementation is a critical aspect in the public policy cycle. This implementation analysis of MGNREGA has provided a number of observations and insights of the ground reality with special reference to District Patiala in Punjab; on the basis of these, the following recommendations are being made. These have been tabulated under the broad headings of administrative machinery, awareness generation, women workers, capacity building of local bodies and transparency and accountability mechanisms of MGNREGA.

1. Administrative Machinery	
Constitution of implementing agencies	• Central Employment Guarantee Council must be constituted as prescribed under the MGNREGA Act. • Punjab State Employment Guarantee Council must be constituted.
Appointment of adequate experts at the state level	• Experts in State Management Team to address issues of social inclusion, strategy and planning, participatory planning process for livelihoods and convergence, knowledge management and learning including research must be appointed as mandated in the guidelines.
Inter-departmental coordination	• Inter-departmental coordination is necessary to implement MGNREGA works; accountability with respect to convergence of MGNREGA works must extend to the concerned officials in other departments also.
Provision of infrastructural facilities	• Need to provide appropriate storage equipment and space for safe record keeping. Also the provision of vehicles for field visits to the MGNREGA officials needs to be organized; if the project cannot support purchase of vehicle an alternative system of requisition be organized.

2. Awareness Generation	
Responsibility of local officials	• Need to hold local officials like Sarpanches and panchayat members strictly responsible for performing awareness generation activities in the villages.
Revival of gram sabha meetings	• The true spirit and practice of gram sabha meetings should be established/revived to include people in the planning and selection of MGNREGA works.
Need to change the apathetic attitude of officials	• Need to bring positive change in the attitude of the officials towards information dissemination. • Need to create a sense of commitment among the officials regarding importance of information dissemination and awareness generation among the people.
3. Women workers	
Individual entitlement of 100 days work to women	• Need to provide individual entitlement of 100 days of work to women instead of household entitlement of 100 days of work. This would avoid negotiation within the household and boost earnings of women.
Inclusion of gender-specific needs	• Need to incorporate gender-specific lifecycle needs such as allowing women time off for breastfeeding and flexibility in terms of women's working hours in order to balance their domestic care and work responsibilities. • Need to include specific policy considerations for female-headed households to increase women participation and make scheme more gender sensitive.
Provision of worksite facilities	• Work-site facilities, especially child care facilities, must be provided as per the provisions of the Act.
Enhancing participation of women in decision-making bodies	• Necessary to encourage women to participate in decision-making bodies like gram sabha and to speak up in meetings.
Involving Civil Society Organizations	• Need for active involvement of NGOs and Civil Society Organizations to mobilize women to come forward and participate in the planning and selection of MGNREGA works and maintenance of assets.
Appointing of women in MGNREGA staff and for worksite management	• Need to include women in MGNREGA worksite management and staff appointments like worksite mates and Gram Rozgar Sahayaks, to achieve gender equality and gender sensitized management.
4. Capacity building of local bodies	
Appointing adequate number of MGNRGEA officials	• Officials like GRS, engineers, technical assistants and Computer Operators-cum-Accounts Clerk need to be appointed in adequate numbers for better work distribution and effective service delivery.
Enhancing capacity of elected officials through outsourcing	• Technical expertise of engineers, accountants etc. can be obtained through outsourced arrangements. This would gear the gram panchayats to improve their competencies for project planning and monitoring; thus in performing their organisational responsibilities better.

	• Local youth, with their expected commitment to local area development and the provision of job opportunity at their doorstep, can be trained to act as social mobilizers. They should be tasked with effecting the involvement of local bodies' representatives.
Compulsory training of appointed officials upon induction	• Compulsory entry-level training for capacity building of APOs and GRSs must be done upon induction.
Skill enhancement for MGNREGA works	• Need to enhance skills of both appointed and elected officials to undertake works under MGNREGA like rain water harvesting, micro irrigation works. For example, district Patiala is a paddy growing region; in this region water harvesting structures should be constructed so that fast depleting ground water may be supplemented. • Need to provide all officials detailed information regarding all the changes in the ambit of works under MGNREGA in order to equip them with all the necessary skills to handle the tasks efficiently and effectively at the beginning of the service.
Conforming with National Capability Building Framework (NCBF) guidelines	• States need to devise a training policy in conformity with the standards laid down in the National Capability Building Framework. This will take into account varied training needs, target groups, institutional structure, and areas/subjects to be covered.
Availability of able resource persons in the training institutes	• Qualified and capable resource persons need to be hired as resource persons having sound knowledge and experience in local governance.
Availability of sufficient funds to the training institutes	• Sufficient amount of funds needs to be provided to the state institutes to hire adequate and best resource persons with sound theoretical as well as practical experience in training.
Adoption of modern training techniques and technology	• Training institutes need to adopt modern participatory training techniques such as group discussions, role-play, brain-storming, experience sharing, case study, games and film based discussions, mock gram sabha and social audit meetings. Satellite based training and communication programme can also be tapped into.
Faculty exchange programmes	• Need to devise a system for exchange of trainers among the training institutes across the country to share good practices effectively e.g. in Assam, the well performing elected representatives of Panchayats were hired as trainers for the MGNREGA training programmes of the elected representatives of rural local bodies. These trainers shared their experiences and knowledge gathered during their tenure and exposure visits outside the state with the trainees.

Quality of the training programmes	• Need to strictly monitor the quality and content of the training programmes. • The trainers must be up-to-date with the recent developments in rural development as well as training techniques. • Trainers need to address the situation on the ground and facilitate the learning process of the trainees through participatory methods.
Attitudinal change towards training programmes	• Need to address the casual attitude of the officials being trained. Officials should be encouraged to take training seriously by incentivising the best performers and identifying and addressing the poor motivation of the apathetic.
5. Transparency and accountability	
Disseminating information through proper channels	• Need to adopt various information dissemination methods prescribed under the Act in letter and spirit to effectively impart information regarding the programme. • Information display boards at the worksites as well as at the public offices must carry relevant (and updated) information. • Frequent awareness generation camps in villages imparting information on various aspects of the scheme are required.
Conducting regular social audits	• Need to conduct regular social audits in accordance with the basic philosophy of the social audit concept. • Specifically address the limitations of apathetic and bureaucratic implementation of social audit rules to strengthen accountability (discussion on p. 199). • Requirement of a strong political will and commitment as in the case of Andhra Pradesh and Rajasthan.
Training of auditors	• Need to train the auditors to look beyond the regular record completion compliance and detect irregularities that are not so obvious. • The independence of the auditors needs to be safeguarded.
Engaging civil society organisations	• Civil society organisations needs to be actively involved for social mobilization; disseminating information regarding provisions of the Act, grievance redressal mechanisms and vigilance monitoring mechanisms; regular and meaningful social audit meetings; people's participation in planning and execution of works and so on.
Enhancing people's participation	• Need to enhance people's participation at all levels of policy making and execution by adopting bottom-up approach through effective awareness generation initiatives by the government and civil society organisations. • A meaningful quorum of members, at-least 80% of the gram sabha in a social audit meeting should be made mandatory.

Active involvement of Vigilance and Monitoring Committees	• Need for active involvement of Vigilance and Monitoring Committees at the village level in the MGNREGA works. • Need to motivate and empower people to participate through these committees in order to maintain transparency of works and accountability.
Appointing Ombudsman	• Need to appoint Ombudsman as per the guidelines in order to make the grievance redressal mechanism functional in the district. • In no case should the office of the Ombudsman be vacant.
Effective Remedial Action	• Credibility of the grievance redressal process has to be established through the actions of the state government as and when the situation demands it.

Endnotes

1. Government of India (2016), Mahatma Gandhi National Rural Employment Guarantee Act, 2005: The journey of a Decade (2016), Ministry of Rural Development, New Delhi, p. 19.
2. *Ibid.*

Bibliography

A. Books

Arya, K.S.; Verma, J.C. and Sharma, K.K. (1985) *Rural Development in India: Some Facets,* Centre for Rural Development, Chandigarh.

Bhatnagar, S. and Chib, S.S. (1987), *Rural Development in India: A Strategy for Socio–Economic Change,* EssEss Publications, New Delhi.

Boserup, E. (1970), *Women's Role in Economic Development,* St. Martin's Press, New York.

Chaturvedi, H.R. (1977), *Bureaucracy and Local Community: Dynamics of Rural Development,* Allied Publishers, Bombay.

Chen, C. (2008), "Transparency: the Key to Better Governance?", in Christopher Hoods and David Heald (eds.), *For the British Academy by Oxford University Press, Oxford, UK, 2006,* (Series: Proceedings of the British Academy number Vol. 135), [Online] Available from: http://online library.wiley.com/doi/10.1002/pad.477/abstract, [Accessed on 25th August, 2015].

CHF (2007), *The CHF Capacity Building Approach,* Cynthia Farrell, Ottawa, Canada.

Chib, S.S. (1987), "Dimension of Rural Poverty and Rural Development in India: An Evaluation of Concepts and Approaches", in SatyavanBhatnagar and Sukhdev Singh Chib (eds.), *Rural Development in India: A Strategy for Socio-economic Change,* EssEss Publications, New Delhi.

Connell, R.W. (1987), *Gender and Power: Society, the Person and Sexual Politics,* Polity Press, Cambridge.

Datt, Ruddar (2008), "PURA: A Road Map for New Rural India", in P. Jegadish Gandhi (ed.), *Dr. Kalam's PURA Model and Societal Transformation: Providing Urban Amenities in Rural Areas,* Deep and Deep Publications Pvt. Ltd., New Delhi.

Dey, Nikhil (2009), "Introduction: The NREGA full Salient Features and Programme Outcomes", in *The National Rural Employment Guarantee Act (NREGA): Design, Process and Impact*, UNDP, New Delhi.

Dreze, J. (2011), "Breaking the Nexus of Corruption", in R. Khera, (ed.), *The Battle for Employment Guarantee*, Oxford University Press, New Delhi.

Dreze, J. (2011a), "Dantewada: Guarantee Withdrawn", in R. Khera, (ed.), *The Battle for Employment Guarantee*, Oxford University Press, New Delhi.

Etzioni, Amitai (1964), *Modern Organizations*, Prentice-Hall, New Jersey.

Florini, Ann (2007), "The Right To Know", in *Transparency for and Open World,* Colombia University Press, New York.

Goetz, Anne Marie and Jenkins, Rob (2004), "Accountability" in *The Social Science Encyclopaedia*, Routledge, New York.

Golding, P. (1986), *Excluding the Poor*, CPAG Publishers, London.

Granzow, S. (2000), *Our dream: A World Free of Poverty*, Oxford University Press and The World Bank.

Hall, Anthony and Midgley, James (2004), *Social Policy for Development*, Sage Publications, London.

Harriss-White, Barbara (2003), *India Working: Essays on Society and Economy*, Cambridge University Press, Cambridge.

Hickey, Samuel and Mohan, Giles (2004), "Towards Participation as transformation: critical themes and challenges", in Samuel Hickey and Giles Mohan (eds.), *Participation: from tyranny to transformation? Exploring new approaches to participation in development*, Zed Books Limited, New York.

Hirschman, A. (1970), *Exit, voice and loyalty: Responses to decline in firms, organisations and states*, Harvard University Press, Cambridge.

Hirway,Indira; Saluja, M.R. and Yadav, Bhupesh (2009), "Assessing Impact of NREGA works in a village based on Village SAM", in *The National Rural Employment Guarantee Act (NREGA): Design, Process and Impact,* UNDP, New Delhi.

Hooja, Rakesh and Parnami, K.K. (2007), *Development Administration and Rural Development*, Aalekh Publishers, Jaipur.

Ingraham, Patricia W.; Phillip, G. Joyce and Donahue, Amy Kneedler (2003), *Government Performance: Why Management Matters*, Johns Hopkins University Press, Baltimore, Maryland.

Kalam, A.P.J. Abdul (2008), "PURA: A Road Map for New Rural India", in P. Jegadish Gandhi (ed.), *Dr. Kalam's PURA Model and Societal Transformation: Providing Urban Amenities in Rural Areas,* Deep and Deep Publications Pvt. Ltd., New Delhi.

Khera, R. (2011), "Wage Payments: Live without Pay?", in R. Khera, (ed.), *The Battle for Employment Guarantee*, Oxford University Press, New Delhi.

Kumar, Rohit (2009), "NREGS: Not just supplementing employment opportunity in Jalore district of Rajasthan", in *The National Rural Employment Guarantee Act (NREGA): Design, Process and Impact*", UNDP, New Delhi, 2009.

Macauslan, Ian (2008), *India's National Rural Employment Guarantee Act: A Case Study for How Change Happens,* Oxfam, UK.

Maheshwari, S.R. (1995), *Rural Development in India: A Public Policy Approach,* Sage Publications, New Delhi.

Norton, Andrew (2011), "Social Guarantees – Rights as Smart Politics", in MaximillanAshwill and Andrew Norton (eds.), *Building Citizenship through Social Policy in the East Caribbean: The Role of Social Guarantees*, The World Bank and Overseas Development Institute, Latin America and Caribbean Region.

Pearson, Ruth; Whitehead, A. and Young, K. (1981), "Introduction: The Continuing Subordination of Women in the Development Process" in Kate Young *et. al.* (eds.), *Of Marriage and the Market,* CSE Books, London.

Prasad, B.K. (2003), *Rural Development: Concepts, Approach and Strategy*, Sarup and Sons, New Delhi.

Raghava, D.V. Rao (1980), *Panchayats and Rural Development*, Ashish Publishing House, New Delhi.

Raghunandan, T.R. (2012), "Introduction", in T.R. Raghunandan, (ed.), *Decentralisation and Local Governments: The Indian Experience, Essays from Economic and Political Weekly*, Orient Blackswan Private Limited, New Delhi.

S. Waisbord (2000), *Watchdog journalism in South America: news, accountability and democracy*, Columbia University Press, New York.

Sastry,Trilochan; Murthy, Rajluxmi V. and Kamath, Rajalaxmi (2009), "NREGA Implementation: Comparative studies of Karnataka and Andhra Pradesh", in *The National Rural Employment Guarantee Act (NREGA): Design, Process and Impact*, UNDP, New Delhi, 2009.

Scott, W.R. (2008), *Institutions and Organizations: Ideas and Interests*, Sage Publications, Los Angeles.

Sengupta, Nilanjan; Bhattacharya, Mousumi S. and Sengupta, R.N. (2012), *Managing Change in Organizations*, PHI Learning Private Limited, New Delhi.

Singh, Hoshiar (1985), *Rural Development in India,* Print well Publishers, Jaipur.

Singh, Katar (1999), *Rural Development: Principles, Policies and Management*, Sage Publication India, New Delhi.

Singh, Shivraj (1989), *Bureaucracy and Rural Development,* Mittal Publications, New Delhi,

Sukhtankar, S. (2012), *What Determines MGNREGA Wages?: Some Evidence on Voice and Exit from Orissa*, University of Pennsylvania, USA.

B. Journals/Consultation Papers/Working Papers/Reports

Ackerman, J. (2004), "Co Governance for Accountability: Beyond "Exit" and "Voice"", *World Development,* Volume 32, Number 3.

Action for Food Production (2009), *Infrastructure Development and Beyond: Exploring the Scope for Sustainable Livelihood Support under NREGA*, Report submitted to the Ministry of Rural Development/UNDP, New Delhi.

Adhikari, Anindita and Bhatia, Karthika (2010), "NREGA Wage Payments: Can We Bank on Banks?",*Economic and Political Weekly*, Volume 45, Number 1.

Administrative Staff College of India (2009), *Quick Appraisal of NREGA in Andhra Pradesh*, Report submitted to the Ministry of Rural Development / UNDP, Administrative Staff College of India, Hyderabad.

Afridi, F. and Iversen, V. (2014), "Social Audits and MGNREGA Delivery: Lessons from Andhra Pradesh", *IZA Discussion Paper Number 8095*, Institute for the Study of Labour, Germany.

Ahmad, J.; Devarajan, S.; Khemani, S. and Shah, S. (2005), "Decentralization and service delivery", *Policy Research Working Paper 3603*, The World Bank, Washington, DC.

Aiyar, Yamini and Samji, Salimah (2006), "Improving the Effectiveness of National Rural Employment Guarantee Act", *Economic and Political Weekly*, Volume 41, Number 4.

Aiyar, Yamini; Posani, Bala; Patnaik, Abhijit and Devasher, Mandakini (2009), "Institutionalizing Social Accountability: Considerations for Policy", *Accountability Initiative Policy Paper 2*, Centre for Policy Research, New Delhi.

Aiyar, Yamini and Samji, Salimah (2009), "Transparency and Accountability in NREGA: A Case Study of Andhra Pradesh", *Working Paper Number1*, Centre for Policy Research, New Delhi.

Aiyar, Yamini; Mehta, SoumyaKapoor and Samji, Salimah (2011), "Strengthening Public Accountability: Lessons from Implementing Social Audits in Andhra Pradesh Accountability Initiative", *Working Paper Series*, Centre for Policy Research, New Delhi.

Aiyar, Yamini (2014), "Re-framing the MGNREGA debate", *The Hindu*, November 8, New Delhi.

Aiyar, Y. and Mehta, S.K. (2015), "Spectators or Participants: Effects of Social Audits in Andhra Pradesh", *Economic and Political Weekly*, Volume 50, Number 7.

Ambasta, Pramathesh; Shankar, P.S. Vijay and Shah, Mihir (2008), "Two Years of NREGA: The Road Ahead", *Economic and Political Weekly*, Volume 43, Number 7.

Ambasta, Pramathesh (2009), "Programming NREGS to succeed", *The Hindu*, 31st October, New Delhi.

Ambasta, P. (2010), "MGNREGA and Rural Governance Reform: Growth and Inclusion through Panchayats", *Paper presented at International Conference on Dynamics of Rural Transformation in Emerging Economies*, Planning Commission, Government of India and Institute for Human Development, New Delhi, India, April 14-16, 2010.

Azam, M. (2011), "The Impact of Indian Job Guarantee Scheme on Labour Market Outcomes: Evidence from A Natural Experiment", [Online] Available from: http://ssrn.com/abstract=1941959, [Accessed on 20th January, 2012].

Banerjee, Kaustav and Saha, Partha (2010), "The NREGA, the Maoists and the Developmental Woes of the Indian State", *Economic and Political Weekly*, Volume 45, Number 28.

Batliwala, S. (2007), "Taking the Power Out of Empowerment – An Experiential Account", *Development in Practice,* Volume 17, Number 4.

Bauhr, Monika and Grimes, Marcia (2012), "What is Government Transparency? New Measures and Relevance for Quality of Government", *Working Paper Series 16*, The Quality of Government Institute, University of Gothenburg, Sweden.

Bauhr, Monika and Nasiritousi, Nagmeh (2012), "Resisting Transparency: Corruption, Legitimacy and the Quality of Global Environmental Politics", *Global Environmental Politics,* Volume 12, Number 4.

Bellver, Ana and Kaufmann, Daniel (2005), Transparenting Transparency: Initial Empirics and Policy Applications, *Policy Research Working Paper*, World Bank, Washington D.C.

Beteille, Andre (1999), "Empowerment", *Economic and Political Weekly,* Volume 34, Number 10-11.

Bhaduri, Amit (2005), "First Priority: Guarantee Employment and the Right to Information", *Economic and Political Weekly,* Volume 40, Number 4.

Bhatia, K. and Adhikari, A. (2010), "NREGA Wage Payments: Can We Bank on the Banks", *Economic and Political Weekly,* Volume 65, Number 1.

Bhattacharyya, R. (2009), *Examining the Changing Status and Role of Middle Class Assamese Women: Lessons from the Lives of University Students,* PhD thesis, Newcastle University, UK.

Bhatty, Kiran (2006), "Employment Guarantee and Child Rights", *Economic & Political Weekly*, Volume 41, Number 20.

Birner, R.; Gayathridevi, K.; Raabe, K.G.; Schiffer, E. and Sekhar, M. (2010), "How to Overcome the Governance Challenges of Implementing NREGA", *Discussion Paper 00963,* International Food Policy Research Institute (IFPRI), US.

Bonner, Kim; Daum, Jennifer; Duncan, Jessie; Dinsmore, Ellen; Fuglesten, Kari; Lai, Leslie; Lee, Julian; Manchester, Katherine; Tadesse, Feker; Quinn, Robert (2012), "MGNREGA Implementation: A Cross-State

Comparison", Paper for *The Woodrow Wilson School's Graduate Policy Workshop*, Woodrow Wilson School of Public and International Affairs, Princeton University, New Jersey.

Bordoloi, J. (2011), *Impact of NREGA on Wage Returns, Food Security and Rural-Urban Migration – Assam*, Report submitted to the Ministry of Agriculture, Agro-Economic Centre for North-East India, Assam Agricultural University, Jorhat.

Bossert, J. T. and Beauvais, C.J. (2002), "Decentralization of Health Systems in Ghana, Zambia, Uganda and the Philippines: A Comparative Analysis of Decision Space", *Health Policy and Planning*, Volume 17, Number 1.

Central Institute of Fisheries Education (2009), *A Study Report on Appraisal on MGNREGA Programme in Thane and Akola Districts of Maharashtra*, Report submitted to the Ministry of Rural Development/UNDP, Central Institute of Fisheries Education, Mumbai.

Centre for Education and Research Development (2010), *NREGA Processes in Andhra Pradesh and Madhya Pradesh: Appraisal and Research Study*, Report submitted to the Ministry of Rural Development/UNDP, Centre for Education and Research Development, New Delhi.

Centre for Good Governance (2009), *Best Practices Notes on Social Accountability Initiatives in South Asia Social Audit of NREGS in Andhra Pradesh*, Hyderabad.

Centre for Research in Rural and Industrial Development (2009), *Appraisal/Impact Assessment of NREGS in Selected Districts of Himachal Pradesh, Punjab and Haryana*, Report submitted to the Ministry of Rural Development/UNDP, CRRID, Chandigarh.

Chakraborty, Pinaki (2007), "Implementation of Employment Guarantee: A Preliminary Appraisal", *Economic and Political Weekly*, Volume 42, Number 7.

Chandhoke, N. (2005), "Democracy and Well-Being in India", *United Nations Research Institute for Social Development*, Geneva.

Chandrashekar, C. and Ghosh, J. (2011), "Public Works and Wages in Rural India", [Online] Available from: http://www.macroscan.org/fet/jan11/fet110111Public_Works.htm, [Accessed on 11th January, 2011].

Copp, James H. (1972), "Rural Sociology and Rural Development", *Rural Sociology*, Volume 37, Number 4.

Cornwall, A. (2004), "Introduction: New Democratic Spaces? The Politics and Dynamics of Institutionalized Participation", *IDS Bulletin*, Volume 35, Number 2.

Dasgupta, S. and Sudarshan, S. (2011), 'Issues in Labour Market Inequality and Women's Participation in India's National Rural Employment Guarantee Act', *Working Paper Number 98*, International Labour Organization, Geneva.

Datar, Chhaya (2007), "Failure of National Rural Employment Guarantee Scheme in Maharashtra", *Economic and Political Weekly,* Volume 43, Number 34.

Dayal,Vikram; Ghate, Rucha; Ghosh, Nilanjan; Chopra, Kanchan and Nagendra, Harini (2012), "Remembering ElinorOstrom", *Economic and Political Weekly*, Volume 47, Number 34.

Decentralization Community (2011), Solution Exchange for the Decentralization Community, [Online] Available from http://www.in.undp.org/content/india/en/home/ourwork/democraticgovernance/decentralization-community—solution-exchange-india.html, [Accessed on 5th September, 2012].

Deininger, K. and Liu, Y. (2010), "Poverty Impacts of India's National Rural Employment Guarantee Scheme: Evidence from Andhra Pradesh", *Paper prepared for presentation at the Agricultural and Applied Economics Association*, Colorado, July 25-27, Colorado,

Dey, Subhashish and Bedi, Arjun S. (2010), "The National Rural Employment Guarantee Scheme in Birbhum", *Economic and Political Weekly,* Volume 45, Number 41.

Dhar, M.L. (2008), "Employment Scenario in India", *Kurukshetra,* Volume 56, Number 4.

Dheeraja, C. and Rao, H. (2010), *Changing Gender Relations: A Study of MGNREGS across Different States,* National Institute of Rural Development (NIRD), Hyderabad.

Dhuru, Arundhate and Pandey, Sandeep (2009), "The Wages of Protest", *The Hindu,* April 5, New Delhi.

Dreze, Jean and Siddhartha (2009), "Flaws in the System", *Frontline,* Volume 26, Issue 01.

Dutta, P.; Murgai,R.; Ravallion,M. and Dominique, W.V. (2012), "Does India's Employment Guarantee Scheme Guarantee Employment?",*Policy Research Working Paper 6003*, World Bank, Washington DC.

Edholm, F.; Harris, O. and Young, K. (1997), "Conceptualizing women", *Critique of Anthropology,* Volume 3 Numbers 9 and10.

El-Bushra, Judy (2000), "Rethinking Gender and Development Practice for the Twenty-first Century", *Gender & Development,* Volume 8, Number 1.

Evans, P. (1996), "Introduction: Development Strategies across Public-Private Divide", *World Development,* Volume 24, Number 6.

Fakuda, Parr;Sakiko; Lawson, Remer; Terra and Randolph, Susan (2009), "An Index of Social Rights Fulfillment: Concept and Methodology", *Journal of Human Rights,* Volume 8, Number 3.

Ferrajoli, Luigi (2001), *The Basis of Fundamental Rights,* Editorial Trotta,Madrid.

Florini, Ann (2002), "Increasing Transparency in Government", *International Journal on World Peace,* Volume 19, Number 3.

Ghose, Ajit K. (2004), "The Employment Challenge in India", *Economic and Political Weekly,* Volume 39, Number 48.

Ghosh, J. (2009), "Equity and Inclusion through Public Expenditure: The Potential of the NREGS", *Paper for International Conference on NREGA,* New Delhi.

Ghosh, J.K. (2011), *Impact of NREGA on Wage Rates, Food Security and Rural Urban Migration in West Bengal,* Report submitted to the Ministry of Agriculture, Agro-Economic Research Centre, Visva-BharatiSantiniketan, Birbhum.

Goetz, Anne Marie (2000), "Accountability to women in development spending at the local level: a concept note", *Paper presented to IDS Workshop on Gender and Accountability in Public and Private Sector,* UK.

Goetz, A. and Jenkins, R. (2001), "Hybrid forms of accountability: citizen engagement in institutions of public sector oversight in India", *Public Management Review,* Volume 3, Number 3.

Goetz, A. and Jenkins, R. (2002), "Voice, Accountability and Human Development: The Emergence of a New Agenda",*Background paper for Human Development Report 2002,* United Nations Development Programme, New York, 2002.

Gopal, K.S. (2009), "NREGA Social Audit: Myths and Reality", *Economic and Political Weekly,* Volume 44, Number 3.

Government of India (1992), *Eighth Five Year Plan, 1992-1997, Volume II*, Planning Commission, New Delhi.

Government of India (2002), *Drought 2002,* Department of Agriculture and Cooperation, Ministry of Agriculture, Government of India, New Delhi.

Government of India (2006), *Unlocking Human Capital: Entitlements and Governance – A Case Study*, Second Administrative Reforms Commission, Ministry of Personnel, Public Grievances and Pensions, Department of Administrative Reforms and Public Grievances, New Delhi.

Government of India (2007), *National Rural Employment Guarantee Act (NREGA): Some Reports from the Field, 2006-07*, Ministry of Rural Development, Department of Rural Development, New Delhi.

Government of India (2008), *Performance Audit of Implementation of National Rural Employment Guarantee Act (NREGA)*, Comptroller and Auditor General of India, Performance Audit Report No. 11, CAG, New Delhi.

Government of India (2009), *National Rural Employment Guarantee Act, 2005: Report to the People 2008-09*, Ministry of Rural Development, Department of Rural Development, New Delhi.

Government of India (2010), *National Capability Building Framework for Panchayati Raj Elected Representatives and Functionaries*, Ministry of Panchayati Raj, New Delhi.

Government of India (2010a), *Report of the Working Group on Transparency and Accountabilityof Central Employment Guarantee Council,* Submitted to Ministry of Rural Development, New Delhi.

Government of India (2011), *Census 2011,* Office of the Registrar General and Census Commissioner, Ministry of Home Affairs, New Delhi.

Government of India (2012), *MGNREGA: Report to the People – 2011-12,* Ministry of Rural Development, Department of Rural Development, New Delhi.

Government of India (2012a), *Report of the Committee on Revision of MGNREGA Operational Guidelines*, Report submitted to the Ministry of Rural Development, New Delhi.

Government of India (2012b), *MGNREGA Sameeksha: An Anthology of Research Studies on the Mahatma Gandhi National Rural Employment Guarantee Act, (2005) – 2006-2012*, Ministry of Rural Development, Orient Blackswan, New Delhi.

Government of India (2013), *Mahatma Gandhi National Rural Employment Guarantee Act (MGNREGA), Annual Report 2012-13,* Ministry of Rural Development, Department of Rural Development, New Delhi.

Government of India (2013a), *Mahatma Gandhi National Rural Employment Guarantee Act, 2005, Operational Guidelines, 2013,* 4th Edition, Ministry of Rural Development, Department of Rural Development, New Delhi.

Government of India (2013b), *TowardsHolistic Panchayat Raj,* Twentieth Anniversary Report of the Expert Committee on Leveraging Panchayats For Efficient Delivery of Public Goods and Services, Policy Issues, Volume 1, New Delhi.

Government of India (2013c), *Performance Audit of Implementation of Mahatma Gandhi National Rural Employment Guarantee Act (MGNREGA),* Comptroller and Auditor General of India Report No. 6 of 2013, CAG, New Delhi.

Government of India (2014), *Report on Capacity Building of Functionaries on Operational Guidelines under MGNREGA*, MGNREGA Division, Department of Rural Development, Ministry of Rural Development, New Delhi.

Government of India (2015), *Mahatma Gandhi National Rural Employment Guarantee Act, 2005, Report to the People: 2014-15*, Ministry of Rural Development, Department of Rural Development, New Delhi.

Government of India (2016), *Mahatma Gandhi National Rural Employment Guarantee Act, 2005: The journey of a Decade,* Ministry of Rural Development, New Delhi.

Grigorescu, Alexandru (2003), "International Organizations and Government Transparency: Linking the International and Domestic Realms", *International Studies Quarterly,* Volume 47, Number 4.

Hazarika, P.G. (2009), *Promoting Women Empowerment and Gender Equality through the Right to Decent Work: Implementation of National Rural Employment Guarantee Program (NREGP) in Assam State (India)—A Case Study,* Institute of Social Studies, The Hague.

Hirway, Indira (2004), "Providing Employment Guarantee in India: Some Critical Issues", *Economic and Political Weekly,* Volume 39, Number 48.

Hirway, I. and Batabyal, S. (2012), *MGNREGA and Women's Empowerment,* United Nation Women South Asia, New Delhi.

Holmes, R.; Rath, S. and Sadana, N. (2011), *An Opportunity for Change? Gender Analysis of the Mahatma Gandhi National Rural Employment Guarantee Act*, Overseas Development Institute and Indian Institute of Dalit Studies, London.

Imbert, C. and Papp, J. (2011), "Equilibrium Distributional Impacts of Government Employment Programs: Evidence from India's Employment Guarantee", *PSE Working Papers n2012-14*, Paris School of Economics, Paris.

Indian Institute of Technology (2010), *NREGA in Districts of Dharmapuri, Erode, Nagapattinam, Perambalur, Thanjavur, Theni, Thoothukudi, Tiruvallur, Vellore, Villupuram of Tamil Nadu*, Report submitted to Ministry of Rural Development/UNDP, Indian Institute of Technology, Chennai.

Institute for Development of Youth, Women and Child (2010), *Impact Assessment of Mahatma Gandhi National Rural Employment Guarantee Scheme on Sustainable Asset Creation and Livelihood*, Report submitted to Ministry of Rural Development/UNDP, IDYWC, Chhindwara.

Institute of Rural Management (2010), *An Impact Assessment Study of the Usefulness and Sustainability of the Assets Created under Mahatma Gandhi Rural Employment Guarantee Act in Sikkim*, IRMA, Anand.

International Labour Organization (2013), *Global Employment Trends 2013*, ILO, Geneva.

Islam, Roumeen (2006), "Does More Transparency Go Along With Better Governance?",*Economics and Politics*, Volume 18, Number 2.

Isunza, E. (2003), 'Construccion de la democracia y rendicion de cuentas: unamiradaregional de nuevas interfaces socioestatales en el contexto de la transicionPolitica Mexicana', *Presented at 2003 meeting of the Latin American Studies Association*, Dallas, March 27-29.

Jacob, Arun and Verghese,Richard (2006), "NREGA Implementation-1: Reasonable Beginning in Palakkad, Kerala", *Economic and Political Weekly,* Volume 41, Number 48.

Jain, L.C. (2005), "Putting Panchayats in Charge", *Economic and Political Weekly*, Volume 40, Number 33.

Jha, R.; Gaiha, R. and Pandey, M.K. (2011), "Net Transfer Benefits under India's Rural Employment Guarantee Scheme", *Journal of Policy Modeling*, Volume 34, Number 2.

Joseph, Shaji (2006), "Power of the People: Political Mobilisation and Guaranteed Employment", *Economic and Political Weekly*, Volume 41, Number 50.

Joshi, Anuradha (2009), "Do Rights Work? Law, Activism and the Employment Guarantee Scheme", *World Development Report 38*, Volume 4, 2009.

Joshi, Anuradha and Moore, Mick (2000), "The mobilising potential of anti-poverty programs", *IDS Working Paper Number 374*, Institute of Development Studies, UK, 2000.

Kajale, J. and Shroff, S. (2011), *Impact of NREGA on Wage Rates, Food Security, and Rural Urban Migration in Maharashtra*, Report Submitted to the Ministry of Agriculture, Gokhale Institute of Politics and Economics, Agro-economic Research Centre, Pune.

Kanbur, Ravi (2006), "What's social policy got to do with economic growth?", [Online] Available from http://www.arts.cornell.edu/poverty/kanbur/SocPolEconGrowth.pdf., [Accessed on 2nd April, 2015].

Kaufmann, Daniel; Mehrez, Gil and Tugrul, Gurgur (2002), *Voice or Public Sector Management? An Empirical Investigation of the Determinants of Public Sector Performance Based on a Survey of Public Officials in Bolivia*, World Bank Institute, [Online]Availablefrom: http://ssrn.com/abstract =316865orhttp://dx.doi.org/10.2139/ssrn.316865, [Accessed on 23rd September, 2015].

Khera, Reetika (2008), "The Black Hole of NREGA Records", *Yojana*, Volume 52.

Khera, Reetika and Nayak, Nandini (2009), "Women Workers and Perceptions of the National Rural Employment Guarantee Act", *Economic & Political Weekly*, Volume 44, Number 43.

Khera, Reetika (2016), "Digging holes, filling them up", *The Indian Express*, February 3, New Delhi.

Khosla, R. (2011), "Caste, Politics and Public Goods Distribution in India: Evidence from NREGS in Andhra Pradesh", *Economic and Political Weekly*, Volume 45, Number 12.

Kumar, P. and Maruthi, I. (2011), *Impact of NREGA on Wage Rate, Food Security and Rural Urban Migration in Karnataka*, Report submitted to the Ministry of Agriculture, Agriculture Development and Rural Transformation Centre, Institute for Social and Economic Change, Bangalore.

Kurtzman, Joel; Yago, Glenn and Triphon, Phumiwasana (2004), "The global costs of opacity—Measuring business and investment risk worldwide", *MIT Sloan Management Review*, Volume 46, Number.

Lam, W. (1996), "Institutional design of public agencies and coproduction: a study of irrigation associations in Taiwan", *World Development*, Volume 24, Number 6.

Lindstedt, Catharina and Naurin, Daniel (2010), "Transparency is not Enough: Making Transparency Effective in Reducing Corruption", *International Political Science Review*, Volume 31.

Louis, Prakash (2006), "NREGA Implementation II: Birth Pangs in Bihar", *Economic and Political Weekly*, Volume 41, Number 48.

Luttrell, C.; Quiroz, S.; Scrutton, C. and Bird, K. (2009), "Understanding and Operationalizing Empowerment", *Working Paper 308,* Overseas Development Institute, [Online} Available from http://www.odi.org.uk/resources/download/4525.pdf, [Accessed on 15th June, 2015].

Mangatter, S. (2011), *Does the Mahatma Gandhi National Rural Employment Guarantee Act (MGNREGA) Strengthen Rural Self-employment in Bolpur subdivision (West Bengal, India)?*, Master's Thesis, Philipps-Universität Marburg, Germany.

McKinsey Global Institute (2015), *The Power of Parity: Advancing Women's Equality in India*, McKinsey and Company, New York.

Mehrotra, Santosh (2008), "NREG: Two Years On: Where Do We Go from Here?",*Economic and Political Weekly*, Volume 43, Number 31.

Mitchell, A. and Bossert, J.T. (2010), "Decentralization, governance and health-system performance: Where You Stand Depends on Where You Sit", *Development Policy Review*, Volume 28, Number 6.

Mitchell, R.B. (1998), "Sources of Transparency: Information Systems in International Regimes", *International Studies Quarterly*, Volume 42, Issue 1.

Mohan, Saumitra (2007), "National Rural Employment Guarantee Programme: How Effective?",*The Administrator*, Volume 50, Number 1.

Molyneux, Maxine (1985), "Mobilization without Emancipation? Women's Interests, the State, and Revolution in Nicaragua", *Feminist Studies*, Volume 11, Number 2.

Morgan, J.P. (2011), "Wages in Rural India Accelerated Sharply Post-NREGA", [Online] Available from India Equity Research: http://indiaer.blogspot.in/2011/10/india-rural-wages-surge-to-support.html, [Accessed on 15th April, 2015].

Moser, Caroline O.N. (1989), "Gender Planning in the Third World: Meeting Practical and Strategic Gender Needs", *World Development,* Volume 17, Number 11.

Mukherjee, D. and Sinha, U.B. (2011), *Understanding NREGA: A Simple Theory and Some Facts,* Centre for Development Economics, Delhi School of Economics, Delhi.

Narayanan, Sudha (2008), "Women's Work Childcare and Employment Guarantee", *Economic & Political Weekly,* Volume 43, Number 9.

Narayanan, Sudha; Ranaware, Krushna; Das, Upasak and Kulkarni, Ashwini (2014), *MGNREGA works and their Impacts: A Rapid Assessment in Maharashtra,* Indira Gandhi Institute of Development Research, Mumbai.

National Federation for Indian Women (2008), *Social-Economic Empowerment of Women under NREGA,* Report Submitted to the Ministry of Rural Development/UNDP, NFIW.

National Sample Survey Organisation (2010), *Employment and Unemployment,66th Round National Survey, (July 2009 - June 2010),* Government of India, New Delhi.

National Sample Survey Organisation (2014), *Employment and Unemployment Situation in India, (July 2011 - June 2012),* Ministry of Statistics &Programme Implementation, Government of India, New Delhi.

Ostrom, E. (1996), "Crossing the great divide: coproduction, synergy and development", *World Development,* Volume 24, Number 6.

Otobe, Naoko (2011), *Global Economic Crisis, Gender and Employment: The Impact and Policy Response,* Employment Sector: Employment Working Paper No. 74, International Labour Organization, Geneva.

Otobe, Naoko (2014), "Promoting women's economic empowerment through productive employment and social protection", *Working Paper 2014/091,* United Nations University-World Institute for Development Economics Research, Helsinki, Finland.

Pande, Varad and Mann, Neelakshi (2014), "MGNREGA: A tale of rural revival", [Online] Availablefrom:http://www.livemint.com/Opinion/tdKbJga16hmXmKs42zHeuK/MGNREGA-A-tale-of-rural-revival.html, [Accessed on 23rd September, 2015].

Pani, N. and Iyer, C. (2011), *Evaluation of the Impact of Processes in the Mahatma Gandhi National Rural Employment Guarantee Scheme in Karnataka*, National Institute of Advanced Studies (NIAS), Bangalore.

Pankaj, Ashok and Tankha, Rukmini (2010), "Empowerment Effects of the NREGS on Women Workers: A Study in Four States", *Economic and Political Weekly*, Volume 45, Number 30.

Papola, T.S. (2005), "A Universal Programme is Feasible", *Economic and Political Weekly*, Volume 40, Number 7.

Patel, Sujata (2006), "Empowerment, Co–option and Domination: Politics of Maharashtra's Employment Guarantee Scheme", *Economic and Political Weekly*, Volume 41, Number 50.

Paul, S. (1992), "Accountability in Public Services: Exit, Voice and Control", *World Development,* Volume 20, Number 7.

Peruzzotti, E. and Smulovitz, C. (2000), "Societal Accountability in Latin America", *Journal of Democracy*, Volume 11, Number 4.

Posani, Bala and Aiyar, Yamini (2009), "State of Accountability: Evolution, Practice and Emerging Questions in Public Accountability in India", *Accountability Initiative, Working Paper Number 2*, Centre for Policy Research, New Delhi.

Pritchett, L. (2006), "Local Information about Schooling: Performance and Costs", *ASER Discussion Series*, ASER, New Delhi.

Raghavan, Karthik; Singh, Niki; Das, Saswata; Bist, Shardul; Das, Subhamoy; Gajjar, Unnati; Singh, Veena; Singh, Vibha and Development of Research and Communication Service Centre (2008), *The National Rural Employment Guarantee Scheme (NREGS) West Bengal: A Study of Sustainable Livelihood Models*, Mudra Institute of Communications, Entrepreneurship Development Cell (MICA – EDC), Ahmedabad.

Rahman, Md. Aminur (2013), "Women's Empowerment: Concept and Beyond", *Global Journal of Human-Social Science*, Volume 13, Number 6.

Rajanna, Mamidipally and Ramesh, Gundeti (2009), "NREGP–Facet of Inclusive Growth: A Study of Karimnagar district in Andhra Pradesh", *Kurukshetra,* Volume 57, Number 4.

Rao, V. Mohan (2008), "Employment Guarantee Scheme is a Lifeline for the Vulnerable Sections", *Kurukshetra,* Volume 56, Number 8.

Ravallion, M. (2012), "Corruption in the MGNREGS: Assessing an Index", *Economic and Political Weekly,* Volume 47, Number 8.

Ravallion, Martin (2014), 'MGNREGA is unwell', *The Indian Express,* October 24, New Delhi.

Ravi, S. and Engler,M. (2013), "Workfare as an Effective Way to Fight Poverty: The Case of India's NREGS", [Online] Available from: http://ssrn.com/paper=1336837, [Accessed on 12th July, 2015].

Razavi, S. (1997), "Fitting Gender into Development Institutions", *World Development,* Volume 25, Number 7.

Razavi, S. (2012), "World Development Report 2012: Gender Equality and Development: A Commentary", *Development and Change,* Volume 43, Number 1.

Razavi, S. and Miller, C. (1995), "From WID to GAD: Conceptual Shifts in the Women and Development Discourse", *Occasional Paper 1,* United Nations Research Institute for Social Development and United Nations Development Programme.

Reddy, C. Rammanohar (2008), "Wake up Call on Rural Employment Guarantee", *Economic and Political Weekly,* Volume 43, Number 4.

Relly and Sabharwal (2009), "Perceptions of transparency of government policymaking: A cross-national study", *Government Information Quarterly,* Volume 26.

Rubin, G. (1975), "The Traffic in women: Notes on Political Economy of Sex", in R. Reiter (ed.), *Towards an Anthropology of Women,* Monthly Review Press, New York.

Sadasivam, Bharti and Ford, Bjoern (2007), "Civil Society and social accountability", *Making Democracy Deliver,* UNDP Democratic Governance Department, UNDP.

Sampath, G. and S., Rukmini (2015), "Is the MGNREGA being set up for failure?",*The Hindu,* May 31, New Delhi.

Sankaran, Kamala (2011), "NREGA Wages: Ensuring Decent Work", *Economic and Political Weekly,* Volume 46, Number 7.

Savale, Sanjay (2006), "Is Local Really Better? Comparing EGS and Local–Managed Rural Work Programmes in Nasik District", *Economic and Political Weekly,* Volume 41, Number 50.

Shaffer, P. (2008), "New Thinking on Poverty: Implications for Globalisation and Poverty Reduction Strategies", *Real-World Economics Review,* Volume 47.

Shah, Mihir (2004), "National Rural Employment Guarantee Act: A Historical Opportunity", *Economic and Political Weekly*, Volume 39, Number 50.

Shah, Mihir (2005), "Saving the Employment Guarantee Act", *Economic and Political Weekly*, Volume 40, Number 7.

Shah, Mihir (2007), "Employment Guarantee, Civil Society and Indian Democracy", *Economic and Political Weekly*, Volume 42, Number 45 and 46.

Shah, Mihir (2009), "Multiplier accelerator synergy in NREGA", *The Hindu*, 30th April, New Delhi.

Shah, T.; Verma, S.; Indu, R. and Hemant, P. (2010), *Asset Creation through Employment Guarantee?: Synthesis of Student Case Studies in 9 States of India*, International Water Management Institute (IWMI), Sri Lanka.

Shankar, S. (2010), "Can Social Audits Count?", *Australia South Asia Research Centre Working Paper 2010/09*, Centre for Policy Research, New Delhi, pp. 1-26.;

Sharma, Amita (2010), "Rights-based Legal Guarantee as Development Policy: Mahatma Gandhi National Rural Employment Guarantee Act", *A Discussion Paper*, UNDP, India.

Sharma, Rita (2015), 'For a better MGNREGA', *The Indian Express*, July 5, New Delhi.

Siddhartha and Vanaik, Anish (2008), "CAG Report on NREGA: Fact and Fiction", *Economic and Political Weekly*, Volume 43, Number 25.

Singh, Raghuvansh Prasad (2008), "Two Years of NREGA", *Yojana*, Volume 52.

Singh, Ritesh and Vutukuru, Vinay (2006), "Enhancing accountability in Public Service Delivery through Social Audit: A case study of Andhra Pradesh, India", *Working Paper Series, Accountability Initiative*, Centre for Policy Research, New Delhi.

Siwach, Raj Kumar and Kumar, Sunil (2009), "Implementing NREGS in Haryana: A Study of Social Audit", *Kurukshetra*, Volume 57, Number 6.

Srivastava, Nisha and Srivastava, Ravi (2010), "Women, Work, and Employment Outcomes in Rural India", *Economic and Political Weekly*, Volume 45, Number 28.

Stasavage, David (2004), "Open-Door or Closed-Door? Transparency in Domestic and International Bargaining", *International Organization*, Volume 58.

Sturges, Paul (2007), "What is this absence called transparency?", Delivered at an ICIE Conference, Pretoria, [Online] Available from: http://www.ifla.org/files/assets/faife/publications/sturges/icie-paper.pdf, [Accessed on 20th August, 2015].

Sudarshan, R.M. (2009), *Examining India's National Rural Employment Guarantee Act: Its Impact and Women's Participation*, Institute of Social Studies Trust, New Delhi.

Sudarshan, R.M. (2011), *India's National Rural Employment Guarantee Act: Women's Participation and Impacts in Himachal Pradesh, Kerala and Rajasthan*, Institute of Development Studies, Centre for Social Protection, New Delhi.

Sudarshan, Ratna (2008), "Impact of NREGA on Rural Labour Market in Kerala: Preliminary Findings on Women's Work", *International conference on "NREGS in India: Impacts and Implementation Experiences"*, New Delhi, 16-17 September.

Sumarto, Sudarno and Suryahadi, Asep (2001), "Principles and Approaches to Targetting: With Reference to the Indonesian Social Safety Net Programs", *MPRA Paper Number 58670*, The SMERU Research Institute, Indonesia.

Tendler, J. (1997), *Good government in the tropics*, John Hopkins University Press, Baltimore.

Tewari, Ruhi (2015), "In MNREGA, Bihar slower than rest", *The Indian Express*, September 10, New Delhi.

The Indian Express (2016), "MGNREGA Message", *Editorial*, January 7, New Delhi.

The Mahatma Gandhi National Rural Employment Guarantee Act, 2005 (2012), Universal Law Publishing Co. Pvt. Ltd., New Delhi.

Tirole, J. (1994), "The Internal Organization of Government", *Oxford Economic Papers New Series*, Volume 46, Number 1.

Tiwari, Nupur (2011), "Reinforcing the implementation and monitoring of the schemes under NREGA through Panchayati Raj", [Online] available from: http:indiagovernance.gov.in/files/Involvement-of-PRIs-in-the-implementation-and-monitoring-of-the-schemes-under-NREGA.pdf, [Accessed on 13th Feb, 2012].

United Nation Development Programme (2004), "Right to Information: Practical Guidance Note", [Online] Available from: http://witt-project.net/IMG/pdf/UNDP_Right_to_Information.pdf, [Accessed on 20th August, 2015].

United Nations Development Programme (2008), *Capacity Assessment Practice Note*, UNDP, New York.

United Nations Office on Drugs and Crime, (2004), "United Nations Convention against Corruption: Priorities for the provision of technical assistance", *Global Programme against Corruption,* [Online] Available from: http://www.unodc.org/pdf/crime/corruption/corruption_gpac_strategy_jul04.pdf, [Accessed on 20th August, 2015].

Vaidyanathan, A. (2005), "Employment Guarantee and Decentralization", *Economic and Political Weekly,* Volume 40, Number 16.

Vaidyanathan, A. (2005a), "Need for Involvement of States", *Economic and Political Weekly,* Volume 40, Number 33.

Verma, S. (2012), *Labour Markets Dynamics in Post-MGNREGS Rural India,* Unpublished note shared with the Ministry of Rural Development, New Delhi.

Vij, Nidhi (2011), "Building Capacities for Empowerment: the Missing link between Social Protection and Social Justice-Case of Social Audits in Mahatma Gandhi National Rural Employment Guarantee Act",*Paper for the International Conference Social Protection for Social Justice,* Institute of Development Studies, UK, 13-15 April, 2011.

Vishwanath, Tara and Kaufmann, Daniel (1999), "Towards Transparency in Finance and Governance", *Policy Research Working Paper,* World Bank, Washington D.C.

World Bank (2003),"Making Services Work for Poor People", *World Development Report, 2004,* Oxford University Press, New York.

World Bank (2006), *Capacity Development Resource Center- Perspectives and Definitions,* World Bank Africa Region.

World Bank (2008), *Realizing Rights Through Social Guarantees: An Analysis of New Approaches to Social Policy in Latin America and South Africa*, World Bank, Washington DC.

World Bank (2011), *Social Protection for a Changing India*, World Bank, Washington DC.

World Development Report (2012), *Gender Equality and Development*, World Bank, Washington.

World Bank (2015), "*The state of social safety nets 2015*", World Bank Group, Washington DC, [Online]Availablefrom:http://documents.worldbank.org/curated/en/2015/07/24741765/state-social-safety-nets-2015, [Accessed on 21st September, 2015].

Websites

[Online] Available from http://nrega.nic.in/nrega/writeraddata/circulars/nrega_doc_faqs.pdf, [Accessed online on 28th may, 2015].

[Online] Available from: http://www.transparency-initiative.org/about/definitions, [Accessed on 20th August, 2015].

[Online] Available from: www.issai.org, [Accessed on 20th August, 2015], "Principles of transparency and accountability," The International Standards of Supreme Audit Institutions, (ISSAI), issued by the International Organization of Supreme Audit Institutions.

[Online]Availablefrom:http://nrega.nic.in/Netnrega/WriteReaddata/Circulars/1072Letter_CFT_02_07_2015.pdf, [Accessed on 15th January, 2016].

[Online] Available from: http://ssrn.com/abstract=1941959, [Accessed on 20th January, 2012].

[Online]Availablefrom:http://www.livemint.com/Opinion/tdKbJga16hmXmKs42zHeuK/MGNREGA-A-tale-of-rural-revival.html, [Accessed on 23rd September, 2015].

[Online]Availablefrom:http://documents.worldbank.org/curated/en/2015/07/24741765/state-social-safety-nets-2015, [Accessed on 21st September, 2015].

[Online]Available from http://www.odi.org.uk/resources/download/4525.pdf, [Accessed on 15th June, 2015].

[Online]Availablefrom:http://www.unodc.org/pdf/crime/corruption/corruption_gpac_strategy_jul04.pdf, [Accessed on 20th August, 2015].